WE ARE THE TROOPERS

WE ARE THE TROOPERS

THE WOMEN OF
THE WINNINGEST TEAM
IN PRO FOOTBALL HISTORY

STEPHEN GUINAN

hachette
BOOKS

New York

Hachette Books
Hachette Book Group
1290 Avenue of the Americas
New York, NY 10104
HachetteBooks.com
Twitter.com/HachetteBooks
Instagram.com/HachetteBooks

First Edition: August 2022

Published by Hachette Books, an imprint of Perseus Books, LLC, a subsidiary of Hachette Book Group, Inc. The Hachette Books name and logo is a trademark of the Hachette Book Group.

The Hachette Speakers Bureau provides a wide range of authors for speaking events. To find out more, go to www.hachettespeakersbureau.com or call (866) 376-6591.

The publisher is not responsible for websites (or their content) that are not owned by the publisher.

Print book interior design by Jeff Stiefel.

Library of Congress Cataloging-in-Publication Data
Names: Guinan, Stephen, author.
Title: We are the Troopers : the women of the winningest team in pro
    football history / Stephen Guinan.
Description: First edition. | New York, N.Y. : Hachette Books, 2022. |
    Includes bibliographical references and index.
Identifiers: LCCN 2021055201 | ISBN 9780306846939 (hardcover) | ISBN
    9780306846922 (ebook)
Subjects: LCSH: Toledo Troopers (Football team)—History. | Women's
    Professional Football League—History. | National Women's Football
    League (U.S.)—History. | Women football players—United
    States—History. | Football—United States—History.
Classification: LCC GV956.T65 G85 2022 | DDC 796.3320973—dc23/eng/20220104
LC record available at https://lccn.loc.gov/2021055201
ISBNs: 978-0-306-84693-9 (hardcover), 978-0-306-84692-2 (ebook)

Printed in the United States

LSC-C

Printing 1, 2022

For the players and coaches,
who followed a dream

CONTENTS

CONTENTS

AUTHOR'S NOTE

I grew up in Toledo in the '70s, watching my dad slap his knees and shout at the TV as his beloved Detroit Lions were getting shellacked. A devout football fan, he rooted with extreme prejudice for the teams of his youth, having grown up in Detroit, as well as those of his acquired hometown of Toledo. On weekends he left the *Toledo Blade* sports pages strewn about the kitchen. As I was learning to decode those headlines covering all manner of football from the NFL to college to the short-lived World Football League (WFL), one day I read about a team called the Toledo Troopers stomping the Detroit Demons. I asked my dad about it. "They're a women's team," he said. "And they're the best team in the country."

One can never trust a father's appraisal of his sports teams, but my dad's tone was reverential. And the more I read, the more coverage I saw from the likes of Orris Tabner on Channel 11 sports, I came to understand that Dad was right. Toledo could pride itself as the home of the best.

And just as they were emerging in my consciousness, the team disappeared. No *Blade* stories. No nightly news segments. No championships. They were simply erased from existence.

Years later, by blind chance I sat next to a stranger in my high school cafeteria. "My dad is the winningest coach in football history," he said.

"Your dad is Don Shula?" I asked. "Tom Landry?"

"His name is Bill Stout," he said. "He coached the Toledo Troopers."

"Winningest?" I asked.

Best winning percentage all-time, he told me. "I know," he said. "I was the waterboy."

The headlines came flooding back to me, as did the images of women in green and gold on the gridiron. But the picture was incomplete. In my mind the team had played for so long and had accomplished so much. There must be a history there.

Over the years, I would learn it. The waterboy and I became friends. Guy Stout would introduce me to the winningest coach himself, a barrel-chested force who related to others through bluster and busting chops. Later, I met the coaches Carl Hamilton, Jim Wright, Jerry Davis, and Mike Stout. When they spoke about the Troopers, I could hear an echo of my own dad's pride: "It was the best time of my life," Carl said.

And then I met the players.

Throughout the '70s, eighty-two women suited up for the Troopers. Some played only a season. Many played for several years before injuries or pregnancies or career paths took them away from the game. Two players, Jackie Allen and Pam Schwartz, played all nine seasons. Together the Troopers represented the most diverse demographic you could draw up, except for three common traits: They were women. They were from Toledo. And they were football players.

In researching the book I've been touched by their stories, as well as those of their opponents in Detroit, Buffalo, Philadelphia, Dallas, Columbus, Middletown, Fort Worth, and Oklahoma City.

As the movement for women's equality reached the halls of Congress in the form of Title IX, these women took to the most violent of American sports. They understood the game at a primal level as only one who has suffered its brutality can. They bore scars and sprains and broken bones. They did not see themselves as agents of change, but surely they were part of it.

Today they share an inspired reverence for the memory of their playing days and of a camaraderie found only in football locker rooms. They speak with misty-eyed pride about what it means to be a champion, and how the lessons they learned playing football and preparing for it would impact the rest of their lives.

"I was a Toledo Trooper," Gloria Jimenez told me. "And it was the greatest thing I've ever done."

I hope that telling this story honors what they did.

When my dad told me about the Troopers, I asked him who he would root for in a contest between his favorites Toledo and Detroit. He didn't hesitate.

"Toledo all the way," he said.

PROLOGUE

The simple notice was a rectangular blank stare: Helvetica type, 1/32 of a page, in black and white.

Players and Coaches Wanted for
Professional Women's Football Team

In June 1971, the advertisement appeared on page 34 of the *Toledo Blade*, in the sports section, camouflaged by ads for Firestone tires and Imperial Lanes all-you-can-bowl and the postings for the horses at Raceway Park.

Lee Hollar had just clocked out of her shift at the Libbey glass plant, a four-acre churning furnace north of downtown. After work she liked to read the *Blade* on her porch in the thick evening air. When she saw the ad, she had no words. She read it over again and again, in disbelief. The ad struck Hollar not as a sign of the times but another sign, a calling whose specificity hit her like music. Her entire life she had known she was different. She never paraded around in dresses or dated boys, like her three sisters had. And while she had joined many of her classmates on the volleyball court or the softball diamond, she had always wanted something more. She had always dreamed of being a football player.

Gloria Jimenez never thought she belonged in a beauty parlor, but for the daughter of migrant farm workers, the term *career path* didn't apply. At least cutting hair at the Northshore Salon beat picking tomatoes, which she still did on weekends to help the family make ends meet. Plus she could gab the day away with her pal Dorothy Parma, who one day showed her an advertisement for a women's football team. Having grown up with nine brothers and sisters, it was easy to imagine, hitting, tackling, bashing. *Now that's where I belong,* Jimenez thought.

One of eleven children, Pam Schwartz had grown up on Toledo's east side, where the air smelled of burning oil from the refinery and tomatoes from the Hunt's packing plant. With four brothers and six sisters, Schwartz learned to eat fast, like a pup at feeding time. Get what you can, and get it quick. When she saw the ad in the *Blade,* she could hear the world shout at her like a playground dare: *I'll bet you can't do that.*

Davelyn Burrows was thirty-four and worked at Frank's Nursery transplanting trees and stacking bags of mulch and feed. Her six-foot, two-inch frame carried 220 pounds. *Finally,* she thought, after reading the advertisement, *a shot in a sport she was built to play.*

The Skiles sisters, Diane and Debbie, grew up in Genoa, in a foundationless house their father had built with materials he'd found. Part Shawnee, he'd raised his twin daughters to ignore what people said you were supposed to do and follow the spirit that flows in your veins. They never owned a TV, never got the message that women were not supposed to play football. When the sisters heard the call for female football players, they didn't think twice. They had spent their autumns in the prairie behind their makeshift ranch doing what every girl presumably did: playing football.

Over the next nine years, more than eighty women answered the call in Toledo. They would practice on an abandoned lot west of downtown and play games in stadiums across the country. In dank locker rooms and torn-up football fields, clad in armor of plastic and pads and athletic tape, they would forge a sisterhood that would last the rest of their lives and find meaning in transforming into football players at a time when the culture around them was also changing. In the tumultuous decade that followed, the Toledo Troopers would not only prove that women could compete in a traditionally male-dominated sport but also they would define what it means to be a champion.

And so before the decade of dominance, before protests and the lobbyists, before the debates and the amendments, before the marches and the mandates, there was only an obscure advertisement in an obscure corner of the heartland and the women who answered it.

It was the birth certificate of the winningest team in football history.

PART I

CHAPTER 1

THE GREAT BLACK SWAMP

For centuries, geology, climate, and westward expansion conspired to create a region nobody wanted. The flat, unclassifiable town with dubious origins was born nameless and then grew into a surly adolescent only to endure a nasty custody battle between irreconcilable parents. It lived with a chip on its shoulder, a middle child that did not get along well with others. It had its heroes, those industry barons who amassed empires on the mantle of manufacturing, men whose promises foresaw into the future just distant enough to forge lasting myths of the riches men were capable of acquiring. It was the geologic center of the Midwest—Toledo, Ohio. A circle drawn with the Glass Capital at its epicenter encompassed New York to the east, the Great Plains to the west, the upper Great Lakes to the north, and the Ohio-Mississippi confluence to the south. Wider still, the forgotten city was literally the crossroads of the country: Build a road from Boston to San Francisco, and another from Sault Ste. Marie to Miami, and they'll intersect in Toledo at the I-90 and I-75 junction.

In the crosshairs evolved an everytown and a nothingtown, a region renowned for its obscurity. As though perpetually on the cusp, the city was neither this nor that. It was a town of wannabes fine with who they were. City yokels and urban bumpkins. The place itself was the butt of the joke. A region whose name had no clear derivative, and where the river flows backward. A patch of the map overlooked by the burning petrochemical-scented giants expanding around it. If Chicago was the second city, Toledo was the hundred-and-second city.

When the glaciers that covered the Midwest receded, they left behind the Great Lakes and a wetland known as the Great Black Swamp, a flat marshland that resisted settlement but for itinerant Native American tribes. In 1615, the Europeans established routes up the St. Lawrence and into the Great Lakes, and the gradual commerce of fur trading along Lake Erie and the Maumee River gave rise to sporadic settlement. The swamp wasn't exactly home to the Erie and Wyandotte, but they abandoned the region when the Iroquois took over in the Beaver Wars and began a peaceable relationship with the European invaders. The global conflict between the French and British in the eighteenth century created fissures in the uneasy frontier alliances. By the time the United States came into its own, the French had chosen to retreat from the Maumee River and regroup into their northern holdings. When Great Britain and the young United States divided up the territory, there were no Native Americans at the table. Under the Western Confederacy, the Natives stood their ground, and President George Washington ordered the frontier Revolutionary War general Anthony Wayne to confront them. With God on his side, and superior weaponry, "Mad Anthony" routed the Native Americans at the Battle of Fallen Timbers, named after the trees that had been tackled by a recent storm. Eight years later, Ohio, the birthplace of football, was born.

It wouldn't be for another generation, and the advent of canal-digging technology, that the region would grow populous enough to gain a commercial identity. Settlers named the swamp settlement after its denizens: Frogtown. At some point in the next century, common courtesy dictated a different moniker, and, for reasons unknown, a new name evolved. It wasn't named after a person. It wasn't named after an explorer, fur trapper, or general. Nor has the name any roots in Native American culture, language, or geography. Some credit Washington Irving's brother, who boasted receiving letters from his famous kin traveling in Spain of all places. Others say it was christened by a popular merchant who liked the sound of it. People went about their business unsure of what to call one another. Over time, multiple towns along the Maumee River became known collectively as the Toledo Strip.

The Strip was just that, a swath of land ten miles wide extending from Lake Erie to the western border of the state on a straight plain, like skin under a bandage. Slipshod surveying soon led to disputes about the border between Ohio and the young upstart territory to the north called Michigan. As boomtowns along canal routes sprouted up, Michigan feared being left behind. Its brash young governor argued that his reckoning of the swamp was as valid as any other, and he claimed custody of Toledo by threatening to throw anyone who abided by Ohio laws in jail for five years hard labor. The Ohioans pushed back—but not on account of their own claim to a precious stake of hot swampland. They just didn't like being told what to do. A Michigan militia ambushed an Ohio survey party and attempted to arrest them for illegal trespassing. Three Ohio boundary commissioners, including Colonel Sebried Dodge, escaped in the standoff. Shots were fired in the incident known as the Battle of Phillips Corners. Although there were no casualties, the event was hyped as the Toledo War. President Andrew Jackson intervened and negotiated the treaty, giving Ohio full custody of Toledo, reasoning that Ohio was a state, and its electoral votes lay at stake, should the citizens view the ruling favorable. As a rather imaginative consolation that has confounded cartographers ever since, Michigan was given the Upper Peninsula. If football is any indicator, today half the population of the city of Toledo maintains allegiance to the State Up North.

With its wetland, lake-effect summertime humidity, the city grew, like a swamp. The Miami and Erie Canal, a 301-mile dredging that connected the Ohio River to the rest of the planet, attracted agricultural and manufacturing merchants. For a time, the town was dubbed Corn City. When larger steamboats hit bottom in rival harbor towns like

Manhattan and Tremainsville, the next wave carrying Polish and German immigrants chose the deeper port on the Toledo Strip. Throughout the mid-nineteenth century, more and more carriages trafficked the downtown streets, oriented not to the compass but to the river that ran a west-to-east diagonal, like a checkmark. Streets running parallel to the Maumee were named after the Great Lakes; streets running perpendicular, after the presidents. By the railroad revolution, Toledo had established schools, a telegraph network, gaslights, a sewer system, and buildings tall enough for elevators. The Strip was poised to become more than a stopover on the transcontinental grid. The Irish joined the wave of immigrants hired to construct canals. Between 1840 and 1870, the population of Toledo grew by a factor of ten. In 1867, Jesup Scott, an East Coaster by birth who made a fortune in real estate, had a vision. The editor of the *Toledo Blade*, Scott had tasted the power of suggestion. He published a pamphlet describing his revelation titled "Toledo: Future Great City of the World." By 1900, Scott predicted, Toledo would become the largest city in the United States.

The oracle would endure—not despite the festering swamp that was the landscape, but because of it. The marshland's by-product was a natural resource about to become inconceivably valuable. In 1888, Renaissance man Edward Drummond Libbey moved his father's glass manufacturing company from Massachusetts to Toledo to access its massive deposits of sand—quality sand. From the swamp, Libbey produced glass, and inventor Michael Owens created the machine that could blow it. The mechanized production of drinking glasses, bottles, and jars gave way to windows and windshields for the automobile. More markets opened under the umbrella of the glass industry, including insulation and fiberglass. Collectively, the economy spawned by the swamp would give Toledo yet another name: the Glass Capital. For the next century, Toledo mayors and dignitaries like *Toledo Blade* publisher Paul Block proudly stood on the mantle of the glass industry. In 1950, Block declared September 22 to be "Glass Day," pronouncing that "it was the most important day in the city's history. It marked Toledo as 'the glass center of the world,'" said Block, echoing Scott's grandiosity.

If there was a hyperbolic optimism expressed by dreamers Scott and Block, female pioneers worked in the here and now. Harriet Whitney, the first woman to teach in a Toledo school, made her history in a one-room log cabin on the extension of the Maumee called Mud Creek. Others like Pauline Perlmutter Steinem, the first female head of the board of education, supported suffrage efforts. She also passed along her activist spirit to her granddaughter Gloria.

Meanwhile, the resistance to women's advancement in the nineteenth century came from the highest platforms and farthest reaches. Women had their place, as expressed by Woodrow Wilson, who believed that women acting in men's traditional spheres was "ludicrous." After witnessing a suffrage rally, Wilson wrote that he gained "a whimsical delight at watching women speak in public." Women performing in roles of leadership was to him a joke.

Likewise, women playing sports inspired the same species of condescension and ridicule. In the 1896 Olympics in Athens, all 245 athletes from fourteen nations were men. Women were expected to lend their applause, not their athletic skills. The perception would continue into the twentieth century. In 1928, the *New York Times* reported that long-distance running for women was "too great a call on feminine strength." The Olympic officials believed that running would cause a woman's uterus to fall out. They banned women from running in any race longer than 200 meters. It wasn't until 1960 that women were allowed to run for 800 meters straight. The marathon, 1984.

* * *

In 1918, a twelve-story chimney rose from the western horizon like a burning lighthouse. The Overland Smokestack became the beacon of the city and its factories churning out the residuals of the automobile:

plastics, fiberglass, carburetors, windshields, mirrors, spark plugs. The hope embedded within the twentieth-century American Dream—that the masses, with nothing but the shirts on their backs from blighted counties or countries, could arrive, find work, and ultimately create a legacy—existed because of places like Toledo with its tent-pole industry sprawling enough to spread opportunity around. At the turn of the century, the city boasted the third-largest railway center as well as one of the largest inland ports in the country.

A mile west of the headquarters of these industries, Libbey engineered brick-lined neighborhoods of behemoth mansions, a fairy-tale village with carriage houses, servants' quarters, and cupolas from which you could see ocean liners steaming in from the bay. Across Monroe Street from his living room window, Libbey established a museum to showcase the history of art in glass. Some of his neighbors in the Old West End caught a whiff of the legacy phase of the dream, like Thomas DeVilbiss, who invented a gun that sprayed paint and pooled his riches into one of the largest endowments for a museum that would befit a future great city.

The production of the automobile became the roots of an economy empire that soon sustained four high schools, drawn in an arc around the river: Scott, Libbey, Waite, and Woodward, named after the men who shepherded the city into the twentieth century. DeVilbiss and Whitmer soon followed, their stairwells filled with second- and third-generation immigrants with no reason to look beyond the opportunities afforded by the engineering of freedom on four wheels.

During World War II, Toledo's factories ran ceaseless, three-shift days. The Willys plant was refitted to produce a four-wheel-drive door-less reconnaissance vehicle that would be used by every Allied country in the war. They called the eyesore a vehicle for Government Purpose—GP for short. Jeep, for shorter. The design of the vehicle bespoke the attitude of the people who made it: all square angles, feisty as a buzz saw, and durable as rock. It didn't care what it looked like, but it got the job done. In a nearly inconceivable feat of mechanical and social engineering, during the war years the Willys-Overland plant produced three hundred jeeps every day. The twenty-acre machine belching smoke and four-wheel-drive wagons never slept. At first, men filled the lines, while women took the jobs they left behind, such as mail carriers, surveyors, city managers, and other civil service positions. When more men shipped overseas, women didn't bat an eye on the assembly lines, stamping out the car that was the vehicular symbol of the Allies across both oceans.

The neighborhoods in the perimeter of the Overland Smokestack became the second and final destination for the great migration, the movement of hundreds of thousands of Blacks from the Jim Crow South, who first found jobs in Detroit and Cleveland, then continued an inward spiral to the Midwest's lowland center. They took up in the neighborhoods by the massive airline junction rail yards and sent their children to the schools named after the titans Libbey and Scott.

The postwar appetite of the Greatest Generation for the automobile kept the factories booming. While Detroit earned its moniker as the Motor City, Toledo saw its Overland factory unfold west into a massive industrial landscape painted with smokestacks against an orange horizon. The glass industry grew in lockstep, and a manufacturing center along I-75 morphed into a sprawling shimmering city unto itself known as the Toledo Complex, a term that could also describe the region's inferiority neurosis. Despite its competitive standing among automobile manufacturing giants, Toledo was overlooked in favor of the metropolises around it, and Jesup Scott's dream in the nineteenth century of a great city never caught up but was replaced by a different dream, one that gave rise to another Great Black Swamp global export.

* * *

The game was a century in the making, a sport cultivated in the petri dishes of recreation clubs, newly founded universities, and city athletics organizations, places for men to demonstrate physical prowess and compete against other clubs in an array of events: boxing, baseball, rugby. Princeton and Rutgers are credited with playing the first game known as football, but the makeshift rugby event would be unrecognizable as football to anyone born after the spectacle. The sport acquired the name *pigskin* because first-generation recreational equipment consisted of the inflated gallbladder of a pig. There was no line of scrimmage. No quarterback. No downs. No forward pass. These innovations would come later, at the turn of the century, as safety precautions for the game that took on the name *the gridiron*, echoing ancient gladiator brutality.

Among the legacies of the nineteenth-century dreamers like Scott stood one that could be drawn from the early days of organized sports through the twentieth century to the modern Super Bowl: An audience equaled profit. In autumn, school-session Saturdays brought out the student body, families, and spectators looking to fill time that a summer baseball game might kill. College leagues formed around the fall football season. Profit margins from ticket sales attracted the attention of university brass, mainly in the Midwest. At the turn of the century, tens of thousands of Toledoans paid to see a horse billed as the world's fastest run in a circle. The thoroughbred named Cresceus broke the world record for trotting the mile in an event billed as the Champion of Champions race, paving the way for Toledo's harness racing hub.

Crowds continued to gather to witness feats of athletic prowess, animal or human. In 1896, the presidents of seven Midwestern schools convened to christen their profiteering and came up with the Intercollegiate Conference of Faculty Representatives. The official name of the organization would remain for ninety years, until the conference incorporated itself as a nonprofit entity, in 1987, as the Big Ten.

As glass became the region's primary export, the sport known as football and its box office tagged along. Seen as a regional cultural export, the game didn't always sell. In 1902, the first Rose Bowl was staged, an exhibition as part of a parade in Pasadena, California. The

University of Michigan, emerging just north of Frogtown, squared off against Stanford. The game was so lopsided that the parade organizers gave up on football altogether in favor of ostrich races. It wouldn't be for another fourteen years before the Parade of Roses would pilot the staged violence again.

Others took a more adamant stance against the game, on ethical grounds. In 1905, at least eighteen men and boys were killed playing football, and scores more were seriously injured, not counting the untold others who sustained brain damage. Like a Roman Colosseum death match, the game was carnage. The only strategy was a slaughter called the Wedge. Imagine a group of young men in a formation like a spear charging headlong into another group in full sprint to stop them. There were no helmets or pads. Splattered blood and broken bones were common. Death came as a result of spinal cords fracturing or, in one case, a broken rib perforating the heart. The *Chicago Tribune* called the year 1905 college football's "death harvest."

Some demanded that the game's savagery be outlawed. Other clubs and universities already tied to profits apologized that the voluntary violence was an unfortunate cost of doing business. The president of the United States intervened. Teddy Roosevelt enjoyed the blood sport and demanded that a committee be formed to institute changes that would save the game. The next year, the meeting of more than sixty universities called itself the National Collegiate Athletic Association (NCAA), the organization formed principally to reduce football's body count.

The agenda item of supreme importance was a proposed rule change called a forward pass, a maneuver recently demonstrated by Walter Camp at Yale that had successfully stabilized his roster. Following the institution of the rule, a pioneer of the play emerged in northwest Ohio. The first collegiate legal forward pass was performed by Bradbury Robinson, born in Bellevue, Ohio, a train stop east of Toledo. A Norwegian student at Notre Dame named Knute Rockne made the pass a salient feature of his team's offense and then founded a summer camp at a gusty Black

Swamp beachhead on the lake, so Notre Dame players could develop the technique of launching a football accurately through the swirling air.

Certainly football had not inspired Jesup Scott's vision of greatness, but the high school that bore his name achieved preeminence when high school football became a national phenomenon. After dominating every team in the region, the Scott Bulldogs looked elsewhere, not only to play the game but to showcase Toledo's finest and to attract the all-important ticket-paying audience. The team traversed the continent by train, stopping off in Chicago, Kansas City, Los Angeles, San Francisco, Portland, and Seattle to clobber opponents. The term *barnstorming* gained currency in the early twentieth century to describe the distribution of theatrical performances or athletic events or campaign stops, in which a promoter secured a venue on short notice of the spectacle. After conquering the West Coast, the Bulldogs invaded Canada playing games in Vancouver, Banff, Medicine Hat, and Moose Jaw, Manitoba. The jewel of Toledo's high schools was crowned the best football team in the state in 1916, 1918, and 1919. Seeking even greater hype, in 1922 the Scott Bulldogs defeated a team from Corvallis, Oregon, 32–0, to become a national champion, as surmised by a growing circle of state athletic associations. The Bulldogs repeated the feat the next year, dispatching both Washington High School of Cedar Rapids, Iowa, 24–21, and Columbia Prep of Portland, Oregon, 20–17.

In fact, the only team in the country that could dethrone the champion from Toledo was another team from Toledo. Scott's primary rival among the city schools was Waite High School, named after Morrison Waite, swamp native and Chief Justice of the United States. Waite took the title in 1924, and again in 1932. The team played successive Fridays in Portland, Maine, and Portland, Oregon. As the train carrying the team crossed the continent, Toledo was cementing its claim as the cesspool from which a new, land-acquisition pastime was forming.

Professional football organizations soon followed. The Toledo Athletic Association formed a version of a football team and, in 1902, joined the

Ohio League, an aggregation of clubs from around the state including Akron, Canton, and Youngstown. The first professional forward pass was likely delivered in the Ohio League. In 1906, the same year the NCAA was formed, the Toledo Maroons played in ballparks and open fields of college campuses, and at Swayne Field on the corner of Monroe Street and Detroit Avenue. They didn't have to travel beyond Ohio's borders to find the best football teams in the world, including the Canton Bulldogs and their pan-athlete star Jim Thorpe, who led his team to three Ohio League championships.

By 1920, classes of able-bodied men no longer called to the front lines came of age on lines of scrimmage in Midwestern cities like Pittsburgh and Buffalo, when they applied for membership to play against the Maroons. The Ohio League expanded its brand to the American Professional Football Association, but by 1922 the name proved to be too much of a mouthful to compete with rival leagues. The Toledo Maroons' affiliative organization adopted something shorter. It dubbed itself the National Football League. To enhance brand recognition, the new league named Jim Thorpe as its first president.

That year, the first man to steal a million dollars did so, at the post office in Toledo, Ohio. Joe Urbaytis from the Polish neighborhood off La Grange Avenue proved that Toledoans could mastermind a heist of unprecedented proportions, ascend to the top of the Federal Bureau of Investigation's most-wanted list, and do hard time at the federal prison on Alcatraz Island.

For the more risk averse, money-making schemes presented themselves around large gatherings. In 1919, boxing promoter Tex Rickard chose Bay View Park on Summit Street north of downtown Toledo to hold the world heavyweight championship. Forty thousand paid to stand in 110-degree swampland to watch the challenger Jack Dempsey beat the tar out of the champion Jess Willard. Rickard took his profits from the slaughter to New York to finance a permanent venue for sporting events called Madison Square Garden.

Promoters like Rickard made killings drawing people out of their homes for any spectacle, no matter the gender. In 1931, forty thousand Toledoans came out to behold the opening of a bridge, one that was a prototype designed by the company that would unveil the Golden Gate six years later.

Soon after the High Level Bridge elevated the Toledo skyline, a promoter saw potential in making women the top billing in a football game. Dick Lazette, a former manager for the Toledo Mud Hens baseball team (so named for a forlorn Black Swamp pheasant), used the Bulldog model to stage full games between all-women teams. Sidebar: Lazette is also credited with inventing the baseball umpire's pocket broom. Annoyed by the cumbersome and unsightly full-size brooms behind every batter's box in America, the Toledo Mud Hens manager created a pocket-size version. Lazette's innovation caught on.

So did his brainstorm of women playing football. First, he recruited two Toledo legends to establish a brand. Herman "Bus" Metzger from national champion Scott and Tom Keefe from Central Catholic were high school football standouts in the NFL's nascent years. The *Toledo News-Bee* described Tom Keefe as the most outstanding gridder in Toledo's scholastic history. Knute Rockne watched Keefe play in an exhibition match against Notre Dame's junior varsity (JV). Rockne liked what he saw and convinced Keefe to sign with the Irish. That spring, Rockne's plane went down in a cornfield over Kansas, killing him and six others, so Keefe changed his mind and finished his career at Ohio State.

Lazette supplied the equipment for his all-women teams by raiding the Shank-Colby boys' league and convincing a local sporting goods distributor to sponsor the shoes. For two years, his games at Swayne Field attracted sizable crowds and made money. But many of those who came out did so to jeer and to protest. It was a double-edged sword, said Lazette. The more recognition they received nationally, the more complaints arrived in the mail. This time it wasn't the president of the United States who intervened, but his wife. First Lady Lou Henry Hoover wrote a scathing letter of rebuke, claiming that Lazette was "exploiting womanhood." The operation folded soon after. Women who wanted to hit would have to wait.

A few blocks away, a four-story, brown brick castle called Thomas DeVilbiss High School opened, joining the bedrock members of the Toledo city league. The boys from the western edge played their home games in the brick-and-mortar cathedral of Page Stadium and wore a distinctive orange and black to distinguish themselves from the primary-colored rivals.

Like the glass industry that sprouted from the natural resources of the swamp, so, too, football itself emerged to supply the regional demand. In 1941, the ball, a permutation of rugby's egg, was designed and developed and engineered at the Wilson Sporting Goods factory in Ada, due south of Toledo. More missile than sphere, the *prolate spheroid* design had a front and a back. Its laces became an essential trait of its function. The ten-thousand-square-foot aluminum-sided pole barn in Ada became the only factory in the world that exclusively manufactured footballs. Since 1955, every Wilson football placed on every tee in every game, college or pro, was manufactured, boxed, and shipped from the swamp to other cities seeking a professional football identity.

* * *

Over the next thirty years, weekend clashes between city-league titans DeVilbiss, Libbey, Scott, Waite, and Woodward became the greatest attraction for Toledo's Greatest Generation. The nuclear family powered by the automobile industry sent its sons to play the sport and its daughters to cheer them on. State and national titles became afterthoughts to the highest prize, the city-league championship, attended by tens of thousands each year on Thanksgiving Day.

Football redefined the region's future greatness, as concentric circles of the sport's pioneers were being drawn around the city. The state that prided itself as birthplace of presidents now claimed to be the cradle of coaches. The legendary Paul Brown, the owner of the Cleveland Browns and then the Cincinnati Bengals, was born in Norwalk, a Toledo outlier. John Heisman was born in Cleveland and started his coaching career close by at Oberlin College. Throughout the twentieth century, football came of age and television spread its gospel, and a line of others would follow, dreamers who grew up playing backyard football in the shadows of automotive plants, glass factories, and oil refineries. Jack Mollenkopf. Woody Hayes. Don Shula. Chuck Noll. Followed by a generation of names like Les Miles, Joe Tiller, or Jim Harbaugh and Urban Meyer, born seven months apart in the same Toledo hospital. The sport became a ladder, with rungs of white hash marks on a green field, under an overcast sky, from which men could climb from the swamp.

In the summer of 1971, a year before Title IX, it wasn't only men who conceived of climbing it.

CHAPTER 2

THE PROMOTER

Sid Friedman's white Cadillac DeVille announced the arrival of a man who saw the big picture. His overcoat was big, his fedora was big, his vision of a league of female football players was big. His former client, football star Jim Brown, was big, perhaps Cleveland's biggest. Friedman was the founder of the All-Star Theatrical Talent Agency, and he used newspapers and radio and television to promulgate his product: buzz. Brainstorms such as boxing matches, child dance troupes, and disco dance contests struck him from the blue, and he followed the scent of an audience wherever it would take him. He did not discriminate when it came to clients but tended toward women or events for which he could promote their sexuality. He was an advocate for the go-go dance community and trafficked along the line between beauty pageants, the nightclub, and the strip club. He was an organizer of the Miss Universe Pageant, believing the solar system and the Milky Way to be insufficient venues. To Friedman, if the dream wasn't big, it was no dream.

In November 1966, when Friedman read the news, his eyes grew wider still.

The two leagues that dominated football's landscape were merging: the National Football League (NFL), born down the road from Friedman, bringing with it four decades of regulated violence, pageantry, and veneration; and the American Football League (AFL), a collection of second-rate teams comprised of cast-off players playing in decrepit stadiums. Friedman's hero was the upstart AFL founder Lamar Hunt, for Hunt saw the big picture. He attracted fans with circus-like pomp: AFL games featured halftime concerts for B-list singers and dancers, marching bands, and, in some cases, literal circus acts with trained elephants, trapeze artists, and bedecked ringmasters. Hunt's AFL also expanded the role of the cheerleader—the once male-only fraternity spirit troupe—to the role of sideline female provocateur.

Friedman foresaw AFL's bolder, grungier version of the sport. At the time of the merger, football was witnessing stratospheric growth, fueled by the emergence of television. The value of Friedman's home-town Cleveland Browns, for instance, had skyrocketed over a fifteen-year period from $600,000 to $14 million, a 2,000 percent increase. Competition for the market share was surging. A Gallup poll revealed that football had overtaken baseball as the sport Americans preferred to watch. North of the border, two regional divisions of nine teams were joining forces to span the continent in the Canadian Football League (CFL). The United Football League (UFL), another contender for the growing football audience, had the previous year looked beyond international borders and rebranded itself as the Continental Football League (COFL), boasting two divisions, three countries, and seventeen teams, such as the Montreal Beavers and the Akron Vulcans. With Happy Chandler, the former head of Major League Baseball (MLB), at the helm, and bankable front office names like Jackie Robinson and Doak Walker, the COFL envisioned American football like the European version, a 365-days-a-year merry-go-round of staggered leagues.

Through the merger, the NFL was defending its turf, as well as running an end around antitrust laws. In 1966 Senators Everett Dirksen of Illinois and Russell Long of Louisiana (New Orleans was among the proposed expansion teams) introduced a bill that would protect the proposed league from monopoly charges. The senators argued in hearings that football was not interstate commerce; that the current arrangement was suicidal for the industry; and, to ensure fair competition among teams, that football must eradicate competition among leagues. The bill stalled in committee. Then Dirksen and Long attached a rider to the 1966 Investment Tax Credit bill that not only exempted the NFL from antitrust claims but established the NFL as a nonprofit entity. Friedman noted the merger defined the National Football League as a nontaxable organization. The bootlegged legislation launched the Super Bowl and set the course for the game born in Ohio to grow into the billion-dollar global economic, social, and cultural industrial complex it would become. As one writer put it, the merger effectively gave owners a license to print money. Yet at the time, few predicted its growth or its historical significance. While the first Super Bowl doubled the audience with a single kickoff, it would take three years before anyone decided to video-record the championship for posterity.

But Friedman saw it coming. And by his estimation, the new league was ignoring half the market. As he set out to stake his claim in the wide-open industry of spectator sports, he courted investors with a question:

"What's better than watching some beautiful women play football?"

* * *

"You're puttin' me on," said his first recruit.

It was Marion Motley, the Canton native and Cleveland legend who'd just been inducted in the Pro Football Hall of Fame. Motley was confused, thinking Friedman sought to play women against men.

Friedman made his case for his Women's Professional Football League (WPFL): In the first phase, he would create a sideshow at halftime events, in which audiences would witness the women's game. In an NFL contest that lasted three hours, actual football game play comprised only eleven minutes. There was the lag between plays, between possession changes, and between quarters, and, of course, there was halftime. With stratospheric television contracts like the kind the new NFL signed, Friedman wondered how those intermittent periods of football could be exploited. His answer could be traced back to his promotion of beauty pageants: "I think football fans are sick and tired of watching marching bands," Friedman said. "It's time for entertainment at halftime shows."

* * *

Once he created his base, he argued, the sideshow would become the main show. He hinted that the NFL would be involved, claiming he was in talks to hold exhibition games as halftime entertainment for four NFL teams—the Pittsburgh Steelers, the Philadelphia Eagles, the Buffalo Bills, and the Miami Dolphins—along with one Canadian team, the Toronto Argonauts. He said two NFL teams had agreed to showcase WPFL games: the New York Giants and the Detroit Lions.

Motley had spent the last thirteen years trying to get back in the game since blowing out his knee. He'd sought several coaching jobs, but after less experienced white coaches won positions he'd applied for, he got the picture. Coaching was no job for a Black man.

"It's time for something different," Friedman said.

Motley was listening.

* * *

In the spring of 1967, Kathrine Switzer was attacked by a male race official for running in the Boston Marathon. The photograph of Switzer being physically forced off the course by the race's co-director, Jock Semple, became an icon, and her story a casus belli for advocates of the Equal Rights Amendment. For Friedman, it was publicity he couldn't buy, and he used the momentum to promote women playing good ol'-fashioned American football. "Women play for keeps," he said in a press release.

He bristled at the notion of the "football widow": wives neglected by their husbands watching football on Sundays. "Women hate football because they can't pry their husbands away from the TV." The problem, in the showman's estimation, was marketing. "Do you know how many of these same women would join their husbands at it? We'd probably draw a larger audience than the game itself."

He began with four teams, kicking up interest in Cleveland, Pittsburgh, Toronto, and Detroit. The advertisement he paid for read *"Okay girls, here's your chance to be liberated. The rough and tumble football way."*

Interested women were to respond by mail or phone. He received dozens of applicants, as well as calls from men who thought the advertisement contained a typo. According to his initial roster, the football hopefuls ranged from 18 to 46 years old, and from 117 to 285 pounds. While they didn't all meet his beauty pageant standards, they could run, pass, and punt. And they could hit. Motley drew up plays and formations he'd run with the Browns years before, and the women took to the game. Motley was impressed. "You'll be surprised," he told a reporter that Friedman had lured to their practice field. "These women will kill you."

Friedman accepted more hopefuls than he needed, hypothesizing that he could increase the talent pool as well as solve the attrition problem. Next, he invented names. Cleveland would be the Daredevils. Detroit the Petticoats (later changed to the Demons). The Pittsburgh All-Stars (later Powderkegs). And the Canadian Belles.

By 1969, Friedman won the attention of a *Sports Illustrated* writer, who confirmed Friedman's vision. Friedman's WPFL had legitimate stars: Marcella Sanborn was dubbed "the Josephine Namath who is expected to put the league on the map." Sanborn could throw a pass 40 yards and punt 50.

Friedman reached out to former Cleveland showman Mike Douglas, now taping his variety program in a Philadelphia studio. In July 1969, Friedman brought Sanborn and a handful of Daredevils to the City of Brotherly Love to take the stage on *The Mike Douglas Show*. Running back Linda Rae Hodge confirmed that women could play: "It's just a wonderful feeling, to go all out. You feel invincible."

Friedman was keenly aware of the lesson of the NFL: By declaring that his organization was not for profit, he stood to maximize it. His bread and butter was billing the games as charity, then walking off with half the box. As a founder of the WPFL, he could determine his own value. He booked high school stadiums, placed promotional ads for the games in local newspapers and radio—and the games drew thousands of spectators. Often the games were held late Saturday afternoon or Saturday night, when there was no professional sports program to compete against. It's tempting to imagine Friedman measuring his success against the early years of the AFL. He imagined going coast to coast.

To achieve continental dominance, he would need a champion, a winner that fans would either get behind or root against. His hometown of Cleveland was the obvious choice. He had witnessed the popularity, and the value, of the Cleveland Browns skyrocket when Paul Brown won three championships in the '50s.

With the pieces of a champion coming together, and a vision of franchises in cities coast to coast, Friedman needed stepping-stones, rungs on the ladder his centerpiece team would climb to prominence.

He needed a patsy to kick around.

CHAPTER 3

THAT KIND OF CHARACTER

When the advertisement ran in the *Toledo Blade* in the summer of 1971, a Connecticut judge was mulling over a suit filed by a group of girls seeking equal opportunity to play sports. The judge rejected the complaint, ruling, "Athletic competition builds character in our boys. We do not need that kind of character in our girls, the women of tomorrow."

At the base of the conveyor belt on the floor of Edward Drummond Libbey's glass factory, Lee Hollar waited for a window to emerge. Hollar worked the bottom of the line, hoisting sheets of raw, soft glass and locking them to A-frame racks to cool. Storefront windows, windshields, skyscraper siding, all born of an industrial cauldron of pressure and heat. As the only woman at the white-hot center of the Glass Capital, Hollar absorbed the taunts of the men around her. *Shouldn't you be in the kitchen?* They laughed. *Must be that time of the month.* Hollar didn't flinch. She understood it was the way of things. It was a man's world, and she chose to work in the depths of it. Along the lines of the relentless, screaming machines, the discourse was exempt from the proprieties of civilian life. Launching a complaint about abuse was not her place. Besides, to whom would she complain?

She was the outlier, the anomaly. Among her three sisters, Hollar was the only one who didn't wear dresses, who didn't play with dolls, who didn't scream at the rock 'n' roll idols crooning on the radio. When she was twelve, her parents didn't like that she preferred to play in the streets with neighborhood boys. They didn't like her propensity for jeans, T-shirts, and sneakers. They didn't like the name their three other daughters called her: *tomboy*. They enrolled her in the Patricia Stevens Finishing School. After a six-week course on how to walk into a room, how to sit while wearing a dress, and how to move your hands while speaking, the instructors gave up. "She's not for us," they told Hollar's parents.

"I'm just not into the frilly shit," Hollar said.

The declaration confirmed what Hollar had known all along: *I am not like them*, she said. Her father understood. He allowed her to follow in his footsteps, into the garage. She learned to change oil, to replace brakes, and to reassemble an exhaust system. Her hands were calloused, her fingernails painted with dirt. Before her first year of high school, she and her father built an engine from the crankcase all the way to the cylinder head of a '56 Buick Special.

After she stacked tons of sheet glass for eight hours, Hollar played center field at night, under the lights. Detwiler Park, downriver from the factory, hosted men's, women's, and co-rec leagues. When games had finished, Hollar would remain to practice, for the joy of it, finding a fly ball rise above the lights of the refinery and tracking it to her glove, then shifting into the technique she had mastered and uncoiling a line drive, on one hop, into the catcher's mitt. She dreamed of throwing a football, like she used to when she was a girl in pickup games in the neighborhood sandlot.

* * *

In between first and second shifts at the factory, the *Toledo Blade* arrived. In 1971, the daily was the dominant media bar none. The map of the *Blade*'s reach stretched from Monroe, Michigan, to the Indiana border to Sandusky, Ohio, in the east and Lima in the south. It landed on the hundreds upon thousands of doorsteps in the city, and in small towns like Swanton and Port Clinton and Clyde. Unfolded, the paper was nearly a square yard, on durable bond paper averaging thirty pages. It was not only news of every kind but entertainment, advertising, and classifieds. The sports desk at the *Blade* ran a dozen writers deep. Their readers gobbled up stories of the major professional sports, especially the NFL and Major League Baseball, plus stories on the next tier: golf, boxing, tennis, bowling. With Toledo being a stepsister to Cleveland and Detroit, its newspaper's beat writers covered the professional teams for both markets: the Indians, Browns, Tigers, Lions. You could count on a story of Toledo's International Hockey League team the Hornets, as well as stories from Toledo's high school giants like Libbey, Whitmer, DeVilbiss, and Scott. The *Blade* was the medium in which Hollar followed Chuck Ealey and the University of Toledo's incredible three consecutive perfect seasons.

One day before heading to the fields Hollar sat down on her front porch to unwind in the breathable evening air. She unsnapped the rubber band from the *Blade* and found the sports pages. She couldn't believe the words she was reading. It was like a dream come true.

* * *

At the time of the Connecticut ruling, one in twenty-seven high school girls played sports. For university students, the number was lower. Lower still was the number of women after college who could be counted as athletes. Like Hollar, women who competed didn't mind that they were a minority, or that they weren't supposed to build that kind of character.

Deb Brzozka played volleyball in high school, albeit only through intramurals or gym class offered by the Catholic schools in which she was brought up. For Brzozka, the Girls Athletic Association (GAA) was the official-sounding organization that served girls who wanted to compete, like a designated bathroom or drinking fountain. Brzozka might find a page in a yearbook devoted to the GAA's activities as she would for clubs that sang or made pottery. The page may or may not have published the GAA's stated mission: to give female students the chance to participate in physical activity, like camping or going on bike rides. At the end of the volleyball season, Brzozka turned in her volleyball jersey only to pick out the same jersey for basketball. The season consisted of a single game against the other GAA team from her high school. Tetherball and four square were sanctioned sports under the GAA, whose moderators volunteered to give their time to organize games out of the goodness of their hearts. It was common for the GAA volunteer to double as the coach, the commissioner, and the referee. Crowds for GAA games were nonexistent. Waiting for her turn to enter the game, Brzozka looked around the gymnasium: *There is no one here*, she thought, as though girls competing in groups was not to be watched. Virtually no records were kept of statistics or scores or of events having taken place. Because why would you? And when the girls finished in the gymnasium doing their girl things, they were scooted along to make room for the boys and a committee of coaches and assistants to practice for the game on Friday night.

Pam Schwartz could never go all out. GAA volleyball felt like extended gym class. Participation was encouraged but not competition and winning. Keeping score was optional. The version of basketball she played forbade anyone from taking more than three dribbles in a row without passing. She felt as though she was on a leash, unlike the no-holds-barred games she played after church with the neighborhood boys, unlike the pad-popping physicality of her high school's football games. She knew there was something more to sports than the inhibited, quadrille-like experience of the GAA.

Schwartz had grown up with four brothers and six sisters, crammed in a house on the other side of the river, between the oil refinery and the Hunt's tomato-packing plant. On patches of green earth adjacent to the alley behind the house, the neighborhood kids convened. A caste system formed as it did at church, with the boys at the top, dictating teams, rules, lineups. As arguments broke out over the relative balance of teams, Schwartz waited her turn in the paltry shade of a chain-link fence. One day the game regressed into primitive, every-man-for-himself rugby: Schwartz jumped into the fray, desiring not to carry the ball but to use her height, her strength, and her wit. She grabbed hold of a boy by his shoulder, leveraged her weight, and buried him.

Sharing a bedroom with five sisters meant Schwartz could only shower on certain days. Dinnertime was a free-for-all; the last child at the table was left with the scraps. Same for laundry: a clean school uniform for Most Blessed Sacrament Elementary or Cardinal Stritch Catholic was up for grabs. After dinner the girls cleaned up while the boys huddled around the black-and-white television. One night her brothers told Schwartz to come look: There were *women football players*. They were watching Marcella Sanborn and Sid Friedman's Cleveland Daredevils on *The Mike Douglas Show*. Someone said the women looked funny, dressed in shoulder pads and football pants, trying to be like men. *They're not trying to be like men*, she thought. *They're trying to be football players.*

* * *

Instead of promoting girls' team sports, schools like Whitmer opened their doors for one-night showcases, featuring tumbling, jumping rope, or vaulting. Marsha Dobbins and Nanette Wolf performed a gymnastics routine at the event that promoted a healthy, feminine display of sports. It was called the Circus.

And then there were the uncounted. Many girls avoided the half-baked measures of the GAA. Earning a blue ribbon for tetherball did not inspire imaginations like the full-scale productions the boys enjoyed, nor was it enough to risk the stigma of being labeled different. As the judge ruled, the court or the field or the pitch wasn't a woman's place. Instead, they played in the margins, out of sight, in playgrounds and back alleys and overgrown city parks and country pastures. Jackie Allen played in the fields around her farmhouse out in Delta. In the spring, she played basketball and football in driveways or empty fields, like the one behind the Colony Theater. Observed from afar, there was little evidence suggesting that what Eunice White was doing had any significance. There were no coaches instructing, no assistants tracking progress, no referees judging, and no audience cheering. There were no seasons, no tournaments, no leagues, no statistics, no official games. Yet if a congregation of boys agreed to smash into one another on a vacant lot, that was where you would find White, spending endless summer afternoons playing the indigenous sport of tackle football.

These athletes, like Lynn Juress, hadn't considered football necessarily a gender-specific activity. It was the only sport Juress had ever played, in backyards in Jackson, Michigan. She'd also spent ten years of her life among men welding together torque converters in the Chrysler plant.

One of the designer footballs manufactured in the swamp featured bleached white leather, easier to see at night, under the lights. In 1945, the ball was used in an exhibition game between the Green Bay Packers and a team of all-star veterans. Nancy Erickson was nine years old, and she would remember the game for the rest of her life. Her uncle, an All-American who served in the navy, played in it, and after the game he gave her a scuffed white football autographed by both teams. The next day she was the most popular kid in school, showing off the football signed by champions. She kept the prize in her room, like a trophy for the sports she never had the opportunity to play. For Erickson, the ball was a treasure, a sign of the future.

But the best Erickson was offered was baseball, and her uncle found her a place on an all-women's baseball team in Kalamazoo. The Lassies had barnstormed the Midwest during the war, and the story of their league would be told in a movie years later, about a group of female baseball players and their curmudgeon coach. The title of the film, *A League of Their Own*, bespoke the desire of women like Erickson to carve out a place in a sport they weren't supposed to play. Over the next thirty years, she bounced around a string of teams in the Amateur Softball Association, the only organization to stage sports for girls in the open air. She amassed scores of trophies over the years but none as memorable as the autographed football. One day as she arrived at the Detwiler diamonds, her teammate Lee Hollar was discussing not the upcoming softball game but another sport, the one Erickson had been waiting thirty years to play.

"Well, it's about time," Erickson said.

Some felt disparity in other ways. Lora Jean Smalley had also played GAA volleyball and basketball at Whitmer. She won recognition as one of the best athletes in the school. She did not win a scholarship, like many boys received, but paid her own way at Ohio University in Athens, where she played club basketball. She also won the affections of a man who would watch her play on the hardcourt. After dating him for a few months, Smalley tried to break it off upon returning to campus for the winter semester. On a mild January night in the courtyard outside her Copeland Hall dormitory, Smalley attempted to sever ties. Her boyfriend told her if he couldn't have her, no one would. He pulled out a .22 caliber revolver he'd brought from home in Cleveland, raised it point-blank, and shot Smalley four times.

The first bullet hit her in the chest, the second in the mouth as she turned to run. The third struck her in the back, and the fourth in her neck. She collapsed in a pool of her blood, convinced she was dead.

She woke up in Sheltering Arms Hospital, where she would remain for weeks, enduring astonished looks from doctors and nurses at her incredible survival. The bullets had by some miracle avoided her vital organs or were slowed by her muscle structure working like Kevlar. The surgeons removed three slugs on the operating table, but the fourth round, the one that pierced the second vertebra in her neck, was fused into the bone. Extracting the lead would likely break her spinal cord. So the doctors left the bullet in place, where it would remain for the rest of her life.

For Smalley, the slug haunted her as a cruel memento. She marveled less at her recovery from four gunshot wounds than at the consequences facing the man who gave them to her. Her ex-boyfriend pleaded not guilty. During the pretrial hearings, a psychologist hired by the defendant's family testified that the man who unloaded four rounds into the woman breaking up with him was incapable of causing harm. The defendant told the judge he had no intention of killing her. Judge John Bolin allowed him to plead to a lesser charge, "shooting without malice." He was sentenced to one year in the county jail, four months of which he'd already served.

When Smalley read the *Blade*, the idea of suiting up in football armor came to her. She wasn't thinking of beauty pageants or go-go dancers. She wanted to hit someone.

CHAPTER 4

CHAOS

Bill Stout arrived home at five o'clock looking for good news. His *Toledo Blade* lay on his doorstep, where he could hear his children crying over the buzz of the window air conditioner unit. He swallowed, wiped the sweat from his forehead. Inside, chaos awaited. Two screaming children in diapers, a catalog of unpaid bills, and the emotional black hole of his marriage.

He had just lost his paycheck in a game of liars' poker. Each Thursday, the men who worked the lines assembling carburetors at the Tillotson factory on Berdan gathered in the break room to take one another's money. They measured manhood by the ability to bluff. It became a ritual, like the lottery, the men calling out numbers into the cigarette smoke, the stakes rising to the ceiling of the entire paycheck.

It wasn't the first time he'd lost everything. He had recently cleaned out his family's savings in secret to buy a horse he hoped would vault him to elite status at Raceway Park on Alexis Road, the showcase venue for harness trotters. All those nights at the track taught him that mere wagering ultimately led nowhere. No matter how well you know the horses, over time, odds will even out; there is no stay against losing as much as or more than winning. However, if he owned a horse, he could control one more variable of the equation. Standardbred owners, having

31

the inside dope on the field, came and went as they pleased, drove Cadillacs, and ate at Cousino's Steakhouse.

The scheme never panned out, despite Stout's insistence to his wife, Sue, that he hadn't stolen the money, he'd *invested* it, that, so to speak, the beans for which he'd exchanged their life savings were magic and would soon yield a golden egg. But the beans were not magic. The standardbred could muster only bottom-tier finishes, and bottom-tier finishers were not long for the industry. Stout couldn't cover a torrent of upkeep costs. His fantasy of pulling up to the owners' parking spaces at Raceway Park dissolved into the reality of relentless charges, a discolored horse that would not compete, and the hard truth that he was sunk in the worst form of unlucky. He soon sold the horse to the slaughterhouse.

* * *

Now they were behind on payments for the washer and dryer, for the house insurance, and the color console TV. Paltry as his paycheck was, for his forty hours sweeping the floor in the sweatbox of the carburetor factory, he had nothing to show, nothing to match the nickels Sue was saving to dig out of the holes he'd dug. Creditors called so often it'd become a nightly ritual to suffer the phone's intermittent metallic ring, until it stopped.

"Where's our money?" she asked point-blank.

"Next week," he told her. In his hands he held the newspaper, his only dopamine against impending doom. *"I'm due."*

That night Stout read stories about the Pentagon Papers, the over-turning of Muhammad Ali's draft evasion conviction, and the founding of the National Women's Political Caucus by a group that included Gloria Steinem, who'd grown up on the north side of town. He read the results from the harness races at Raceway Park, the payouts for the daily double, the trifecta, the perfecta. Confirming what he knew, for a moment, overtook the gut punch of his blown check.

Then he read the ad.

Players and Coaches Wanted for Professional Women's Football League

He didn't think much of the women's movement. His upbringing tended to the traditional, and, all things being equal, it was best that the sexes kept to their roles. After all, Toledo was not the vanguard of social change. It was not Woodstock. It was not the cutting edge of the civil rights movement or the antiwar movement. It had avoided the violent unrest of its Midwestern big sisters Detroit and Chicago. At the same time, when it came to his own interests, Stout was quick to rock the boat, to challenge accepted conventions. He had a soft spot for stories of standing up to the man. Regarding the civil rights and antiwar movements, he was deep down sympathetic, but he wasn't one to follow a crowd, no matter what it was chanting.

He folded up the paper into a bundle and threw it in the trash.

But the advertisement didn't let go. Perhaps it was the disastrous state of his household, collection agencies calling, no prospects on the horizon. Perhaps it was the game of football itself that called him, the thing he knew better than anything else, and the sound of the hit and the chaos he created came back to him.

* * *

It was what he was best at.

When he was a child his forte was disruption. His parents, Depression-era survivors, mandated absolute adherence to rules and tradition. Sunday service at the Episcopalian church was automatic, followed by a dinner that resembled a Norman Rockwell painting: His mother cooked a roast and delivered it to the head of the table, where his father sat, waiting to carve out measured portions to restless children.

However, if the parents demanded propriety, their second child defied it. He was short and stocky, a runt in comparison to his tall and lean older brother. From the beginning, Stout was not granted the privileges bestowed to the firstborn, and so became the terms of his upbringing. He was seldom satisfied, and he hoarded any advantage he could leverage. He was boisterous, rough-and-tumble. He would destroy the house playing ball, so his mother signed him up for sports, like basketball and football and baseball. She sent him away to church camp to give the boy an outlet for his restless energy. While he loved to play, he was often undersized. But he never backed down from physical contact and developed a chip on his shoulder, the consequence of suffering a childhood as the fat kid.

To his younger siblings, he was the consummate big brother. They were his audience, his fawning subjects. His little brother Mike looked up to him and sided with Stout in family squabbles. By the time he arrived at DeVilbiss High School, Stout had become the full-blown opposite version of his older brother and his father. He was the class cut-up, the jokester, the kid who flouted the rules and the authority while staying just inside them, except for a few notable occasions. One night, like many suburban myths, Bill convinced a teammate to take his family's Corvette for a joyride. The car wound up upside down off I-475, and Bill and his two friends were happy to escape with their lives.

DeVilbiss was one of the largest high schools in the city, drawing from the Old West End to Old Orchard a massive demographic of the American working class: sons and daughters of urban apartments, Jeep factory workers, Champion spark plug manufacturers, restaurant owners, university academics, real estate surveyors, and housing contractors erecting neighborhoods along Monroe Street, which ran northwest. Football Friday Night had its origins as Stout's generation came of age. Boys dreamed of suiting up in orange and white, charging under the Page Stadium lights to the roar of a packed house and beskirted girls waving pompoms.

Among his classmates, Stout was popular, a satirist whose brand of humor tended toward the off-color, if not altogether crude. As a student,

Stout worked the system. He could read the room and apply his wit toward getting around the toil of schoolwork instead of engaging. He was better than proficient if he had to be, and survived the day by street smarts until four o'clock, when football practice began.

Among the horde of white practice helmets glistening in the sun, Stout was hidden. He was a pug, short and barrel chested. When coach Dave Hardy sized him up, he thought, *Too small.* Then he saw the pug play. The kid had a motor, as though he bore a personal vendetta against the sad sack who lined up across from him. Next to an offensive guard or center, Stout looked out of place, diminutive. And then the snap, and Stout would best him with animal abandon. If he didn't whip them the first time, he popped back up and went at them again. He had a low center of gravity that he used to his advantage. It wasn't his skill and it wasn't his size, but something else Hardy saw. It seemed only a matter of time before Stout got the best of his opponent. He was not the blow-dried, Lassie-dog collie of the show, but the pit bull chosen for its particular skills should circumstances call for them.

Football called for them. Stout could have carried the ball, but a football team needed a certain character at an important position. The sport required a man to create chaos, to wreak havoc, to absorb the blow, to be the first to engage the enemy, the first to charge out of the surrounded garret. That man was called the off guard. Not only did the off guard absorb the tip of the spear, but he did so on every play. Some positions go several plays feeling little or no contact with the enemy. Ordinary linemen are occasionally spared the beating, depending on how certain schemes play out. Not the off guard. For all the unknowns of a football play, there is the certainty that the off guard will get pummeled or dish out a pummeling. If daylight was the open field, Stout's character was forged in the darkness of the line of scrimmage. At the moment of the snap, the off guard takes on the entire team at the point of attack, and at the whistle, the off guard is getting up off the ground, either on top of someone or underneath. During the years Stout played, the position gained a signifier more descriptive of its position on the face of the defense: the nose guard.

The boys of DeVilbiss like Stout were guided by legends like Bob Chappuis, who, after donning the orange and white, played at Michigan and was the runner-up for the Heisman Trophy, or Princeton half-back Dickie Kazmaier, who graced the cover of *Time* magazine as the Heisman winner in 1951. So when he stepped onto the field of Page Stadium, an austere Depression-era enclosure of red brick, it was Bill Stout vs. the world. He proved not only that he could compete against the bigger guards and centers, but he could beat them with his cinder-block physique and a style of play that his teammates described as *mean*. On every play he was going to give you everything he had, his teammates said of him, plus a little bit more. He developed tricks from the short-handed arsenal he was given, such as using his face mask as a weapon, driving it like a Van Helsing stake into the chest of his victim. Within the explosion of collision, he could detect weakness and then pick it apart. He tormented. If a lineman betrayed any vulnerability, such as their weaker hand, or a tendency, let alone a limp or a bandaged knee, Stout went after it. His priority was to abuse. He played with a devil in his eye, his teammates said. Stout was right at home doing the dirty work of blowing up plays, sacrificing his body for the team, and giving linemen more than they could handle. He would hit anyone standing, before the whistle blew the play dead. Opponents had to account for number 77, a junkyard dog without a chain. His team repeated as city champions his sophomore year, and in his junior year, Stout was recognized as the best defensive player on the team.

In his senior year, he added to his repertoire of techniques and perfected the timing to apply them. There were the standards, such as stepping on fingers, twisting ankles on the bottom of the pile, or throwing an uppercut into the gut of an occupied guard. Stout had a knack for knowing in what direction the referee was looking and maximizing his attack. He took pride in knocking players out of the game. Woundings were not uncommon in a sport whose rules encouraged head slapping. Later in games, after the field was torn up, Stout targeted the most clean-faced victim, lined up in front of him, and then lodged his hand inside the boy's face mask with a handful of rank DeVilbiss earth.

He also learned about pain. He'd had his shins kicked. His elbow hammered. Fingers jammed. Eyes gouged. Underneath the piles of bodies, Stout seemed to suffer perpetual sprains, whether the ankle, the knee, wrists. Getting the wind knocked out of you was a particular kind of torture you learned about only through experience. Stout learned to suffer pain, to navigate its threshold, and to bounce back after every beating.

His game featured something more than toughness. Running back Rick Salem went against Stout in practice and learned the lesson of beating Stout. One day Salem got away, leaving Stout in the dust. The next play Stout latched on and didn't let go, then body-slammed Salem to the turf to make a point: One pays a high price to get the best of Stout, and it makes no difference how long it takes, the repayment shall be extracted, with interest. *He would rather die than give in*, Salem said, as he watched Stout run roughshod over defenses, glad that number 77 was wearing orange and white.

In 1961, each win took on greater meaning, more chips in the pot. Stout's family followed his success like groupies. In the Page Stadium stands, they watched proudly as their son and brother owned the line of scrimmage. The DeVilbiss Tigers' defense was the best in the league. On a cool cloudless Thanksgiving Day, the Tigers played to a packed house for the city championship, the Shoe Bowl, and paraded off with the trophy.

The year belonged to him. All-city on a championship team. The anti-hero of his family's story. The alpha among his teammates. He'd found a place within the arena of a game and stretched the conventions to suit him. Football was a system this baby-faced buzz cut had dicked. The Shoe Bowl trophy, the proof in his hands. For his Tasmanian-devil record of destruction at nose guard, the *Toledo Blade* named him the best player in the city.

His success and hope for a career grew hand in hand. He'd watched his quarterback Danny Simrell win a scholarship to Toledo, where he landed a coaching job on the sidelines. His teammate Jim Detweiler ran fullback for the University of Michigan and would be drafted in the first NFL-AFL draft. Boys from Toledo could become Heisman winners. They could score touchdowns in the Ohio State–Michigan game. And they could forge a career trolling the sidelines of a football field.

Stout had had his share of tackles and sacks, but so did his teammates who benefited from other teams scheming away from the buzz saw in the middle of the field. Had there been statistics for humiliations, double teams, or obscene put-downs, Stout would be going Division I on a full ride. But for all the holy terror he was on the field, no scout could justify recommending him based on the raw numbers. Five feet, nine inches. One hundred ninety-five pounds. Numbers you couldn't get around. Players he bested were winning scholarships, while Stout earned only a tuition waver at the Mennonite college in Bluffton and an invitation to walk on at Kent State, a middling Mid-American Conference (MAC) outfit.

At Kent, talent was a dime a dozen. On the practice field, there were scores of players as good or better, and more would be lining up in the future. His antics weren't enough. At Kent he heard the faint echo that he had peaked, that a city championship was as good as it would get. He wasn't the leader in the huddle, the caged animal unleashed on underclassmen. He was replaceable. And as though it was a foregone conclusion, Stout knew early on his stint as a Golden Flash would not last. His plan B was to return to northwest Ohio, where he phoned the coaches at Bluffton College and came crawling back.

He had another reason to return to northwest Ohio. He'd begun dating Sue Guy, a classmate from DeVilbiss. She was fun-loving, game, a doting audience for his zig-when-they-zag attitude. She'd spend weekend nights with him in secret down in Bluffton. To Sue, he remained the pirate, the kid who refused to grow up. Once, his parents left the house for a week and forbade Stout to come home, except to mow the lawn. Bill and Sue and their friends spent the week at the house, leaving doors open and taking what they wanted from the refrigerator. Stout was not going to be like his parents. But he would honor his agreements, on his terms. At two thirty in the morning, hours before the family returned, Stout lit the lawn with the headlights of his Plymouth, fired up the lawn mower, and finished the job.

At Bluffton, he was out of his element. The incessant praying before and after practices and games was not his vibe. And he had no patience for the classroom, suffering lectures that had no bearing on his life. College was a con of someone else's design. He also harbored the notion of cutting out the middleman and trying out for the Detroit Lions, but the better bet was returning to Toledo, to his audience, to Sue.

Bill Stout and Sue Guy married in 1965, their wedding a prickly affair befitting Stout's iconoclastic bent. Sue's father demanded that the wedding be in a Catholic church; her sister promised never to speak to her again if it wasn't. But the old guard at the church didn't make it easy. The monsignor at St. Patrick's demanded that Stout undergo a full conversion, sign papers promising that his children would be raised in the Church, and swear off birth control. Stout was not one to take orders. Not by a teacher, not by a parent, not by the government, and not by a Catholic priest. It was the thing Sue both loved and hated about him. They would say their vows in the nearest Episcopal church, and if you didn't want to come, don't come.

His wedding in July symbolically ended his football-playing career. He was still a kid, he rationalized. He could answer the call if it ever came. Meanwhile, he would start a life. And, for a time, Stout and Sue held it together. He landed a job replenishing vending machines; she filed and mimeographed reports at the bank. After work, their lives revolved around sports. There was bowling, softball, the horse races. They spent nights sitting across from each other playing Foto-Electric Football, a board game using lights and diagrams strategically placed to determine the outcome of a play. Six months after they got married, Stout tried on a pair of shoes only to discover that his feet were a half size larger. A realization came over him: He was married, he was done with football, the prime of his life was behind him, and his body was still growing.

The first child took Sue's maiden name as his first name. The second took one from Stout's side. Guy and Stefanie. The stress of raising the two was a dose of reality on the young couple taking on the world with only a chip on their shoulder. When stocking Twinkies didn't bring in enough to cover the month, Stout landed a gig at Tillotson Carburetor, which featured a cigarette smoke–filled factory break room filled with factory employees, an audience that welcomed Stout's brand of swagger into its conversations about gambling odds. Stout bet the races and the spreads, a combination that accelerated the strain on his marriage. Meanwhile, Sue was stealing toilet paper from the bank, unsure if her husband would be bringing home any money at all.

* * *

Now he was in the wilderness. He was in the wrong place among the lowlifes in a factory break room. His house on Westbrook Drive, a stranger's house. His dream of a happy marriage, the once noble city now abandoned, eroded, and overgrown. His paycheck was gone on a bad beat.

The ad wouldn't let go. He had thrown it away, but it became a burning ember, a hazy dream of making a career in the area of his expertise. Like the action in Foto-Electric Football, the game existed in his mind, a fantasy, a dream. He'd always known his street smarts would one day find traction, like they had for some of his true-blooded teammates. Danny Simrell was a full-time coach at the university, his classmate Joe Johnson was the head at Bowsher High School. Stout believed he was at least their equal.

And like Friedman he had followed the stratospheric growth of the sport. Leagues were forming, football games were taking over every day of the week, and there was no telling how big the audience would grow. He'd seen football franchises emerge in middling Great Lakes cities like Buffalo and Green Bay to overtake the Detroits and Clevelands and Chicagos. Why not Toledo? And if the women's movement was for real, why not take a chance?

Like a gambler, he rearranged reality to suit his story: Was this the dope that would lead to the big hit?

His daughter was screaming in a high chair. His son was throwing the ball in the house like a previous version of himself. His wife was asking how they would pay the bills, and the phone was ringing.

Stout went to the kitchen, lifted the lid from the trash can, and fished the newspaper out.

CHAPTER 5

THE COMPROMISE

Sid Friedman talked fast.

The Women's Professional Football League (WPFL) was growing. "Women's libbers"—Friedman's term for the untapped demographic of players and fans—were spreading across the country. Cities were adopting franchises, just like the NFL. His league would "grow bigger than the men's game," he said, wearing a suit and holding court to a handful of hopefuls who showed up for the meeting at the Harley House Hotel, on the other side of the river.

Stout had arrived first, sporting a coat and tie. He took a seat by the door and watched as Friedman handed out mimeographed plans for the WPFL. Toledo would compete against the likes of New York, Los Angeles, and Dallas, all of which would be forming teams. Just look at the NFL, Friedman touted: Millions of people watched Super Bowl V. Thirty-second commercials during that game cost tens of thousands of dollars. Football for men started in Ohio, and in Ohio it would start for women. The WPFL was the start of something big.

To build his league, Friedman said, he needed more. More teams, more players, more coaches, more people, and, ultimately, more money. Friedman, who seemed perpetually on the move, announced that his league also required more owners. He had ground to cover. His ad had run in the *Columbus Dispatch*, the *Buffalo News*, the *Pittsburgh Post-Gazette*, in addition to the mainstays the *Plain Dealer* and the *Free Press*.

That was when he delivered the catch: The price of the Toledo franchise was three thousand dollars.

Two candidates walked out. Weighing the angles, Stout felt the urge to follow them, for he had no money to invest. But neither did he have a college degree or other prospects on the horizon. Certainly, getting in on the ground floor had appeal. A start-up league might be his break. It was a gamble, to be sure. The longer he sat, the more he felt as though the train had left the station, the wheels were in motion. He conjured up the feeling that attractive odds gave him, like a lucky break. Then he gave a quick study of the remaining candidate for the job: a six-four grizzly bear of a man who was as quiet as he was big, a poker face. Stout pegged him as a former player like himself.

* * *

Like Stout, Carl Hamilton wanted to get back in the game.

In the summer of 1964, Hamilton had just graduated from Glenville High School in Cleveland, and the last thing he wanted was to go back to school. Hamilton hated the classroom and could not face grinding out more time in courses even more difficult than the ones he'd barely escaped. On the other hand, the great unknown of the future seemed approachable through the door of the armed services. He had spoken to recruiters, who tended to find more luck among lower-income families and minorities. The recruiter told him the GI Bill would pay for college. He would return a hero, and the conflict in Southeast Asia would be swift and victorious. It was a bankable option, the way they put it, in a sea of unknowns. The army would never go out of business, and they were accepting applications.

Finding comfort in numbers, Hamilton rode with his Glenville football teammate and best friend Jerry Woodall down to the recruiter's office that summer. But as they signed up for boot camp in Fort Jackson, Hamilton was nervous. In most circumstances, speaking wasn't necessary. His six-four, 240-pound African American frame did the talking. Still, being administered a physical in a government office wasn't sitting well with him. They had him undress, they checked his eyes and his throat, stuck an instrument in his ear. And then they checked his blood pressure. The doctor shook his head and read the results. Hamilton's numbers jumped off the page as unacceptably high. His application to the army was rejected.

Hamilton's mother was alarmed. Perhaps it was the jolt of the abrupt change of course, but the following day she dragged him to another doctor, this time the family physician, for she knew there existed a history of strokes in the Hamilton family. She didn't want her son keeling over, on a battlefield or not. But now there was no poking or prodding. Just Dr. Richardson, who he'd known all his life, telling him that there was no sign of high blood pressure. He was perfectly healthy. He must have been nervous, Dr. Richardson said. If the army physicians had waited ten minutes for Hamilton to relax, he would've passed his physical exam and been on his way to Fort Jackson.

His only option now was the one he hated: going to school. If there was a silver lining, it included football. At Glenville, Hamilton had held his own on the defensive line by listening to coaches describing his helmet and face mask as a bull on his shoulders. *Look, a bull doesn't use his arms to tackle, he uses his head.* Hamilton used his helmet like a bull and won the attention of Bowling Green and Kent State. If nothing else, he had the size and athleticism on par with linemen in the Mid-American Conference. Instead of heading south to boot camp, Hamilton headed west to football camp at Bowling Green.

Woodall, on the other hand, left for Fort Jackson and then Vietnam. One week shy of serving a full tour, Woodall was with his platoon on patrol. Among the dozens of men to choose from, the sniper chose Woodall. The news of his death, and the heartbreaking timing of it, hit Hamilton hard. He knew that could've been him taking a sniper's bullet, but for a false high blood pressure test. It gave him perspective. Not long after, Hamilton's life took on a clear direction. He married his high school sweetheart, Judy, and committed to finishing what he started at Bowling Green. He kept growing, and despite his ho-hum posture toward the game, he was good at it. He learned to see where the play was going before the ball was snapped.

A yearning in him grew. The feeling of a crowded stadium about to let loose. The locker room was pure, undiluted excitement and energy. Never had it occurred to him that the feeling, all nausea and needles, was not gender specific. And the release was the daylight, the grass, the open field, the hit. At Bowling Green, he honed the technique he learned at Glenville. He didn't love the game so much as he purely loved defense. Stopping other men from doing what they were trying to do. Causing chaos. Putting a body on the opponent. Using his bull head. Wrapping up. Taking down.

He earned a reputation as a bull who would play through the whistle. He was sometimes flagged for unsportsmanlike conduct when he couldn't stop his momentum and annihilated a quarterback late. He was a train that had left the station, he said, and there was no stopping it.

Nor was there stopping the course to settle down with his family, which after graduation included a daughter and a son, and a job as a deputy sheriff at the courthouse in downtown Toledo. Not even an invitation from the up-and-coming Dallas Cowboys could pull him away from the life he understood to be a miraculous gift. He should be dead, like Woodall.

Football on Saturdays and Sundays worked on him, like the sheaf of a nerve. He became sensitive to the itch. There was nothing like the feel of a football field in autumn, its chill, the sound of pads popping. He considered coaching high school but knew that more schooling in the form of an education degree was an impossible route. And then, in June 1971, he read the same advertisement that Bill Stout pulled out of the trash.

* * *

The field of candidates was down to two, and Friedman kept talking.

He played politician: They both could have the job. "Co–head coaches," he suggested.

"Not a chance," Stout said. "I'll be in charge, or I walk." It wasn't a bluff, but he was trained in steely confrontation. He let his offer fill the room.

Hamilton folded, turned to leave. Friedman stepped in: "We can work this out," the salesman said. He adored Hamilton's experience, living on the defensive line at Bowling Green. A MAC school, a Division I school. Where Stout couldn't cut it.

Friedman conjured up a compromise: Stout would be the head coach. Hamilton, the defensive coordinator. As for the price tag, Friedman would work out the financing.

The handshake among the three men sealed the deal. Three men founded the Toledo franchise of the Women's Professional Football League. Stout, a white factory worker with a high school diploma, and Carl Hamilton, a Black sheriff's deputy and former MAC defensive tackle, would be coaches for the all-women Toledo Troopers.

Now they needed players.

CHAPTER 6

FIRST DOWN

On a steamy Saturday afternoon in July 1971, a group of women gathered on the Bancroft Street field, an expanse of dry grass kept by Gesu Church for the city's Catholic school league. The sky above the swamp was a horizon-to-horizon seasick-green haze. The heat hung heavy in the air in the late afternoon as the cars draining the factory parking lots buzzed by.

The women who drove to the tryout climbed out of their cars slowly, not wanting to stand alone. Lee Hollar came dressed to play: sweatshirt, tennis shoes, athletic shorts. Pam Schwartz had persuaded her mother to use the family car with a lie: *It's like a summer job*, she'd argued. *I'll get paid*. Others arrived in groups. Judy Verbosky hitched a ride with her GAA softball teammate Patsy Farrell and lied about where she was going. Verbosky had just finished her sophomore year at Rossford High School, across the river. Her mother and father were the ma and pa of Verbosky's Market, a stand-alone family-run butcher shop and general store established in 1926. Verbosky understood that she was expected to help run the grocery store, not play football. Plus there were not many girls in the St. Mary Magdalene Catholic Church community of Rossford suiting up in football pads. Best to endeavor the trial of sports anonymously.

Many of the women trying out had recently graduated from high school and played in the Detwiler summer softball leagues. A few were older, in their thirties. Some were married. Karen Kelly was a twenty-five-year-old mother of two who loved watching a new TV program called *Monday Night Football*, after a day of work decorating cakes. Her husband preferred that she not drive the car, so he dropped her off.

Some like Sheila Browne and a few of her softball teammates came as a group. Mary Jo Dobbins had seen the ad and tried to convince her friend Nanette Wolf to come out with her. The month before, Wolf had given birth to her first child, a son. She weighed her options and concluded that football might provide a suitable break from nursing a newborn. Jackie Allen drove from Swanton. She worked in an accountant's office and thought playing football would get her in shape and perhaps make her a few bucks on the side. Lora Jean Smalley had a bullet in her neck and the Virginia Slims jingle in her head: *You've come a long way, baby!* None had read *The Feminine Mystique* nor were any members of the National Organization for Women.

A balding man in a tie and a fedora framing his forehead like a halo welcomed each woman with a photocopied application. Sid Friedman introduced himself as "the temporary owner" of the team before bouncing around the legal end of the tryout. The salesman collected the forms, sizing up what he believed to be the talent among the tryouts. He announced that any payment the players and coaches received would be contingent on ticket sales. "Technically, you'll be professionals," he told them. "In the only league of its kind."

The form requested the player's vitals: age, height, weight, and marital status.

A woman with sunshine-blond hair pulled back by a newspaper rubber band stepped forward. Connie Miller surveyed the form. Under marital status, she wrote *single*. *It wasn't right,* Miller thought, the descriptor juxtaposed to her signature. *Miller* was the name of the man she had married, the man who had left her single when her daughter was born with myelomeningocele. For the four years her daughter was alive it was a name she loathed, a cursed signifier she did not have the money to change back. Just scribbling her name in the thick humid air, she broke out in a sweat.

Then came the liability waiver. Players assumed financial and psychological responsibility, should they sustain an injury while playing for Friedman's Women's Professional Football League. Before cruising off in his Cadillac to the Buffalo tryout, he handed the baton to the two men he did not call by name, but chirped that they were "the coaches."

Miller, scanning the gathering of women, counted thirty tryouts. She hadn't been in a classroom in six years, since graduating from the all-girls Catholic school, but she recognized the feeling: the first day of school.

* * *

The teacher stood in the center, a trash can of a physique, alongside his assistant, a hulking giant with a hangdog, no-nonsense gaze. The two men did not dwell on introductions but spoke in direct terms. "Women. Ladies—" He hesitated. "You will be expected to block, tackle, and hit. All of you will be playing by NFL rules. Like the men."

Verbosky couldn't keep a smile from her face. The sound of it—"*block, tackle, and hit*"—cast a spell and, paired with the unifying "*all of you,*" suggested a portal from isolation to something greater.

The hard, sun-caked field divided by faded lines of chalk and flanked by the H-shaped goalposts created a sense of order. Hamilton placed a single orange cone at 40 yards, and one at a time the women lined up and ran in the swampy air. Stout noted the times using the second hand on his watch—no 40-yard standard existed to measure them against, except each other—and then he underlined the names of those who ran under six seconds.

Next came the most fundamental football acts: catching and throwing. Hamilton lofted crossing routes to each woman at 20 yards. Verbosky brought the ball in easy, with flair even, knowing full well a tryout is a horse-and-pony show. She imitated Paul Warfield, holding the ball like a loaf of bread. Deb Brzozka betrayed zero experience with a football, how to hold your hands, how to turn your body to meet the ball. Likewise, many didn't have the knack for throwing something called a spiral, the smooth, spinning, missile-like beauty of a ball artfully thrown. And then Lee Hollar stepped up. At five-eleven she was among the tallest. And she was lean and long, like a swimmer. She picked up the ball, wrapped her fingers around the threads like an edge of plate glass, cocked, and fired a bullet back to the teacher.

Then they were ordered to run. Schwartz estimated that three times around the perimeter of the Gesu fields approximated a mile, but after stumbling through a lap under the relentless sun, Schwartz felt the weight of inertia. She had only known the sporadic sprinting of the basketball court, not the sustained grind of long distance. She and Burrows trailed the pack, wheezing alongside Bancroft and the traffic beside her. Other women slowed and stopped. Something in her kept her legs pushing over the dried-out grass, defying the pull to rest. Then she heard a voice spray from a passing car, *Get back in the kitchen!* as though her upbringing was calling her back. Schwartz didn't look back but kept her legs moving.

Not everyone was inspired by spite. Some were tentative, embarrassed to go all out. Dobbins sank back in the heat, unable to breathe. Smalley forever navigated the line between strength conditioning and a broken neck. Nanette Wolf barely made it back, dragging her body across the cones. She was pushed by something inside, she said. She was no phys ed student dogging it, forced into physical activity. She was there by choice, and she would finish what she started.

* * *

Before heading to Buffalo, Friedman had demanded that Stout keep a roster of at least thirty, giving special consideration to the pretty ones.

His Cleveland franchise was forty deep, as insurance against deserters. "Better to have too many than not enough."

In the parking lot Stout and Hamilton narrowed on a number, the fewest with which they could mold a team. Exchanging their notes, they spoke in the coded language of football: *Size up front. Speed. Athleticism.* In their speech they confirmed each other's imagination. The list would include offense, defense, and special teams. In a scheme like a Venn diagram, many of the players would play two ways. Some three ways. Conservative from the start, they decided better to have fewer strengths than many weaknesses.

The next afternoon, in the fading light of the parking lot, under the drone of summer cicadas, Bill Stout stood with his back to the sun, emulating the formal ritual of the high school cut. The women sat on the parking lot guardrail to hear the names of those who were welcome to come back to practice on Monday. Pam Schwartz. Patsy Farrell. Peggy Dauer. Lynn Juress. Debbie and Diane Skiles. Lora Jean Smalley. Like classroom attendance roll, the teacher called Jackie Allen and Sheila Browne and Connie Miller. He did not call Mary Jo Dobbins but did call her friend Nanette Wolf. He also called Lee Hollar, Deb Brzozka, and twelve others, including Judy Verbosky, who had yet to legally drive a car.

Verbosky was thrilled to hear her name but kept the news a secret. After Karen Kelly made the team, her husband agreed to drive her to practice, but only if she hid in the back seat until they cleared the neighborhood, so no one would see her in shoulder pads.

All there was to start was a list of names. They had no pads, no helmets, no jerseys, no colors, no field to call a home. They also had no certainty that they had what it takes to be football players.

* * *

When Stout insisted on keeping a team of only twenty-five players, Friedman shrugged. "Suit yourself," Friedman told him. A lower payroll was just as well. Friedman, the constant moving target, didn't ask for their names or the paperwork. "You keep it," he said. "You're the coach. You're in charge of the Toledo Troopers. Your first game is in three weeks."

Friedman called it a scrimmage. "A preseason game. Just like NFL." The team should have plenty of time to prepare. And about the equipment, Friedman only had to close the deal with a local Pop Warner league from which he was copping helmets and pads, and the gear would be on its way.

* * *

To Lee Hollar, arranging the afternoon into segments of football training bore the spark of novelty, the repetitions revealing the sport's DNA. The practice agenda consisted of walk-throughs, lessons in football 101. To the music of muscle cars roaring by, they repeated the regimen of the tryout: running, calisthenics, skill training, and running again. The penetrating velocity of a thrown football. The expanse of 10 yards, as viewed from the ground. The held-breath moment before the snap, holding statue-still before the explosion. When a play starts and ends. Hollar learned a new language. The ready position. The set position. The neutral zone. Linemen learned what they could and couldn't do with their hands. The huddle itself was a chapter, an arrangement as formal as a wedding photograph: 10 yards behind the line, the center, the bride-groom, flanked by the tackles, guards, and ends. The backs to each side. And Hollar at the front, calling the shot.

The shot she would call required understanding of basic formation anatomy. Backs were assigned numbers: Quarterback number one. Full-back number two. Halfback number three. The gaps between the linemen on the left side were odd-numbered. Even-numbered to the right. When Hollar called the 33, for instance, Verbosky was to take the handoff and explode into the hole between Schwartz and Farrell.

The coach seemed agitated by the pseudo practices, wanting to instruct his expertise in chaos. When another day went by without pads and helmets, Stout administered a lesson on the most fundamental act of the football play: the snap. Hollar at quarterback, Sheila Browne at center. He couldn't resist the joke of delivering a baby, but it fell flat; Hollar found nothing funny in the exchange of the football. The proper snap of a football between players was a sleight of hand, with force. One player delivered the blow and the other absorbed it, puzzle pieces snapping together. As for handoffs, Hollar and Verbosky's courtesy frustrated Stout. So he did what he could without equipment. He took the ball and slammed it into Verbosky's gut. The two stood for a moment, connected by pigskin. "That's how you handle a football!"

* * *

The helmets and pads and jerseys never came. Friedman figured it would save money to have the team pick up their gear in Cleveland on the way to the game against the Buffalo All-Stars. He had secured a stadium in Roaring Spring, a sleepy one-school town six hours away in the hills of central Pennsylvania.

On September 11, 1971, twenty-four strangers boarded a coach bus with only a vague notion of where they were going, and vaguer still what would happen when they got there. They had no equipment, and they had no Verbosky, who couldn't lie her way around being away from the family store for two days.

"Beats flying," Stout said, referring to the 727 that went down in Alaska and killed everyone on board the week before. Hamilton told him there was nothing anyone could do to get him to set foot on an airplane.

When the bus rolled into its destination somewhere in the Pennsylvania prairie, Hollar was astonished at what she saw: cars lining the parking lot. *What's going on here?*, she thought. She took a deep breath. Friedman had secured Central High Stadium in Roaring Spring and had promoted the game in the newspapers and on the radio. Patsy Farrell said there must be a thousand people come to watch. They filled the stands and stood along the fencing surrounding the track. Friedman had talked a big game when describing the sport's popularity, and now he was delivering. In the locker room, Hollar could sense the size of the crowd, chanting, awaiting their entrance. This was no GAA event, no Detwiler softball game attended by a scattering of family. There were actual people, in the stands, who had come to see her play a game she had never played. On a field with chalked lines, in a stadium with a scoreboard and a committee of referees.

In the locker room the equipment was waiting. Hollar tore open a box and distributed the presents: White helmets, white pants. White plastic shoulder pads. White jerseys. White mouth guards. It was the point of no return, the reveal of the bride in lily white. Hollar rifled through the gear, searching for the proper sizes. The helmets were identical, glossy cue balls with the double-bar face mask bolted on both sides. The pants included a pad above the knee, the thigh, the tailbone, and a slot on each side for pads to cover the hips. Farrell discovered the tailbone pad and deduced that it belonged in the front. To the untrained eye, shoulder pads were also reversible. Pulling her shoulder pads on like a sweater, lacing them up tight, Jackie Allen felt the urge of a football player. Wrapped in armor, her first inclination was to hit something. The second was to hit it again, harder. Her fists bound in tape, her cleats echoing on concrete like talons.

The mouth guard was a final coronation, a hard C-ring of universal size that fit no one, its hard plastic drawing blood from their cheeks and gums. It hurt to wear, made breathing difficult and intelligible speech impossible, but Hollar coveted it because biting down inspired thoughts of the violence she was about to experience, collisions that would penetrate the body and remove teeth. A moment ago she was on a bus in the middle of nowhere. Now she was putting on football pads for the first time. Throw in the packed stadium she could hear like a nearby falls, and a chaotic panic set in. She became nauseous. In the locker room mirror, she saw a woman she had never seen looking back at her, all dolled up. But the pads felt good, the helmet snapped tight, and in a glance, she began to see herself.

The women gathered at the threshold, remaining close, like pack animals. The feeling was pure thrill, following their coaches, walking out of the tunnel into the daylight, the crowd cheering, the public-address announcer echoing the voice of God.

* * *

The women in pristine white broke huddle with a mismatched clap and wandered to the line of scrimmage. Sheila Browne looked down at the ball, then back at Hollar. "You ready for this?" she asked. Hollar mumbled something about not going back.

The crash at the snap was instantaneous. The All-Star line smashed through like a no-knock raid. The nose guard knocked Browne into the backfield. Hollar crumpled, felt the weight of a pile of human bodies and the taste of grass. A whistle stopped the violence but only until the next snap. On third down Hollar managed to deliver the ball to Dauer, who took the onslaught. On the sideline Browne wasn't embarrassed to ask: *Are they allowed to do that?*

They learned the only way, the hard way. The All-Stars were apt teachers, having played the previous season as well as the previous week against the Canadian Belles, Friedman's Toronto outfit, and demonstrated a baseline understanding of the rules of engagement. They knew how to line up. They knew both how to block and how to avoid one. They were experienced at the game's rhythm and understood that their obligations included the infliction of physical pain. Buffalo was also better equipped. They wore uniforms that fit, and the players showed off an array of additional wraps and bands and pads, each a layer of confidence heading into the hit. They knew how to pace themselves in full pads. On the Trooper side, the relentless beat of the game and hauling the payload of the helmet, shoulder pads, and wrong-size pants through the thick Appalachian grass wore the players down.

The All-Stars also knew how to run in the direction of the end zone, which was more than the Troopers could say. In the third quarter Peggy Dauer picked up a fumble and, Jim Marshall–like, ran the wrong way. Farrell tracked her down before she made it to the end zone and righted the course. It was all Dauer could do to make it back to the line of scrimmage, stumbling across the acreage of Pennsylvania countryside for a net gain of a yard.

Hamilton, standing next to Stout, put it bluntly: "They don't know jack shit," he said.

Stout shook his head. His team was the five-ten off guard getting bullied by the Division I–bound center. Stout blamed Friedman for the debacle, the cut-rate equipment, the lack of organization, the lack of detail. *Stay low!* he commanded, searching for mental cues on the fly to describe what he saw. The assemblage showed no regard for nuance or for specialization of positions. Instead, wisdom came from gravity, and keeping balance. The line of Schwartz and Burrows and Browne showed a learning curve: They began to leverage if only to avoid the torture of getting back up. They began hitting, but without technique or timing, like bar-fight drunks.

Desperate for action, Stout attempted to improvise a screen pass to counter the relentless blitz. Hollar looked confused: *What screen?*

The final score was 40–0, a mere footnote to the brutal lesson of the line of scrimmage.

That night in the hotel in Altoona, the women suffered the aftermath. They were beaten, battered, bruised. They made cold presses with plastic bags and ice from the machines. They groaned, wobbling and limping about. At one point, Delores Anderson collapsed. Her teammates revived her with cold water, a candy bar, and fresh air. "Well, now we know," Dauer said.

"Know what?" said Anderson.

"The feeling of getting the shit beat out of you."

* * *

At the hotel in Altoona, Stout and Hamilton divided the duties. They would need to specialize their coaching. Stout would handle the skill positions, the backs and wide receivers. They would bring in assistants: Jim Wright, a former lineman, would teach the offensive line. They would also need a trainer, a manager, a showrunner to wrap ankles, repair equipment, troubleshoot. Stout thought of calling his brother Mike. This time he wouldn't be asking for money.

The bus ride home was quiet, a Sunday. The women dozed off, their movements igniting a deadening pain that told the story of each bump and bruise. Hollar sat awake, now fully returned from the transformation, and recalled the game like a movie. She saw the missed blocks, the unfinished tackles. The wide-open field waiting to be attacked. The team was awful, she concluded. She climbed out of her seat, found Stout staring out the window.

"Coach," she said. "When's next game?"

CHAPTER 7

THEY'RE FOOTBALL PLAYERS

In the fall of 1971, Gloria Steinem, who had graduated from Toledo's Waite High School on the east side, published the first issue of *Ms.* magazine. The cover featured an illustration of a woman with several arms holding items representative of her work: a telephone, a typewriter, a steering wheel, a skillet, and a garden rake, marching across a rolling field of green. She was not carrying a football. But as Steinem prepared to launch her journal of women's empowerment, sixteen-year-old Judy Verbosky was lacing up shoulder pads and snapping on a football helmet in Steinem's hometown in preparation for the Troopers' first official football game.

Verbosky was familiar with the tools representing women's work, spending nights and weekends at her family's general store. She stocked, she cleaned, she landscaped, she kept inventory. She had grown early; with her shag sandy-blond hair and a confident five-foot, five-inch frame, she walked like a grown woman. Her parents told her she could be whatever she wanted to be. Still, she was afraid to tell them where she was headed. Her softball teammate Patsy Farrell had her equipment waiting for her in the trunk of her car. Now on the Gesu practice field, she stood in shoulder pads and a helmet as her coaches Stout and Hamilton set the course of action.

"From this point forward, we are demanding two things," Carl Hamilton preached. "One. You have to have desire. Two. You have to tackle. I don't care who you are. If you don't do these, then you might as well go home right now."

By *desire*, Hamilton meant conditioning. If the team of women were to have a chance on a football field, each player, each link in the chain, must be tempered like steel. They would need to withstand ill-fitting uniforms, the unmanicured grasslands of Friedman's venues, and the grind of the line of scrimmage from the first play to the last.

They began with the mile, followed by 40-yard dashes, followed by seven-second sprints, the average life span between snap and whistle. Then they ran the mile again. And they ran fully loaded in pads held together by ragged T-shirts.

They performed military-style calisthenics, in formation. Jumping jacks. Sit-ups. Leg lifts. It was a chicken-egg question: In order to have desire, the body must demonstrate endurance. Or was it the reverse? After getting their asses handed to them in Pennsylvania, the Troopers answered with the surest return on their investment: sweat.

At dusk, swampland mosquitoes swarmed the field, creating motivation. "If you keep moving," said Hamilton, "you won't be eaten alive."

One more, came the mantra from Stout, delivered flatly, automatic. He ordered *One more* at the end of each drill, finding the limit and then adding a rep for good measure. After a seven-second sprint, a recruit named Marilyn Robinson stooped over, wheezing. She pulled her face mask up and heaved. She fell to a knee, crying. Her teammates knelt to console her. *One more*, the order came. A moment of hesitation drew a line between the coach and players. Hamilton gave Stout a look.

The nose guard pulled the whistle from his mouth. "They're football players."

* * *

The second order of business was hitting. Verbosky had watched the sport in her high school bleachers, but what she couldn't learn from afar was that hits were car crashes in miniature. "Hit me as hard as you can," Hamilton said to her, a yellow shield of foam and neoprene attached to his forearm. *All the way through*, as though the target floated three feet beyond the runner. She charged at him, discovering that she had more to give, as well as the hammerlike force of the shoulder armor. Verbosky fell on all fours, her lungs burning. *"My grandmother hits harder than that,"* Stout said. *"And she's dead."*

Hamilton explained the method as technical as a platform dive. Wide stance for balance. Chin up. Wrap up. And keep your feet moving. He repeated the mantra: *Hit. Low.*

The last drill of the night was a test, with one item. Win the leverage battle against Stout, and pass. The has-been nose guard hunched in the set position as each player, desperation in her eyes, lunged. Miller, an acrobat, understood, plunging her helmet into his gut, then pushing him back. Verbosky repeated. Then Allen. Schwartz. Burrows. They were getting it, the low explosion and drive. Brzozka, sapped of strength in the late-summer heat, threw her hands onto Stout's shoulder. By instinct he slapped them aside. "Get back here and get your pads down!" Stout screamed.

Brzozka couldn't lower her head and shoulders at the point of contact. She sank her teeth into her mouth guard, squeezing shut the panic. She resisted diving in missile-like. "Pads down!" he screamed. "Or we'll be here all night!" When she got blown back again, the tears began.

"Hit low," he said, "and I'll stop yelling."

When Brzozka went out for the team, she had nowhere to go. She was twenty years old and married, to a lieutenant in the National Guard who spent weekends as a soldier. She wanted to do something besides sitting at home and staring at the floor. She'd played in a few basketball games that her all-girls Catholic high school staged, but never on a sustained team, with a season. The experience was torture—the exhaustion, the humiliation. She felt sweet relief when the last drill ended in the waning light, only to have another feeling take hold: the anticipation for the next gathering of the women she called teammates to start.

* * *

When Jackie Allen was twelve, she ran away from a fight. Among her classmates Allen stood out because her grandmother was a beautician and her mother a seamstress. She had the finest clothes, hair, nails. One day she received a note that she was going to get beat up. Allen hid in the school bathroom while her attacker and a crowd gathered outside. A friend found her cowering in a stall. "They will never stop picking on you," she told Allen. "If you don't get out there and fight, I'll fight you right here." Terrified, Allen entered the circle, where she learned to strike first. She attacked, landing punch after punch until the bully was on the ground. Then she got on top and kept swinging.

Hamilton watched Allen strike first, throwing herself into the hit. She didn't bend around it, or push it aside, but went straight through, with demented eyes. "I've got a place for you," Hamilton told her.

The same principle held for carrying the ball. Against Buffalo, Peggy Dauer had given up yards to avoid contact, or at least eased her way into the defender's charge. Now she was being instructed to burst through tacklers, to invite the contact in order to explode to the other side. Dauer had never experienced a sanctioned hit while jumping rope or playing four square for the GAA. Now she was commanded to hurl her body, not just into others but through them. Now she was suited up in battle armor in the open air. Now she was tasting the hit for the first time, and it tasted good.

* * *

Hamilton designed a 5–3 formation, a crowded, box-stuffing, I-dare-you defensive alignment. Nose guard, two tackles, two ends, three line-backers, three blitzing corners. Living on the line at Bowling Green, Hamilton had seen giants even bigger than he torn apart by smaller, faster attackers. He put Connie Miller and Nanette Wolf as middle linebackers. Neither stood taller than five-three in cleats. Miller hadn't specialized in her sport but answered the call of whatever organization needed players. Her strengths would've shone on a gymnastics floor, had anyone bothered to direct her to a mat. On a flat surface she was a ninja, able to sprint, flip, and fly. Now she was a slashing cruiser among the churning battleships of the line. From the middle linebacker position, Miller began to see gaps, anticipate the movement of the play. She found purpose not in scoring but in havoc creation.

* * *

On the other corner of the field, Stout applied the lecture to the offensive line. To win the battle, an offensive lineman had to dominate. She had to blow off the ball, keep pads low, and drive. Squaring off against one another, the women came set, they held statue-still, then exploded into one another. Verbosky became accustomed to the unmistakable clap of plastic echoing over the field. Each took their turn, including the backs and backers. Wolf and Miller gave up twenty pounds to Burrows and Schwartz. Disparity didn't matter. Stout blew the whistle. Schwartz blew Wolf out of the picture, without mercy, and a nickname began to take root: *Nasty*.

They rehearsed a basic playbook, but the offensive practice equated to punishment. An automatic sentence of running was handed down for mental mistakes. If Schwartz came off the snap left when the play was right, she ran. If Lora Jean Smalley didn't beat her man to the block, she ran. If Verbosky missed her gap, she ran. Sunk in the three-point stance, Burrows waited in dull pain as Stout detected poor form. He kicked her fingers free from the dirt, toppling her to the ground.

"Line UP!" became the mantra for special teams. The choreography of kickoffs, punts, and field goals was pounded in by brute force repetition. Friedman differentiated his version of football from the men's game with a wrinkle of the extra point: 2 points for kicking, and 1 point for crossing the line with the ball.

Practice ended with a vocabulary lesson: the pop-up drill. A circle formed around two women lying on their backs, head to head, as though stargazing. On the ground, Hollar endured a moment of disorientation, alone, exposed. To her football was a catechism, and she was beginning to see the light. The moment she had set foot on the gridiron, Stout pegged her as a quarterback, and not just because she could throw the football 50 yards. An instinct blossomed; each new set of circumstances of play required focus on the task at hand, a higher level of consciousness. She'd watched unflashy, mistake-free field generals like Bart Starr or Johnny Unitas, and now emulated them. She understood that moxie wasn't learned but beaten into you, and when her turn at the pop-up drill came up, she hit the ground, looking into the green sky hoping to be the hitter. She heard the whistle, popped up, drove her shoulder into Dauer's waist, and brought her down. Then she trotted back in line, lifted her face mask, and spit.

After practice, the women sat for a moment in their cars in the last light of day, savoring a moment of rest. They could barely grip the steering wheel, their forearms shaking, and later, their cores drained of strength, they collapsed into their beds and fell into a deep coma. Like hunter-gatherers, they were toughening in their sleep. In the morning they woke rewarded, their bodies tight as a closed fist.

* * *

After the debacle in Pennsylvania, Stout sought to correct a fundamental flaw. Football teams rushed the open field en masse to marching bands playing fight songs and cheerleaders waving banners and face-painted fans cheering slogans. A team was united by its emblems, signifying its tradition and its turf. The colors gave meaning to land acquisition, elevated the endeavor of playing to a cause greater than the self. Against Buffalo, the women played in top-to-bottom white, anonymous and unconnected. If the women were to become a team, they would be bound by colors.

At Friedman's suggestion, Stout went down the list of city high school football programs, including his alma mater, looking for equipment. It was Start High School who called back. Their donations were game-worn but in suitable shape. The Spartans: forest green trimmed in white numbers. Helmets were not included, so Stout collected the white practice helmets, lined them up on the embankment wall in his driveway, and spray-painted each a glossy dark green. With automotive accent tape he added a double white stripe down the middle. As a finishing touch, he adorned the side with an emblem of transecting double *T*s.

On a cool September morning, the women who would animate the colors awaited a Buckeye charter at the Gesu Church parking lot. An early-fall cold snap blew through, the air near freezing. The women stayed sharp and warm by running through a basic set of plays and formations to dull the nerves. Hollar kept moving, running over the formations in her head: Odd numbers ran left, even right. Verbosky cleared herself to play, knowing she would return, like Cinderella, before midnight. They stuffed their helmets through the shoulder pads and grabbed the face masks as a handle, carrying their gear in a bundle, like a lunch pail. Nanette Wolf said goodbye to her husband and handed over her infant son, David, with a bottle and blanket. Then she climbed on the bus with the rest of her teammates.

For Verbosky, the bus ride bore mystery. She had no idea what she was getting herself into, besides being chum for Friedman's Cleveland Daredevils. On the three-hour jostle across Ohio cornfields she could sense a bond forming. Verbosky was one of twenty-four women, united by green and a higher power. When they arrived at the stadium in Carrollton, she walked tentatively on the concrete. The locker room, a doorless dank cell, crumbling and smelling of urine, served as another portal. Miller said it matched the sordid photographs from the Attica prison riots, which they had all seen the week before. They dressed quickly, having learned to protect themselves. Schwartz had dusted off elbow pads from volleyball.

Kelly brought ankle braces and knee pads. They would wait seven years before the invention of the sports bra; for now, they used Ace bandages wrapped around their chests.

Mike Stout, the new farmhand, waited outside with the medical kit, a toolbox with dividers for Band-Aids, compress bandages, braces, gauze, nail clippers, and tweezers. And rolls and rolls of athletic tape.

The turnout for the first official game for the Toledo Troopers did not live up to the mayhem of the exhibition against Buffalo. A smattering of family and Daredevil followers made the trip, a threshold of eyeballs in the home stands. And there were Friedman's Daredevils themselves, awaiting en masse, a platoon of red jerseys and white helmets, running plays and formations.

Hamilton knew that pile driver Marion Motley would be coaching the Daredevils, but surveying his first opponent he recognized a small world: Flanking the Hall of Famer were his assistants, his sons Ray and Phil, who had been Hamilton's teammates at Cleveland Glenville. The Motley brothers, Cleveland football royalty. Hamilton was squaring off against his superiors, as though at a class reunion, to measure their careers against one another.

* * *

"Make it personal," Hamilton said to a rapt circle before the kick.

Verbosky was absorbing the language of the sport, the mental cues that turn a civilian into a football player. She stood in a strange place, on a prairie hours from home, the grass between the hash marks chewed up and spit out by the high school game the night before. The referee was beckoning the players with his whistle for the coin toss, and standing on the other side of the field was an army of Daredevils in red. She did not channel her energy but exuded it, reacting to the moment. Jackie Allen and Pam Schwartz imagined applying the tackling lesson, now with referees and an audience, when it counted. Lee Hollar fought back the hiccups, her body physically ejecting the anxiety. Sheila Browne also felt the terror of the limelight. They were suited up, taped up, revved up. All caged energy seeking release.

Hamilton's dictum revealed the desperation: *"If I see anyone arm tackling, I'm gonna sit your ass on the bench!"*

The collective disorientation dissolved on the first possession. The Troopers broke huddle and trotted to the line in glorious new colors, like Cinderella transformed for the ball. Hollar took a clean snap and gave the ball to Verbosky, stumbling forward into the chaos of the line. She found room, purchase for her pounding legs. Browne and Diane Skiles and Schwartz heaved forward. Skiles gave up a hundred pounds to the Daredevil tackle, but Skiles was quicker, having only to maneuver to buy the running back time. Behind Burrows at guard, gaping holes formed. Hollar found rhythm alternating between Verbosky and Dauer. It was a crude machine, a basic engine with first-generation parts that sparked, coughed, and chugged. Deep in enemy territory, the Daredevils were exhausted. *One more*, Hollar said in the huddle. She took the snap, waited for Dauer and Verbosky to plunge, then followed them, a wall of green toppling forward into the end zone, the first Trooper touchdown.

No one knew what to do. They'd never practiced celebrating. The women mobbed Hollar out of pure joy, and that was what Verbosky remembered best. She had played on GAA teams, but never in helmets and pads, when what is at stake is not a certificate or a blue ribbon or a medal. It's the feeling of driving your opponent into the dirt and the unchained emotion of the women flying around her, on the sidelines and in the huddle and on the bus and in the dank fluorescent dungeon.

Verbosky remained on the field for defense, at safety. In the heat of battle, hitting became instinct. She awaited hungrily behind her teammates, decoding. She followed the carnage and flew to the ball, finishing off the work her teammates began.

In the first half, Hollar repeated the drive twice. With the addition of Verbosky, the offense had options and fresh legs. They crashed the putrid locker room like a house party at halftime, looking at one another in disbelief of a two-touchdown lead. The hiccups and butterflies were gone, replaced by euphoria, and a hunger for more hitting.

In the second act Hollar kept pounding. After the jab-cross of Verbosky and Dauer, the factory worker dropped back to pass, saw open field and a bright sky. She launched it over the middle, where Verbosky, running a deep cross, allowed the ball to float into her lap before tumbling down inside the 10-yard line. The touchdown on Hollar's bootleg into the open end zone seemed an afterthought to the truth of the drive. The game clock was irrelevant. They had only one mode of playing, which was blowing off the line, and repeat.

There was nothing to compare it to, Karen Kelly said. "Better than having children," she said.

* * *

To tell her parents, Verbosky would need a different comparison. On the ride home she planned her confession, not out of shame but pride. She wanted to share the experience, and the tiny news clipping proving it, but the words were lost, like the order of a football play exploding into chaos. She remembered following Burrows's green jersey blasting holes in front of her and driving into daylight. She remembered lining up wide, running the cross route, flying through enemy territory into the clear, and seeing the ball fly from Hollar's arm in the scrum like a rocket and soar over the field, and her legs carrying her to catch it. She remembered mud, the tattoos of cold dirt caked into hands and forearms.

"Football?" her father said. Followed by a torrent of questions. *"Who's on the team? Where do you play? Who's the coach? Who are your teammates? What do you know about playing football?"*

On Sunday they scrutinized the recap in the paper, which mentioned her touchdown, her name in black and white. Ma and Pa Verbosky were skeptical. When they said she could be anything she wanted to be, they didn't mean a football player.

"You can come see for yourself," the football player said.

* * *

Of all the places Friedman could've reserved for Toledo's first home game, a rematch with Buffalo, he chose Rossford High School's Bulldog Stadium, on the far east side, which sat less than a half a mile from Verbosky's Market. On Saturday night, Mrs. Verbosky left the store and dodged the headlights on Eagle Point Road to the stadium. Mr. Verbosky stayed behind, left to imagine what was taking place under the muffled echo of the PA announcer and the stadium lights glowing in the orange night.

What he didn't see was revenge, and a crowd of nearly two thousand people, drawn by a warm autumn Saturday. With over a month of training, and appetites whetted with the taste of victory, the Troopers attacked. They were leaner now. Tougher, like a sled dog hardened by toil. And they were playing to their hometown. Jackie Allen applied the method she'd learned against Cleveland, that is, to press. The first score, in the first professional football game held in Toledo in fifty years, was a safety. The line of Allen, Schwartz, Farrell, and Burrows blew up their counterparts while Miller and Wolf diagnosed one of the few plays the All-Stars ran, and shot the gaps into the backfield. Allen trapped the All-Stars running back in the end zone and didn't let go while the rest piled on.

Allen was proving herself as the Bill Stout of the Troopers. At off guard, she picked apart Buffalo's tendencies, a glance, a blink of an eye, and shot to the point of attack. To add to the pressure on the center, Allen's hands were quick as a mousetrap. Just one careless delivery, and number 83 turned organization into a scrum for the ball. The game was easy, Allen said, if you knew what was coming—and if you were quicker than the woman across from you. Off the field, Allen was a caricature of sweetness, greeting visitors to the office with a smile. On the football field she became a junkyard dog, shredding the woman across from her like survival depended on it.

The offense in front of Hollar ground up the field. The drive and the warm night wore down the resistance until Hollar simply followed Burrows into the end zone on a keeper. In Pennsylvania, Buffalo had played fundamental smashmouth football. Now it was the new-look green team serving it back to them.

Not many girls could say they scored a touchdown on their high school's football field. Judy Verbosky scored twice. She looked up into the stands and saw her mother, on her feet, cheering. There's nothing like crossing the plane of the goal line for a touchdown, Verbosky discovered. To carry or catch a football in sacred territory is an experience unequaled in the sports she played. It wasn't always beautiful, but it is the culmination of an orchestrated violence and grace on the part of many, a collaborative miracle. But seeing her mother in the stands was also momentary validation. Daughters could score touchdowns, too. As though to emphasize the point, Verbosky later dodged around the clogged line, then zigzagged back and forth for a 60-yard touchdown, but a holding penalty called the play back.

* * *

Verbosky repeated the performance in the rematch against Cleveland, this time on a cold windswept field of Waite High School, Gloria Steinem's alma mater. After the offensive line had pounded like a heavyweight hammering body blows, Hollar flipped to Verbosky sprinting outside in the clear. Motley's defense didn't know what hit them. The sixteen-year-old led her team of women back to the sidelines after the mob scene. Verbosky wanted to share the feeling. "You should get the ball," Verbosky told Dauer. The fullback shook her head, tapped her on the helmet. "We all got a job to do."

Hollar surprised the Daredevils with a new set of plays. She called for a trap, or the offense's answer to the blitzing linebacker. Now Schwartz broke from the line and barreled laterally toward the Daredevil defensive end to annihilate. "It was a free-for-all," she said. Dauer burst into the hole to meet the oncoming red linebacker. Never had the women been ordered to hit like this, not in basketball, not in softball, not in field hockey. Not in golf or tennis. And when there was no one left to hit, Schwartz and Dauer formed a police escort of blockers for Verbosky. They were methodical, relentless. They were not unstoppable, but to bring down the fullback with fresh legs running downhill, for example, required a decision on the part of a defender that took a toll. It was only a matter of time before Dauer got her chance to barrel-roll into the end zone.

On defense the green team played with a fearsome abandon that seemed against the rules. They did not anticipate the whistle ending the play but gang-tackled. Halftime score: 24–6.

* * *

When they'd been beaten inside and outside, Hollar went over the top. "They're daring me to throw it," Hollar told her coach in the locker room. With the lead, and the wind at her back, Hollar pulled back a handoff to a diving Juress, steadied her feet, and let fly a wobbly rocket that settled back to earth into Verbosky's hands in full sprint. She coolly trotted the rest of the way into the end zone.

Friedman wouldn't be bringing home a winner. In the end he was not a coach or general manager but a promoter, a spinmeister interested most in the bottom line. He'd brought in Hall of Fame names and booked appearances on TV shows. But on the cold Waite field, his outfit stood no chance against the green-and-white machine that seemed to improve as the clock wound down. The Troopers were blowing the doors off his chosen red army, the team he was grooming to be crowned

Cleveland's next champion. In founding the Troopers, he had prayed for an opponent. And his prayer was answered.

Final: Toledo 30, Cleveland 6.

At the last, sustained whistle, the women spilled onto the field in the November chill. They were drawn to walk the torn-up field, to linger between the hash marks, center stage after a show. Helen Reddy's blare-horn voice sang in their heads: *I am strong. I am invincible.* Their season was over after four games. They had suited up and accepted the charge of a game they'd never played. If nothing else, they showed themselves that they could play.

Stout's intuitions were not distracted by small talk or courtesies, a tendency that made him a sore loser and a prickly winner. He wished Motley good luck next year. His team had beaten an NFL Hall of Famer twice. The dream of football glory remained a glowing ember. He would have a year to imagine ways he could improve on the product. He would think about Xs and Os amid the shrieking machines at Tillotson. While watching the Super Bowl in January, played in a college stadium in New Orleans, he would imagine the crowds that had come out to see women play. He would imagine the expansion of Friedman's league to cities whose names adorned stadium scoreboards across the country.

* * *

In December, Stout reserved the Valhalla for Raceway Park winners, the paneled private room at Cousino's Steakhouse, for the team banquet. The end-of-the-year gala had its roots in high school football, a send-off to honor individual achievement, to deliver sentimental speeches, and to clear the air of things left unsaid in the heat of battle. The denouement memorialized the season, an occasion to exchange mud-and sweat-soaked jerseys for a dress or a coat and tie; grunting, shouting, and swearing for reflection, inside jokes, and a reading of poetry. They toasted the award winners: Most Improved Player Pam Schwartz, Best

Offensive Player Lee Hollar, and Best Defensive Player Nanette Wolf. The culminating award was given to the Most Valuable Player. "While our success is a team effort, our MVP did everything for us," Stout said. Then he called the name of the general store clerk who added football to the list of women's work.

Verbosky downplayed the recognition, crediting her teammates for driving down the field and driving her to practices. She shared her anticipation for the seasons to come.

But for her parents, the banquet was the last straw.

After being named the most valuable, she was sweeping up cigarette butts in the Verbosky's Market parking lot. One of the store's employees, a family friend they called Harry the Bread Man, approached her. He began outlining her parents' case. Football was not for women to play. She would get hurt. She would suffer in the long run. The Verbosky's Market community wasn't ready for female football players. The name and the brand didn't need the scandalous news of one of its daughters taking up a man's game.

Verbosky was dazed, realizing her parents had given the duty of delivering their decision to Harry the Bread Man. She finished her pass of the parking lot, made her rounds of cleaning the store. In her mind the message loud and clear was sinking in.

She told her softball teammates. She wouldn't be needing rides to practice or to games or banquets. As glorious as the game was, the MVP was done with football. The women tried to talk sense to her, but Verbosky had made up her mind. She would honor her parents' wishes.

With Verbosky, the team had won every game convincingly. Without her, they lost an exhibition by forty. Her football teammates brainstormed.

Sheila Browne had an idea. She had witnessed the fastest human she had ever seen fly around the bases at Detwiler Park. In her mind she put a football in her hands. "Her name," she told her teammates, "is LJ."

CHAPTER 8

"THEY CAN'T CATCH ME, MOMMA!"

In June 1972, President Richard Nixon signed Public Law No. 92-318, 86 Stat. 235, otherwise known as Title IX of the Education Amendments of 1972 to the Higher Education Act of 1965. Earlier in the month, in the high school named for one of Toledo's founding titans, a humble, soft-spoken athlete named Linda Jefferson walked across the Libbey High School gymnasium stage to receive her diploma.

For Jefferson, and female athletes like her, the stroll across the stage was the end of the line. At that moment, athletics scholarships for women did not exist. It would be the next year that a university would award a tuition waiver to a woman, a golfer from Miami. Jefferson bore no resentment as she crossed the stage. She was not a follower of the movement. She did not hear the clamor of the Equal Rights Amendment, which had recently passed through both houses of Congress, nor had she followed the bill prohibiting sex discrimination that was to be made law of the land. She did not participate in marches or riots. At the moment, Jefferson, the most decorated runner in her high school, was occupied by a more immediate concern than equality. Her graduation fell on her mother's birthday, and she had not prepared a gift. When she arrived home, she flung her diploma in her mother's lap. "Happy birthday," she said.

She'd grown up on Buckingham Street, on Toledo's south side, one block north of the rumble and creak of the boxcar traffic of the Norfolk Southern junction. A Channel 11 news story had called Air Line Junction the most dangerous neighborhood in the city. In daylight, Linda Jefferson learned to play in the treeless streets lined with two-story A-frames and bungalows and the occasional makeshift church. On the summer-scorched pavement she played whatever sport the ball dictated. Driveway basketball and softball long toss and pickup football. As the sun fell, Jefferson's mother made sure her children were inside, safe from gunshots—*or worse*, Jefferson's mother said.

She did not play sports at Lincoln Elementary or Pickett Junior High because there were no sports to play. In the summertime, no rec leagues existed in the near south side, nor were there corresponding organizations to the neighborhood Boys Club.

As a child she was quiet, her shyness not born of a lack of confidence but of humility ingrained by her mother. Sally Jefferson, a single mother of four, demanded discipline and wasn't afraid to use force. When fights broke out between Jefferson and her younger brother or two older sisters, Sally's whip would come down hardest on Linda. *"You should know better,"* Sally said. Linda took it to mean she was special.

With no father figure to speak of, Sally did the work of both. Every night the four children ate dinner around the table, and every night the four children cleaned up. Sally did not tolerate breaches of manners or lazy, improper speech.

An unspoken bond tethered Jefferson close to home, except when she heard the voices of neighborhood kids in the street. When the games formed after school, the boys told her to go back home, not because girls shouldn't play but because they couldn't beat her. She didn't complain or boast or gloat. But when she bounded off her front porch to join the games, she could see their faces drop. One day she came home after besting the boys in footraces. Her mother told her to get back outside and keep her pride in check. Now the boys were testing their prowess throwing a nickel across a parking lot. By the time she came home she'd beat them at the long-distance coin toss.

She did not so much answer a call but an instinct within, a craving, an urge. In fact, being called the fastest only agitated her, the suggestion of a ceiling, as well as a failure to describe the totality of her ability, which burned in her like a superpower.

"I don't care what it is," she told her mother. "I'm going to be best at something."

She stood average height and weight. Her Angela Davis Afro dome bespoke a style that was both cutting-edge and traditional. Sizing her up, her opponents saw nothing that would lead them to conclude that she was one of the best female athletes of her generation. And then they saw her run.

In her first year at Libbey High School, she made the girls' teams for basketball, softball, and track. She had never been trained, never been drilled on technique, never taken lessons or played with select travel clubs. She did not own any equipment besides a pair of sneakers. On the basketball court, she played rover, the position free to cross half court in the 6-on-6 version of the sport. In the open pasture of a softball outfield, she could close on a fly ball and make the catch look easy, and in track she won spots on the elite sprinting team: the 50-meter, the 100-meter, and the 4x100-meter. She loved to compete and survived the school day by anticipating the rush ignited by a whistle or starter's pistol.

She followed the great track stars like Wilma Rudolph, but her idol above all was Althea Gibson. Gibson was the first Black woman to win a Grand Slam, an achievement she repeated three times. A Black woman, the number-one-ranked tennis player in the world—and, when she saw another barrier to break, Gibson became the first Black woman to join the LPGA tour. Even though no tennis court or golf course existed anywhere near Buckingham Street, Jefferson saw in Gibson a hero to emulate.

While she excelled at team sports, especially when Libbey switched over to five-player basketball in 1970, speed was her first love. She made her mark in the sport that showcases individual talent: track and field. LJ was the fastest girl in the school, a piece of news that spread quickly around a wet April dual track meet. She began collecting school records in all manner of track-and-field events. Watching her explode off the block and burn, spectators stopped talking. And because speed is a form of flying, she was also a long-jump champion. She dreamed of going fast. She studied acceleration rates, such as when the 1967 Corvette broke the five-second barrier in reaching sixty miles per hour. Cars became her fantasy. She dreamed of punching the gas and soaring overland, not with any particular destination in mind. Just going as fast as a land-bound object could go.

Game on, Jefferson was ruthless. But once she dispatched an opponent, she turned soft-spoken, humble. Her mother made sure of it. Sally Jefferson shook her head at the undisciplined, mouthy boys who paraded around school and sporting events. She saw their banter and bombast as degenerate, a problem linked to the gang fights breaking out at Friday night football games and other city-league events. The riots became so prevalent that in 1964 the city of Toledo banned night games altogether. Linda was forbidden to make a show of her conquests, her mother mandated, because performance spoke loudest of all.

Off the field, Jefferson's quiet confidence, her contagious smile and cool in her own skin put others at ease. She was a quick study, a student who spoke well in front of a group. She navigated the minefield of a south-side public school in the most dangerous neighborhood and seemed career-tracked, even setting aside her prodigious athletic gifts.

Before she graduated, Jefferson had one last championship and one final score to settle. Roz Stoner from crosstown Rogers had surprised Jefferson her freshman year by breaking the tape in front of her at the last moment. In two more meets, when it came down to the 100, Jefferson was distracted, rattled. Stoner beat her again and again. Now was the last time they would meet, for the city title.

To up the ante, in the spring of 1972, the city league had decided that girls competing were as worthy as the boys. For the first time in the state of Ohio, boys and girls would hold their respective events at the same culminating meet. That year's city championship at Start High School attracted the largest audience in the city league's history, despite the storm that whipped through town delaying the first event. The sky was cloudy, gusty, and warm. The track was soft and slow. Jefferson took her place on the block, next to Stoner. She extinguished all thought and let go. She exploded off the start, but here came Stoner, closing. In a flash it was over, and by the time her earthly consciousness returned, Jefferson had held off Stoner by a tenth of a second.

Next were the 4x100 and 4x200. Jefferson was the anchor for both. She was loose, oozing confidence. Now she was standing next to Brenda Morehead. Morehead, the upstart from Scott who the next year would obliterate city records, would then go on to medal in the Pan Am Games in 1975 and run for the US Olympic team in Montreal. But that would come later. The future Olympian would have to wait. The stands were packed and loud. Jefferson could see her mother, could hear her as though hers was the only audible voice. And here came teammate Colia Lucas around the corner to deliver the baton. In both the 4x100 and 4x200, the others stood no chance, and Jefferson wasn't about to give it away. Down the final leg, Jefferson burned, crossing the finish line going away. Was Jefferson a champion? She'd broken her school's records. She'd beaten her rivals. As a team, Libbey finished third overall, but as Jefferson walked off the track for the last time, the gold medals around her neck gave her the answer.

* * *

That summer she took a job at UPS, saving to pay for college. She spent her nights around the softball diamonds at Detwiler Park, one of very few places female athletes could cross the lines and participate in sanctioned sports. The women who came out to play were not distracted schoolgirls but women who'd been playing under the lights for years. They carried their equipment in designated bags. They cursed and spit. And they put a wallop on a ball like Jefferson had not seen playing with teenagers.

It did not take long to prove herself. At a showcase event, Jefferson notched a time for running the bases that broke all records. She immediately took her place at the top of the lineup and won the admiration of her teammates, who loved the effortless fire with which Jefferson played every pitch.

In the summer of 1972 at Detwiler, the women were not talking about a piece of legislation whose legalese-sounding name bore no relevance to their lives. They supported the Equal Rights Amendment but did nothing to persuade Ohio lawmakers to ratify it. They talked instead about a women's football team that had won all its games. The year before, the team had traveled to other cities. This year they would play Detroit and Toronto and Cleveland and Pittsburgh. One night a man appeared who many of the women knew. The potbellied stranger strolled between the backstops, eyeballing the athletes as they ran the bases. Jefferson's teammates like Sheila Browne called him *Coach*.

* * *

In July 1972, the owners of the Baltimore Colts and the Los Angeles Rams traded their entire teams to each other. Incredibly, the franchises were appraised at the same amount to the penny. The owners had discovered a loophole to avoid paying taxes, one that was legal under the current bargaining agreement, and so they didn't have to bother denying the scam. It was the kind of gimmick that Sid Friedman sought to exploit as he tinkered away at his upstart league.

Friedman ran the business side of the WPFL under a shell entity called Day Enterprises, a nonprofit, just like the NFL. He claimed ownership of the teams in Buffalo, Pittsburgh, Toronto, Cleveland, and Toledo. With an official season under his belt, he refined his pitch: First, the NFL had proved that no ceiling existed for revenues from football leagues with a national following. Franchises could be swapped to avoid paying taxes. Look, he was right all along: Investors were lining up for sports and entertainment ventures that netted seven-figure sponsorships. The World Football League, for example, was now courting investors with a vision of global proportions. The World Hockey Association (WHA) emerged to challenge the National Hockey League (NHL). Boxing matches drew the largest audiences in the world.

Second, female athletes were wresting a crescent of limelight from men, revealing a demand for both male and female audiences. Billie Jean King, for example, filled stadiums around the world. Gymnast Olga Korbut became a household name. Even Friedman's bread and butter—beauty pageants—showed the potential of a bill with women taking center stage. Women's rights marches, the Equal Rights Amendment, and the women's liberation movement to Friedman were free advertising, tea leaves pointing to the profitability of his vision.

"This thing is spreading," Friedman preached. He was telling Stout that the scheme of a coast-to-coast league was taking shape. It was critical now that owners take stock and purchase franchise rights within his WPFL before the league took off.

Friedman set the price at three to ten thousand dollars, depending on the market.

Investors were listening. West of the Mississippi, other cities were forming all-women teams, fueled by reports of Friedman's success in the Midwest. Investors in Dallas, Houston, and Los Angeles were ponying up to launch a West Coast conference of the sport. The athletics director for Hollywood High School, who had equipment and stadium connections, was fronting money for the Los Angeles Dandelions. And just as Lamar Hunt had done the decade before, two Texas brothers were forming teams in Dallas and Fort Worth.

Stout bided his time. He was willing to lay down money on a good bet, as long as the bookie could back it. He and Friedman had forged a gentleman's agreement for the grace period before Stout paid up: Fried-man supplied the uniforms and equipment, and Stout recruited the talent to play in them. Stout also invested what he could from his own pocket, as well as his sweat. Furthermore, in his mind, his investment had built the legitimacy of the brand. Stout brokered sponsorships for the game-day program Friedman was putting together and cut a deal with a local sporting goods wholesaler.

Stout orchestrated a press event all his own. Following the first season, Stout called for a practice at the Lucas County Rec Center, the site of the county fair. When the women arrived, they met two male *Blade* reporters and a photographer interested in writing a piece about playing football with women. The columnists suited up with the women for a scrimmage and were surprised to find themselves on the receiving end of a thrashing. On a sweep, Barry Stephan thought he could sidestep Connie Miller, but the linebacker stood him up, drove through him, and buried him in the turf. "I let you off easy." Miller told him, "In a real game, we hit harder."

The headline spanned nearly the width of the page of the Super Bowl Sunday edition. More than the praise his players lavished on the coaches, Stout could see the story finding legs: Women can play. *These were not girls trying to play football*, Stephan wrote. *They were football players. And when they got a shot at you, it hurt.*

* * *

For the 1972 season, Friedman upgraded the plain-Jane green and white with a motif of gold livening up the new line for the fall: gold pants, gold numbers, and a ring of gold circling the sleeves. The colors brought to mind the Green Bay Packers, the flagship of the new NFL. To Friedman they inspired visions of Super Bowls between rival leagues and packed stadiums. To Stout, the colors inspired the vision of Vince Lombardi, for whom the Super Bowl trophy is named, the greatest coach of all time.

It was critical, Friedman said, that the product on the field attract larger crowds, to build the audiences he'd invested in the first year. For the product to have value, the games had to be competitive.

"My team will be ready to play," Stout said.

"That's what I'm afraid of," Friedman said.

* * *

In the off-season, Hollar phoned Stout every week, stuck in the mode of analyzing both the plays they executed and the ones they woulda-shoulda-coulda. Hollar pleaded with Stout to call her own plays; she hated waiting for the messages to be relayed by substitutes into each huddle. To many, the Xs and Os were a simple arithmetic, a helmet-to-helmet equation. To Hollar, the game became a field of study, the mastery of which required not only strength and speed and machinelike timing but also awareness of the narrative, the coherent sequence built on past events, specific details, and character development.

Just as much as it needs players, coaches, helmets, and pads, a football team needs a home. A franchise needs a place to operate, available at all times, free from the city's Catholic school teams' unpredictable schedules. High school fields and their ram-fed fall sports calendar were dead ends, and Stout preferred his team not drive to some remote location in the identity-less suburbs. He settled on an undeveloped forgotten corner in his old stomping grounds.

Adjacent to DeVilbiss High School lay a small tree-lined patch of overgrown city property. It wasn't a park exactly, more like an expanse of grass that attracted pickup games, picnics, and afternoon family parties. Cigarette butts dotted the uneven terrain, and broken glass glistened amid the leaves collecting along the curbless street. Page Stadium and its brick façade loomed in the distance. The high school's brick boiler tower stood in plain view, and beyond that the Overland Smokestack. To the south, a small neighborhood square had developed on Central Avenue, with a grocery store, a pharmacy, and a theater called the Colony. Like the city itself, the park was born without a name.

There was no placard or marker or map that indicated it existed, but the neglected pasture assumed its identity: Colony Field.

* * *

One Saturday morning in the summer, Stout was in a good mood. He preempted Sue's resentment for not spending more time with his children by declaring he would take Guy and Stefanie to the park. On the way, Stout stopped at the hardware store to buy a shovel, a contractor's level, and several bags of concrete. When the three arrived at Colony Field, Hamilton, Wright, and Mike Stout were waiting. They had brought with them three sections of twelve-foot-long four-inch cast-iron water pipes Stout found at a scrapyard. Together they weighed over two hundred pounds. The coaches spent the morning carving out two craters into city property, then fastened the pieces together with T-joints and concrete footers, as Guy and Stefanie looked on in fascination.

The men weren't concerned that anyone would object. "If the cops show up, it'd be their first time to this godforsaken park," Hamilton said.

Like Iwo Jima, the four of them hoisted the massive black iron H. They held it upright and level with ropes and stakes pounded into the hard ground.

The Troopers had officially laid claim to land.

* * *

Stout's memory of his days at Page Stadium inspired another set piece. He'd seen it rotting away in the practice field at his alma mater and convinced the custodian to have it moved. Doing so required the work of a team of men to hoist the monstrosity onto a flatbed, and a team of women to unload it. A rusted-out tackling sled now awaited the

Troopers like a steel dinosaur carcass. It weighed over a quarter ton, with five upright fingers of corroded steel, and a platform on which Hamilton could stand and shout.

Instead of spending nights at home, Stout accompanied Wright to the softball diamonds at Detwiler. The two men followed the buzz of a speedster who played center field alongside their offensive tackle Sheila Browne.

In the twilight they watched an unassuming batter with a dome Afro step up to the plate. She was small next to the sluggers in the dugout. She was aggressive with the bat, undisciplined, clobbering a grounder to the left side—nothing special. But then they saw her explode out of the box. The shortstop had no chance against her, a dashing blur down the first base line. The next batter slapped a flabby bloop that split the out-fielders, and the speedster was flying again, suddenly rounding second, and then third, stomping on home plate before the defense knew what had hit them.

"That's LJ," Browne said.

The dugout fence between them, Stout introduced himself, told her about the tryouts.

I'll pass, Jefferson said with a nod. She'd never played football, except in the streets. She was nobody's fool.

Browne worked on her next. "It's the real deal," she told her. Browne knew that the desire to play was just that, an opportunity to lace up cleats and step between the lines. The women were not playing football to make a point, she said, other than that they were better than you.

* * *

The same instincts that had drawn Jefferson to the track burned in her. The knowledge of her untapped gift drove her. It must mean something that she could beat every woman she'd ever met.

Her mother wasn't having it. For the past four years Sally Jefferson had sat in stale, stagnant gymnasiums and cold, rainy stadiums watching her daughter, listening to the PA announcer celebrate her name after every sensational score or race. She kept her daughter's medals in a shrinelike pedestal in the living room on Buckingham. Now she was watching her youngest daughter race around the base paths in summer softball, scoring from first on a single. Football, on the other hand, was out of the question. *Under no circumstances are you to play tackle football*, Sally Jefferson told her daughter. *It's a barbaric sport.* She would surely be injured. On top of that, Sally was her mother, and the issue was decided.

The Saturday of the tryout, Jefferson stayed home. She lay on her bed in the unforgiving heat listening to cars passing by over broken glass. She felt the sting of uncertainty. No high school awaited her, no games on the hard court, no races in the spring. She could hear her mother's voice echoing. But in her mind, Jefferson tended toward flight. The feeling of soaring past her competition. She dreamed of speed, of one day moving to a place far away from Buckingham Street, for she knew that nothing could contain her, not the city, not her mother, not anyone trying to bring her down.

* * *

A white Chevy Impala prowled around Colony Field before pulling onto the grass. Gloria Jimenez climbed out, sporting a T-shirt emblazoned with *Super Chicano* in rainbow font. Three of her brothers followed, leaning on the car to watch. Across the field a group of women were gathering. Some of them wore shoulder pads. Jimenez recognized one of them: the chatterbox from the salon, Dorothy Parma, who stood barely five feet tall. *If you will, I will*, each had promised. "You don't have to stay," Jimenez told her brothers.

"We want to watch you get killed," said Louis, the oldest.

"You wish."

* * *

Karen Gould was a physiology student at the University of Toledo. Every day, a bright blonde plopped down next to her out of breath from running across campus. "Yeah, I'm a football player," Connie Miller told her. Gould had grown up in Millbury, Ohio, home of zero sports for girls, unless you count beating up the boys who lived across the street.

* * *

Terry Dale had watched the Troopers play at Rossford and thought, *Where do I sign?* Undersized but quick, Dale was versatile. She also had a cannon for an arm. When she was twelve she was playing catch with her brother. *Is that all you got?* he taunted. Dale showed him what she had. The baseball shattered his jaw and sent him to the hospital, where doctors had to construct a new jaw with special glass.

Gloria Jimenez had also preferred playing with brothers, all six of them, in Mulberry Park on the north side. She also had three sisters, who tended to remain indoors. Gloria went outside. Her parents let her roam free in the streets, as long as she ran with family. On the other hand they were scared for her life within the confines of Woodward High School, where in 1967 a riot had broken out. They pulled her out of school and demanded she select one of the two careers available for women, cutting hair or applying makeup. In 1972 Jimenez was spending her days inside a salon when she read about an all-women football team. *Why not?* she thought.

Olivia Flores was a freshman at Mary Manse College, an all-women enclave run by Ursuline nuns. Flores had tried basketball but tended to get into foul trouble. Her teammate Pam Schwartz, a tough, physical defender in her own right, suggested Flores play a different sport.

In all, the team reloaded with a few specialists, skill players who could throw and catch, and a set of linemen who did not need to be taught to hit people. And then came Sunday.

Some called her Sondi. Some called her Jonsey. She also went by

Sunday, the day she was born. No one called her by her name, which was Vera. Vera Melrose Jones stood six foot one, lithe and sculpted with square shoulders and a long, effortless stride, like a runway model. In fact she looked good onstage, as a backup singer for the Ohio Players, a soul rock outfit out of Dayton. She'd harbored dreams of spending her life on the road, in front of screaming fans, her name in lights. For now, she settled on the chalk on the placard announcing the daily specials at the Peppermint Club, where she sang bluesy covers of Ella Fitzgerald and Etta James, and songs composed from poetry she wrote on her own. At twenty-seven, she was older than everyone except Burrows, a fact one picked up not from her look but from her movement. She exuded cool. Her jaw was hard set, and she looked at you with the eyes of a predator, a menacing glare that remained when you looked away. During the day, like Jimenez, she worked as a beautician. On her days off, she played pickup basketball with the men at Birmingham Park, amid the burning haze of the Sun Oil refinery. On the football field, she showed off her prowess, using her long legs to accelerate past the lumbering linemen. During the receivers' tryout, Hollar dropped back and threw a short crossing route. Sunday extended a single arm and plucked the ball clean out of the air with one hand, tucked it into a cradle, and kept running.

* * *

The Dallas Cowboys broke huddle. The linemen sauntered up to their positions on the line and stooped into the set position, elbows on knees. Quarterback Roger Staubach crouched over center and barked out a signal. Right then, the entire line stood up in Rockette-like unison, then back down into the three-point ready position. Like the game itself, the maneuver was an exaggerated show, a choreographed deception within the rules used to distract and confuse. A trademark of the Cowboys, the Landry Shift was a curiosity for both casual viewers and students of the game, like Stout, who the previous season had watched Dallas in their new state-of-the-art football arena ride the Landry Shift into the playoffs, through conference championship, and over Miami in the Super Bowl. He couldn't get the Landry Shift off his mind.

And so when the Troopers broke huddle in 1972, Burrows, Browne, Farrell, and Kelly trotted to the line. At Hollar's call under center, up the line went in chorus, then back down to the ready, like a breathing giant.

At camp, Stout and his coaches discovered assets they lacked the year before: veterans. Pam Schwartz, Jackie Allen, Lee Hollar, Deb Brzozka, Patsy Farrell, Peggy Dauer, and Davelyn Burrows, among others. They knew what they were in for and they returned, ready for the gauntlet awaiting them. And when practice began, the veterans saw something familiar in the rookies: the look behind the face mask, a look of awe and terror, like soldiers being deployed at the front. The newbies learned to take orders; if the instructions were not executed, on keeping your pads low, for instance, dozens were lined up to enforce the punishments for violating the rules of the hit. Karen Gould caught a screen pass from Hollar and saw Connie Miller and her blond ponytail containing on the end, forcing her back to the middle. Where Pam Schwartz was running full speed. Gould took the hit standing up, and by the time she hit the ground, in the backfield, more white helmets piled on. "You all right?" said Schwartz, the one they called the nicest and meanest person you would ever meet. "Take care of yourself out here, now." And the women popped up and trotted back in line.

So that's how it's going to be, Terry Dale thought, as she stepped up for her turn. She corralled a short pass from Hollar over the middle, then dove forward head down, but here was Jackie Allen targeting the football, and a rookie who wasn't following the instructions on how to hold it. The ball flung, disappearing into the scrum like a trapped rabbit. It was a severe infraction, for which Dale was ordered to run. "Where?" she asked.

"Just start running," said Stout.

Running gave her time to internalize her sin. Twice around the field, Dale stumbled back into the huddle. What ego was left, Hollar finished off: "Kid, hang on to the ball, or I'll never give it to you again. Understand?"

By her third practice, Sunday had read the room. She had tested the toughness of each woman through conditioning, hitting drills, and walk-throughs. She was playing safety, scanning the field for a target. She found Browne following the play and knocked her sideways off her feet. "That wasn't very nice," chirped Browne.

Sunday laughed, another conquest.

Later, during the pop-up drill, Sunday counted off the opposite line, the requisite math to determine her partner. She found Browne looking back at her. "Don't worry," Sunday said. "I'll play nice."

Sunday sang as she lay down head to head with Browne. Stout took his time. "Loser runs a lap," Stout said.

The ball dropped to Sunday. She rolled over and sprang to her feet, to discover Schwartz bearing down. Stunned, Sunday hesitated and as Nasty drove her to the ground, the circle erupted in laughter.

* * *

Hitting was both elixir and teacher. Eunice White had played for the University of Toledo's basketball team, that is, the women's club team. She played hard, and physical. After Jim Wright saw her swing a softball bat at Detwiler, he told her she should give football a try. White was standoffish, tentative. Out of curiosity she showed up at Colony Field, where Wright gave her a set of pads and a helmet. White let her guard down when she met the team. To her they were the nicest, most polite people she'd ever met. She lined up across from Burrows. At the whistle, Burrows knocked her silly; *Blew me back on my ass, peeled me like a banana,* White would later say. Pancaked on her back, she gained a thorough understanding of the purpose of pads.

Flores was next. She, too, would take her lesson from experience's chastening hand. Like White, she lined up. There was the whistle, the pop of shoulder pads, and the hard earth beneath her back. "Is that the best you can do?" Burrows said, shaking her head.

Getting laid out in the controlled environment of practice was one thing, but the meaning of the hit during a game was another. In her first game, Jimenez was inserted at left tackle. She remembered her training for the bulldog position: *"Follow the ball!"* At the snap she saw the whole play before her. The Cleveland left guard pulled and headed her way. She knew it, was prepared for it, knew where the ball was going. Jimenez occupied the guard just enough to fall into the path of the charging running back. She absorbed the blow and hung on. The whistle declared the play dead, and to Jimenez it was the greatest experience of her life.

In the third game, against Detroit, Brzozka was chasing the Demon running back down the sidelines. Out of nowhere came the Demon tight end, delivering a shoulder full speed, knocking Brzozka clean off her feet. Dazed, Brzozka stumbled to the end who'd flattened her. The Demon braced, expecting retaliation. "That was an *amazing* block!" Brzozka said, proud of that woman, from the receiving end of a hard, clean football play.

The hit taught them a truth about the game that cannot be explained. A football player is a supremely conditioned specimen. It may have been Carl Hamilton shouting from atop the tackling sled as the women pushed him across the gravelly turf in the late-afternoon sun. But it was also the call of their own bodies demanding the fire-tempered preparation for the punishment to come. A player began at one end and pushed the sled five times, hitting with equal force each giant rusted finger, or else the sled would turn off course. Rookies like Jimenez began to understand that a far worse fate awaited the player who didn't give all she had on the churned-up, sweat-stained turf of Colony Field.

* * *

Two weeks before the season opener, Sheila Browne showed up to practice with a guest. The stranger was unassuming and remained standoffish on the sideline.

When Stout got around to her, he said, "You changed your mind."

"Looks like fun," Jefferson said with a shrug.

"Oh, it's fun," Stout said. He told her she was welcome to watch. If she was serious, she was also welcome to come back the next day prepared to run.

Linda Jefferson imagined herself a wide receiver. Everywhere she went she'd been the fastest, whether it was at Detwiler Park or the track-and-field city championships. Just like Bob Hayes, the gold medal sprinter turned NFL wide receiver. He'd parlayed raw speed into greatness on the gridiron. In her mind, he'd avoided the brutality of running between the hash marks but soared unscathed along the sidelines. She was happy to steer clear of the maelstrom of the line of scrimmage. That way, she would avoid getting hurt, and her mother would never have to know.

Her first practice she was tentative, deferential as she'd been taught to be. She asked to play on the outside, a wideout. She ran post routes but kept outrunning the ball. "Throw it over her head," Stout ordered. Launched from Hollar's arm, a football could travel 50 yards, but now it was racing against a force that seemed to defy gravity. Jefferson flew past as the ball sank behind her and bounced. Again, Hollar five-step dropped and let fly, and Jefferson slowed down, waiting for the ball to return to earth.

Stout tried her at scatback, the term he used for an undersized running back or slot receiver, the waterbug interpretation of a ball carrier. At first she blew past her blockers into the surprise party of linebackers. "Be patient," Stout told her. "Wait for your line to do their job." Then she began to see. She timed her quickness to avoid Farrell; she danced around and through Allen and Miller, running toward sideline daylight. But she was tethered to the next rep, and so she rarely had the chance to open up the engine all the way. There were signs, though, that she was no ordinary player. Once on a pitch to the right, Dale at outside linebacker tried to contain. She sank her fingers into Jefferson flying outside, but when the green blur vanished, Dale was on her knees, holding in her hand a shred of Jefferson's jersey.

It was later, as Jefferson led suicides, that Wright and Stout compared notes.

"How good is *she*?" Wright said, almost to himself.

"We'll find out soon," said Stout, easing into a smile.

Whether anyone could answer Wright's question would remain a subject of debate. Prior to snapping on a football helmet, Jefferson had faced a line of rivals in particular sports: track and field, softball, basketball. Now she was venturing into territory where none of them would follow.

* * *

The Cadillac nosed onto the practice field. Friedman, armed with a camera, demanded that the women line up for pictures. He provided a hairbrush and a handheld mirror. "Just your good side, ladies," he said.

They posed like NFL players for Topps cards. Helmetless, with groomed hair, they simulated running or blocking or tackling. Brzozka turned back to look at the camera while holding the ball outstretched as though she were hauling in a post route. Miller gave the pinup photographer a Heisman stiff arm, the ball tucked.

The program Friedman produced turned into a twenty-page color catalog of player profiles, statistics, and sponsors. The cover featured a stock illustration of a quarterback looking over a charging defensive line. That is, a male quarterback and male linemen. The centerfold sponsored by Pepsi listed the women's names, their height and weight, and their position.

Friedman added another column to their profile: single or married. It was all he could do to leave out their bra size.

* * *

In September 1972, state governments debated the ratification of the Equal Rights Amendment, Pope Paul VI announced that women could never play the role of men, and the Troopers lined up for kickoff against Friedman's Cleveland Daredevils, twenty miles south of Toledo in Bowling Green.

Jefferson was all butterflies. First of all, she didn't like betraying her mother. It wasn't an overt lie, but Jefferson knew her mother wouldn't see it that way, if she ever found out. Second, she stood on the far sideline, the far right flank of the kickoff defense. She could feel the Daredevils breathing behind her, and the crowd, and the dry heat of late summer. And then a whistle pierced the moment. This was real.

At the kick, Jefferson ran, burning through blockers, tracking the returner. The runner pivoted, running lateral, and Jefferson followed. That was when Jefferson was obliterated, knocked off her feet from her blind side. She thought she was dead. She couldn't move. Couldn't breathe. She felt the paralyzing sucker punch of getting the wind knocked out of her. When her lungs finally let loose, she saw a Trooper looking down at her, her own teammate from the opposite flank who had knocked her senseless. It was Browne. "I told you it's fun," Browne said, helping the rookie to her feet.

As she watched from the sidelines, the notion circled in her mind that perhaps the game wasn't for her. But in a moment, the luxury of thinking vanished. As with a starter's pistol, there was only the snap and its consequences. The defense forced a punt, and Hollar led the offense onto the field. Stout had called the play, a scheme that would offer Jefferson some room, and Hollar delivered it to the huddle: *"Pro set left 3, 27 pitch."*

Jefferson surveyed the field, twenty-one women in front of her about to explode. At the Landry Shift, she took a breath. *Be cool*, she thought, *and let it go*. At the snap, Jefferson broke left, took the pitch from Hollar, and followed Dauer toward the corner. She could see it before it happened, Schwartz opening the end, Dauer wiping out the linebacker, Gould and Jones clearing the way. She saw the opening and flew through, accelerating, leaving only a helpless safety and an expanse of daylight. She was gone, a green rocket down the Trooper sideline.

One touch. One touchdown. The Troopers mobbed her, like a child returning from the first day of school. "Didn't I tell you?" Sheila Browne said. "Didn't I tell you!"

Yeah, I could get used to this, Jefferson thought.

Her teammates would, too. She finished her first game with 98 yards on ten carries and two touchdowns, the other coming on a 65-yard punt return. She was a skyrocket, weaving through the air without decelerating around tacklers. She ran toward open spaces, around edges, where she used her extra gear.

Stout and Hamilton couldn't explain what they saw—no one taught her to see the field. Her talent was speed to be sure, but it was also instinct, a core impulse forged in the relentless sun on Buckingham Street and on the crabgrass-dotted track at Libbey, an alertness against impending threats, and the timing to strike and fly.

Her first game was a field test, a dipping of the toe. Stout didn't exploit his new weapon but stuck to his game plan, keeping the Daredevil defense in a constant guessing game. Hollar was the conductor, no matter what virtuoso played first violin. He used every play in the book, alternating runs by Jefferson, Dauer, Gould, and Brzozka. And right when he saw an exposed tendency, here comes Sunday Jones on a reverse for 16 yards. Predictability was the enemy. Outwitting your opponent is the essence of a game, in liars' poker and in football. In the end, six different backs carried the ball. In the second half, Cleveland stacked the line, so Hollar dropped back, saw Jones running into a safety-less post, and threw over the top for a 47-yard touchdown.

Not bad, Hamilton said, keeping to his side of the sandbox. On defense, the stored-up hope and anticipation accrued in the off-season came pouring out. The line centered by Allen, and flanked by Schwartz and Jimenez, was an impenetrable wall. Jimenez, White, and Farrell dominated the edges. Jones at safety was free to choose her lane of attack and showed Hamilton she could put her head down and spear a runner. Cleveland managed three first downs in the first half, and that was all they would get.

Cleveland tallied 55 yards for the game and did not score. With every earth-churning drive the Trooper offense put together, the defense was goaded to match. Furthermore, no sympathy existed on the line of scrimmage. When Jimenez crouched into her three-point stance, before the ball was snapped, she did not check the scoreboard. In the third quarter, the defense pushed the Daredevils inside the ten. Disorganized, the helpless Daredevils lined up in a formation Jones recognized. She shot through and separated the ball from the quarterback, and Farrell picked it up for a touchdown.

The defense mobbed Farrell, the women arm in arm, uplifted by a joy found nowhere else, and marched back to their side as though coming down from the mountaintop, as though it was the game-winning score, not the one that made the score 36–0.

Hamilton turned away to hide his satisfaction. But they had seen it. Their joy was a tidal wave, and they called him out for the teddy bear he was. "Let's go, Cuddles!" they sang, and the six-foot, four-inch, 260-pound former lineman had a nickname.

* * *

"We need to talk," Friedman said. He collected the cash from the box office and the concessions after every game. After the Cleveland game he cornered Stout. "This is not good for the game." He noted that the fans who left before the final gun were toxic—those are the ones who don't buy concessions and who don't come back. "When you don't let the other team score," Friedman said. "We've got a product problem."

Stout: "Then fix your product."

Both men sensed the crossroads coming. From Friedman's point of view, the addition of Jefferson didn't help the situation. He also sensed that Stout was different from the other men he'd hired to coach his teams. Motley, the Hall of Famer. Charley Scales, the seven-year NFL veteran from Cleveland and Pittsburgh, who coached the Powderkegs.

Stout, on the other hand, had been passed over. He'd never made the big leagues. Nor did he have a college degree that would have enabled him to take the well-worn path to coaching high school or college. Destroying his WPFL opponents satisfied his need to show his worth. Furthermore, he found no traction in other areas of his life. His marriage was dead on arrival. His career had no prospects beyond factory line manager. The Troopers presented a chance to make a mark in something he believed was true.

* * *

The *Blade* sitting on Jefferson's doorstep that morning beckoned like a letter from the principal. Jefferson would have scooped it up, buried the sports page in the trash. Chances were Sally wouldn't dig deep past the scoreboard section, where the Troopers were getting coverage. Chances were Sally wouldn't even check the Sunday scores, now that the stories of her daughter's reign at Libbey had all dried up. Chances were she wouldn't see that her daughter had ignited a Trooper offense with two touchdowns. There would be more stories to come. It was an omen, the newspaper, an inevitable arrival like the sun coming up, a cosmic sign rolled up and rubber-banded, sitting silently on the porch.

She hated keeping the secret. She was eighteen years old. She had graduated from high school and held her job sorting and packing parcels. At the same time, something told her that her mother knew. She had to have known, like a parent knows.

The thing the parent forbids is the thing that bites and doesn't let go.

Jefferson wanted full and open ownership of it, the game. She climbed out of Sheila Browne's Datsun and opened the hatch. For three weeks she'd been hiding her shoulder pads and helmet in the trunk, on the down low. She felt the butterflies again. She grabbed the face mask through the pads, closed the hatch, and headed up the stairs.

Her mother was waiting for her.

"So you're gonna play football?"

Jefferson did not hesitate. "Yep," she said, as though daring her mother. Her resolve was in it, the ferocity with which she sat poised before the pistol, and the snap. *Try to stop me.*

She set her pads down on the porch.

In this mother-daughter game of chicken, Sally balked. Her daughter was an adult. She could make her own decisions. Perhaps Sally sensed the mutually assured destruction of a confrontation. Still, the mother instinct would not capitulate without a say. She allowed her to play on the condition that the game met with her approval. Sally would form her opinion after witnessing with her own eyes what this football nonsense was all about.

* * *

What it was all about was a group of football players drawn by an unstoppable force. It was about running and blocking and hitting and tackling. It was about savagery and precision. It was about executing technique and teamwork in the chill of an autumn night and a white grid on a green pasture. To be sure, it was about women uniting over a game they weren't supposed to play. But what Sally Jefferson saw was a full-scale operation, led by a potbellied curmudgeon shouting orders, a team of women working in SWAT team unison, and a runner who made her stand up every time she touched the ball.

That night, in a clear September twilight against the Detroit Demons, at Sylvania High School Stadium, Jefferson ran for 164 yards on eight carries. By the fourth quarter, she had scored touchdowns on runs of 30 and 56 yards. She also ran back a punt for a 39-yard score. It was clear to everyone in the stadium including Sally that number 48 was a threat to fly into the clear every time she touched the ball. As though any doubt remained, Jefferson wasn't about to stop, knowing the omnipotent face in the crowd.

In the fourth quarter, the Troopers came set at their own 31-yard line. Hollar called *Pro set 38*, a handoff that Jefferson was to take wide to the right, but this time the Detroit defensive end held contain, forcing Jefferson back to the inside. But Jefferson's velocity wasn't about to turn back. She took the wide angle, cutting backward toward her end zone and around, beating the end with enough space to turn and fly along the sideline. Nobody was going to catch her. Sixty-nine yards later she coasted into the end zone, her chin tilted slightly up into the floodlit night.

After the game, Jefferson's mother was waiting for her in the parking lot. Sally tried to temper her joy at what she had seen. "Just don't let them hit you," Sally said.

"They can't catch me, Momma!" Jefferson said, and tossed her gear, shoulder pads, and helmet into the front passenger seat.

PART II

CHAPTER 9

OWNERSHIP

If the 1971 Troopers were a lumbering Toledo-manufactured Jeep engine, clunky and unstoppable, the year-two additions gave the capability of a Mustang GT. Over the 1972 nine-game season, the team averaged 37 points a game. Classic off-tackle backs Dauer and Brzozka tallied touchdowns on misdirections, or by becoming battering rams for short yardage when opponents wore down. And then number 48, relaxed in the backfield, was a home run threat each break of the huddle. Sunday at split end bided her time, targeting linebackers and obliterating them from the outside. The team's objectives on each play internalized in each woman: to knock the opponent off the ball.

Against Buffalo, in a game played in Lackawanna, New York, the outcome of two plays amounted to revelation. Sunday, tackled on a punt return, planted her hand in a nest of broken glass hidden in the willowy grass. Blood covered her hand and ran in beads down her arm. Hamilton removed a shard of amber glass and dressed the wound in a shower of Bactine and athletic tape. "Do you want to go to the hospital?" he asked.

"I want to go back in the game," said Jonsey.

Sunday trotted wide, her hand a taped club. She glanced at her destination in the open space, shot a look back to Hollar. A single pivot and she burst vertical, searching the sky for the plummeting spiral. She allowed it to fall into her hands, tape and all, then galloped into the end zone untouched. Gyrating, she turned to meet her teammates, her arms in the air, like she was saved. The experience was exalted, glorifying. The series she sat out was the only one she missed for the game. On defense, as a free safety, she became a predator who could roam freely, identify the gaps, plan her assault, calculate the angle of the running back, and attack with the intention of taking her head off. She surprised even the veterans, who approved of her nickname that bespoke her work: Dr. Death.

In the third quarter, the All-Stars took the kickoff and attempted a wrinkle. The fullback took a dive off right tackle, but the quarterback kept the ball on play action. Miller at the mike stayed home, as though she'd sussed out the scheme, dropping into coverage. She'd never caught a pass; she'd never even run a route. But the ball was on its way, silhouetted by the lights. The rest was pure action. Miller jumped into the path of that train, and what happened next she would remember the rest of her life. Her hands rose without thought and came down with the football, like a magnet, as well as a single terrifying thought after she corralled it: *I'd better run the right way.* Her legs did. She ran like Jefferson herself, sucked into the clear. Thirty-seven yards later her wits returned to her, and she was crossing the goal line. In the end zone, Burrows lifted Miller on her shoulders and carried her among her teammates like a royal escorted on a throne. It was the team's first pick six.

* * *

To Hollar it was magic to watch. She'd been waiting her entire life to play, and now she talked about the game in terms of execution. On Thursdays, before the Friday walk-throughs, Hollar phoned Stout at home after practice. There were issues to discuss, such as the timing of the screen pass, innovations to the playbook, and positioning of players. She pleaded with him to let her call her own plays. Stout wasn't ready to relinquish control and instead discussed the metaphor he contemplated during his day job making carburetors. It was a combustion engine, an offense, starting up and running, like the motor the Jeep plant was churning out. A football drive was an assemblage of moving parts working in airtight precision. The spark plug of the quarterback, the crankshaft of the lineman, the pistons of the skill players. Hollar comprehended the comparison in all its levels. She like her teammates had played football of the backyard variety, which never boomed with a stadium's PA announcer or with a referee's whistle, and the real thing was like a drug. The more they played, the more they wanted to play. The more they won, the more they wanted to win.

* * *

Friedman wanted them to lose. The league was his brainchild. He was the founder. The owner. His genius was forming an east-west Super Bowl–style championship that would mark the beginning of a national football phenomenon like the one of the previous decade. Because Friedman wasn't the only one to follow the NFL's great awakening. Joe and Stan Mathews in Dallas had watched their hometown dreamer Lamar Hunt transform a start-up into reality, which was now manifest in the form of a single-purpose state-of-the-art iconic Texas Stadium. In fact, the Mathews brothers by appearances were Hunt protégés, bolstering their presence with a ten-gallon hat and a big dream. Friedman had sold them the idea of the West Coast league with reports of box office windfalls in the Midwest. They were on the cusp of major sponsorship, he told them, and now was the time to strike. At the same time, teams in Los Angeles, San Diego, and Houston were taking shape. The Dallas Bluebonnets followed Friedman's start-up model: An ad in the paper inspired dozens of women to show up, many who were nursing students at the El Centro community college downtown.

The brothers from Texas created two teams: Fort Worth and Dallas. They used their ties to Cowboys brass and secured the home of the Super

Bowl champion Cowboys for Friedman's matchup. They would have to wait until the NFL season ended, so they targeted a February kickoff.

In Cleveland, Daredevil skin was hardening. The Motley sons notched wins in games that held the attention of fans who then promoted through word of mouth. But Friedman had learned a lesson: He couldn't stay toe-to-toe with Toledo, even without its new lethal weapon.

While Friedman couldn't order a team of his to win, he could order one to lose.

"Do you realize what you stand to gain by losing?" Friedman asked.

Stout was on the phone in his kitchen. He had returned from New York, having dispatched the New York Pets 34–0. It was their tenth straight win, consistent with the method and pace of the other Trooper torchings: a close first half, followed by a blowout in the second. In all their wins, Stout and Hamilton made halftime adjustments, emphasized basic execution, and relied on conditioning to do the rest.

There was another reason for the lopsided scores. The Troopers never let up. In 1972, they beat their opponents by a combined score of 298–32. After a game in Buffalo a reporter asked Jefferson, "Do you ever think to go easy on teams, once the game is in hand?" Jefferson didn't understand the question. They played every down to dominate. The score was irrelevant. What was true and real was the moment they lined up, the women to the left and to the right, and their shared enemy across the line of scrimmage.

"I don't think you understand," Friedman said. He personally counted the box office returns after every game. Then he worked on Stout—the whole point is putting butts in seats. And competitive games attract fans. Which attracts more fans. Friedman told Stout he'd been promoting events in print and on radio and television since before Stout knew what a football was. He could create *buzz*, and even if couldn't, he could say he could, which in his mind amounted to the same thing.

Stout had read the stories Friedman had planted in the paper, playing all the angles.

"Now the college students are interested," Friedman had told the *Plain Dealer*. "Girls who wanted to be physical education teachers want to learn about football."

"The sport is authentic. It's not a setup, like rollerball," he told the Associated Press.

"Some of these girls are good enough to play minor league men's ball," he told the *Free Press*.

"You have to understand," Friedman told Stout. "I'm a businessman. You're just a coach. When you watch a football game, you see football. I see a business."

Stout's ego bristled. He had witnessed his players taking to the sport at its most basic and brutal. He clung to his faith in the game itself. "You want me to go back on everything I've done?" Stout said.

"Work with me," Friedman said. "Just keep it close."

* * *

It was cold for late October in the swamp. The team performed their ritual, the torn-up turf of Colony Field becoming familiar as home. They ran patterns to stay warm before filing onto the bus. Even for home games at Sylvania High School, the team traveled together to the stadium. They marched out, carrying their pads. They did little things like assemble their gear in the order it would be put on, including socks, right and left. Mike Stout and Hamilton taped up ankles and wrists. They gauged the tightness of string-tied shoulder pads, pants, and shoes, just right for combat. When a snapped shoestring might knock the ritual off kilter, Mike had the replacement waiting. They noticed their breathing and sank their teeth into mouth guards and clenched their bodies tight. Hollar got the hiccups. They eased their nerves by sparring like mountain goats or slapping helmets. They heard Al Green's "Let's Stay Together" coming from the PA system, and the crowd gathering. In the locker room their self-awareness receded, and they became unrecognizable from who they were when they walked in. Then they exploded from the tunnel and into the lights.

From the stands Friedman watched, hoping to see a product that went down to the wire.

On their first drive, he thought Stout was finally getting the message. The Daredevils had contained the Troopers and Jefferson to a few small gains. Then on third and two from the Cleveland forty-one, the Troopers showed their pro set, and number 48 scanned the left flat anticipating the play. At the snap Flores pulled to the left, in front of Hollar, who exposed the ball for the exchange. Jefferson danced to the outside, hiding behind the stretched-out line. That moment was all Hollar needed to break free, into the void, on the naked bootleg right. She tucked the ball in and took it all the way to the pylon for the first score. It was as though Stout had deeked Friedman himself.

Over the next four quarters, the Troopers put a hurting on Friedman's team like never before. They ran up 592 yards in putting up a 64-spot on the scoreboard. Jefferson scored six touchdowns, all on plays longer than 20 yards. Twice she scored on play-action screen passes that Hollar delivered just before going down, floating the ball to her in space, and the rest was academic. The Daredevils didn't know what hit them. Stout did not take his foot off the gas, even ahead by 50. Hamilton's line kept pushing until there was no space left to push, and Allen took down the Daredevil quarterback in the end zone for a safety.

Stout would rather die than give in.

The gaudy score was Stout's language, spoken at Friedman. Let there be no doubt that Stout was in control of the moment. If anyone thought otherwise, they were welcome to come down here and line up across from him.

But not total control. Late in the game, Connie Miller succumbed to sloppiness. She let herself go, not diving low but attempting to pull a runner down from her shoulders. Her leg twisted, snapping her tibia. The fractured bone couldn't take on any weight. Hamilton and Stout managed to carry her off the field, Miller apologizing for her lapse of concentration. *"I shouldn't have done that,"* she said.

* * *

In the dungy Sylvania locker room, amid husks of sweat- and grass-stained athletic tape that lay strewn on the floor like shed skin, the women recounted the highlights and hits, finding validation in one another. Then they changed into outfits for the next play, namely celebrating another win, another perfect season. To Jefferson it was as though they owned the city, riding in Sunday's Cadillac to the Peppermint Club or the Ottawa Tavern or the 19th Floor, the Holiday Inn's rooftop lounge downtown. Jefferson, accustomed to the UPS late-shift hours, kept her same game-face cool throughout the night, when others faded. Sunday lifted a glass for the victory: *"To the Troopers,"* she said, *"and to living by the light of the moon."*

The lyrical toast struck a chord, expressing their dominance on the field, and off it. Sunday extended the toast to Jefferson: *"To Moonie,"* she said, and the star's nickname was born.

* * *

The University of Toledo Rockets had finished three consecutive un-defeated seasons the year before. In the NFL, the Miami Dolphins were narrating a season of perfection. And as though perfection was the standard, the Troopers completed their second year, winning every game decisively. The parallel was not lost on Stout, who boasted of his wins in the break room at Tillotson and made references to Don Shula, as though they were equals. And with every win, Stout gained more ammunition against those who looked at him with skepticism in their voices, or in their eyes. *Go ahead*, the five-foot, ten-inch pug would shoot back, *doubt me*. He relished proving haters wrong, and that was what he toasted, when after the game he and his coaches fell into their booth in the back at Cousino's.

* * *

For men like Friedman, there was no last word. He would make his announcement soon. He had successfully brokered a game with Joe Mathews's outfit in Dallas, the Bluebonnets, to be played in Texas Stadium, home of the Landry-Shifting Cowboys. Among the teams in Friedman's league, which included Cleveland, Toronto, Buffalo, New York, and Pittsburgh, the outfit from Toledo was the only choice. Not only had they earned their rightful spot atop the standings, their dominance in every facet of the sport was the best promotion of it. The Glass City would be a tougher sell for Friedman, but if an event in the sport's preeminent venue would legitimize his business, then he would invite his league's legitimate champion. What remained was the question of ownership. Friedman was the founder, who had made good on his promise to unite teams across the Mississippi. Now he could put the squeeze on Stout to honor the deal and pay for his franchise or fire him outright.

* * *

Winter in Toledo was an abyss of gray. In the argument of worst winter city among Detroit, Cleveland, and Chicago sat the town connecting them. The Maumee froze over, thawed, churned into rubble, and froze again, like a glacier left to die and decompose. A National Weather Service report called Toledo the most miserable city in the country. It reflected the atmosphere inside the house on Westbrook Drive. Stout's and Sue's unspoken pledge to survive the holidays had timed out, and with the new year any past on which their marriage could stand faded away. In January the phone rang.

"Congratulations," Friedman told Stout. "You're going to Dallas." The deal was finalized. Speaking quickly to limit long-distance charges, Friedman said the Troopers would represent the eastern division of the WPFL and play in the holiest megachurch of the sport. The *Plain Dealer* announced the game as a "Super Bowl for Girls Football." The Mathews brothers would underwrite the flights and accommodations. All Stout had to do was get his team ready to play. That and pay up the $3,000 for his franchise.

* * *

For Stout, the idea of bowing out existed for a moment in the winter gloom. After all, he didn't have the money. The returns from Raceway Park and liars' poker were not panning out. On top of that, what did he have? Yanking the Troopers from under Friedman meant burning the bridge to the WPFL. Without Friedman, there would be no league, no season, no opponent, no stadium, no game, and no glory. But on television, all was golden sunshine, palm trees, and ninety thousand people in the Los Angeles Coliseum watching the Miami Dolphins complete the only undefeated season in NFL history. He watched, enrapt, as Don Shula rode into the sunset on the shoulders of his team.

Still another impossible barrier confronted the Troopers. Colony Field was a sheet of ice, the tackling sled a frozen iron shipwreck. At practice, the women wore winter coats and gloves. Hollar attempted to lead calisthenics, but the crushed bed of ice under their cleats was no place to train. Then Sunday had an idea. She remembered the Presbyterian church on Collingwood, where she'd grown up with the neighborhood boys playing basketball on dark winter afternoons. It was no Cowboys stadium, but it was a space to run. And the floors were dry.

* * *

In the empty gymnasium of the Presbyterian church on Collingwood, the women ran under flickering fluorescent lights. At half speed they ran through the playbook. Stout reminded them that the last time they held half-measure practices they got blown out. There was no substitute under the sun for raw, full-contact hitting. He tried to anticipate every contingency, but the unknowns were adding up. How would the team handle airline travel for the first time? Would the women be distracted by playing in an NFL stadium? Would the Dallas Bluebonnets show up as advertised, a hard-hitting horde befitting their male Dallas counterparts? Would he return to the Tillotson break room having failed to live up to Shula's undefeated run? The only certainty was the disaster that was his home life on Westbrook. He avoided setting foot in the house if he could, and kept the women late at practice, to run an extra suicide for every problem he could imagine. Stout blew the whistle, and the women worked off the rust in helmets and pads, the hardwood creaking under them in the dim gymnasium.

One night he saw his team half-assing it, their pop muted by the soft rubber mats they pounced on. He stepped in to demonstrate a proper hit. Across from him was Nanette Wolf. Frustrated, jittery, he exploded, and caught Wolf flat-footed. She stood up slowly, dazed. The hit got their attention, and the women found their footing, retreated into their armor, tightened up the ship.

It wasn't until she got home that Wolf saw the blood. The news she heard at the hospital hit her harder than Stout had. She'd miscarried. She held her hands over her womb to feel what was no longer there. Physically, she could recover. The conditioning endured at a Trooper practice was harder on a body. But guilt was a different opponent, and Wolf withdrew. She announced to her team that she wouldn't be coming to practice, or to the championship game.

It was tragedy added to the injury on top of insult. Wolf's absence compounded Miller's, and a hole appeared that the team tried to ignore. Then Wolf apologized. She understood that the duty to finish what they started was a higher calling. She asked for forgiveness and prayed that God would bless her teammates when they took the field in Dallas.

* * *

When the phone rang at the end of the month, Stout braced for more bad news. This time Friedman insisted on payment for what belonged to him. He told Stout, "I've held up my end of the deal." Now Stout was to honor his. The two-year gentleman's agreement had expired. For exclusive rights to the Toledo Troopers, including rights to play in Dallas, Stout was to pay up. It was his final offer. Otherwise, Day Enterprises was cutting ties then and there.

"You think you own the team?" Stout said. "Show me where it says you own the Troopers." And when Friedman balked, Stout found his foothold and kept pushing. His bottomless spite was in it. The notion of getting shitcanned by a blowhard like Friedman made him clench tighter. "You gonna fire me, Sid?" Stout said. "You gonna fire Carl? You gonna fire everybody?"

Cut away all but what a man is willing to fight for, and you have the essence. It wasn't the trademark Stout fought for. It was the team, and the women who wore its colors.

"You have nothing," Stout said.

Friedman's only leverage was the uniforms he had himself purchased. He demanded that Stout return the jerseys, or he'd be slapped with a cease-and-desist. "The uniform doesn't belong to you," Friedman said. "It belongs to the league."

Stout didn't give in: "You can have your goddamned jerseys."

Stout hung up the phone, not realizing what he had done. He lit a cigarette, let his agitation burn away. He was no stranger to the bluff, but as he settled, he felt anxiety of a different stripe. He had cut the line to the anchor that was Friedman. Now he found himself adrift on a lifeboat with a women's football team. They had their practice jerseys. They had a cold, badly lit gymnasium. They had their plane tickets. And there was nowhere else to go, except Dallas.

CHAPTER 10

WORLD CHAMPIONS

In 1971, Texas Stadium opened as a symbol of the AFL-NFL merger, in brick and mortar, iron and steel, asphalt and AstroTurf. No longer would professional football teams have to share their home with colleges, other professional sports, or Olympic events. The gunmetal fortress rising from a sea of pavement in the suburbs was the focal point of the newborn league. The designers left a hole in the roof to allow God to see men play. In January 1973, Texas Stadium hosted the Pro Bowl. In February it hosted the Toledo Troopers and the Dallas Bluebonnets.

The party of twenty-one women and four coaches schlepped their bags onto a Southwest airliner from a staircase wheeled onto the tarmac. It may have looked like the first time a team of paid female athletes was climbing aboard a plane. Because it was. They were by turns giddy with excitement and sober with anxiety. Olivia Flores passed out the moment the wheels left the earth and the fuselage ascended into the clouds. Hamilton had never thought he would board a plane in his life, not even as a player for Bowling Green. Human-made things like furniture, automobiles, and doorframes were not manufactured to accommodate him. By extension, neither were passenger aircraft. The turbulence the 727 hit over the Mississippi confirmed his fears. He hung on to the seat for his life, even after the plane touched down on solid ground.

Hamilton's conniption softened their jitters, and they fell into a spell of reverence for what they saw. Unlike Friedman, Joe Mathews understood that to make money you had to spend it, and he rolled out the carpet for his visiting opponent. A transit bus driver met the team at Greater Southwest Airport, helped load their baggage, and drove them to their hotel. Then came the tour of Texas Stadium, the concrete-and-steel edifice rising on the horizon, diabolical in its size. The Bluebonnets catered a barbecue on the concourse, like the field, bigger than anyone had ever seen. Dressed in slacks and blazers and ankle boots, the team strolled down the service ramp that opened onto the field. The men wore striped ties and blazers. They stayed together like schoolchildren on a museum tour. The jumbotron's golden glitz read *WELCOME TROOPERS.*

They gazed up at the sky through the oval hole and knelt down to feel the manufactured earth with their hands. In the sun, the turf glowed a fluorescent green. They remarked on how the field sloped down from the center, like the roof of a house. Sixty-five thousand blue seats stared down at them, indifferent. Stout, Hamilton, and Wright were drawn to the center of the football megachurch, to the 50-yard line. They stood atop the NFL logo and took a picture. None had made it onto an NFL field, until now.

The term *locker room* failed to signify what the women entered. A high-ceilinged gallery carpeted wall-to-wall. The stalls were interlocking wardrobes crafted from dark hardwood. Some had nameplates. Linda Jefferson found one. She stood in front of Bob Hayes's locker for a moment with her hands in her pockets. Deb Brzozka found Roger Staubach's and hung her coat up on the hook.

Some lockers had chalkboard name plates, a reminder of how easily the dream could get erased.

Stout nodded, understanding that the slate could be wiped clean. He felt as though he was about to be erased. He moved on through the tour in a daze. That night, walking the hotel hallways to enforce curfew, he began to see the forest for the trees. Perhaps Dallas would be the end of the line. He could take his winnings of headlines and blowouts and a trip to Dallas and walk away from the table.

* * *

When she took the field, the first thing Hollar realized was the truth of AstroTurf: It was hard, ungiving, like the proverbial parking lot. The novelty of the plastic grass wears off quickly, like skin on their elbows and forearms once burned on the turf. The second was the army of Bluebonnets that came charging out of the tunnel. They kept coming. The Trooper sideline could have been a bus stop of itinerants in tattered green and grass-stained white. The Dallas side was an army, dressed top to bottom in spanking-new black and blue. Their dark helmets sparkled from the rows of lights along the roofline. Hollar estimated there must have been fifty players. As they executed their warm-up drills, the echo of their popping pads throughout the stadium confirmed their reputation promulgated in their PR of hard hitting. Brzozka felt something she'd never sensed before a game, a kind of slow-drip lonesome dread. *We are going to get killed*, she thought, as she could feel tears welling up inside.

One player stood out among the mass of helmets. She was six feet tall and weighed nearly three hundred pounds, according to the program. The Bluebonnet Goliath was Bobbie Grant, towering over the dark army preparing for battle. On the field, she seemed to plug the entire span between the hash marks, just by standing there.

They could hear an unmistakable chant coming from the Dallas sideline, just like the commercial: *Everything's better, with Bluebonnet on it!*

The Troopers began to sink under the Texas-size enormity of the moment.

Stout and Hamilton could see it on their players' faces, their body language. Their heads were spinning. They recognized the butterflies they felt back in Buffalo, when they'd been destroyed. The Dallas side had its share of fans but very little on the Trooper side. They were all alone. Their composure was collapsing into a just-happy-to-be-here passivity. Dressed in their mismatched practice jerseys, they did not feel like the imposing force they'd been back home. Hollar sensed it and withdrew. The heartbeat of the moment was the game itself. The buildup. The hype. The staredown before the fight. It was everything, the half-covered dome and the jumbotron and the NFL logo in red, white, and blue. Performance was a matter of posture, composure, and facing down what wasn't real.

Jackie Allen had felt it before, too. But not on a football field. She'd seen fights in school: physical, fist-flailing throwdowns. She knew that the first person to back down was the sorry sucker to get bloodied. She felt the collective tremble of fear. She stood in the center of the circle of teammates, staring down that fear in their eyes. *"There may be a hundred of those bitches over there. But we only have to play eleven of them. That's all we got to do!"*

The first snap proved the rumors true: The team in blue hit harder than any opponent. The coach across from Stout, Rick Benat, had prepared the Dallas women on the game's machinelike timing. The line shot off in sync, and Troopers braced for the wave. Dallas quarterback Barbara O'Brien had grown up on sandlots and barnyard basketball courts. Broad-shouldered and athletic, O'Brien could've played fullback. She was a quick study, and the Troopers were apt teachers. Schwartz, White, Farrell, and Allen clung together on the fundamental physics of keeping pads low. Ballhawks like Jones and Jimenez piled on. Getting hit by the Troopers, O'Brien said later, felt like getting hit by a tank.

Mary Meserole lined up at fullback for the Bonnets. Like her teammates, she was a stranger to the game but an old friend to hitting. She'd played with her brothers growing up. Her mother told her not to come inside unless she couldn't stop the bleeding. She'd fallen off horses, jumped off balconies, hung from TV antennas. Once, she bit off her own tongue on a fall. But she'd never felt the force like the wrecking ball of Schwartz's helmet. At the whistle, Meserole opened her eyes and thought her femur was broken. A dizzy relief washed over her when she saw the concave thigh pad. It had been knocked inside out at the hit.

On offense, the Trooper engine sputtered. The Bluebonnets keyed on Jefferson and relied on the human battleship in Grant to blow up any hope of finding room up the middle. It was as though Grant's presence gave the Bluebonnets an extra helmet to fly into the backfield. Hollar seethed in the huddle, her team unable to execute.

The concrete turf gave the game a harder edge. It became another defender, the hard surface, a teammate on the side of whoever earned leverage on the hit. Brzozka thought it felt like getting hit by a car. She'd never been hit so hard. Right tackle Linda Williamson got stood up, then T-boned from the side. Her foot stuck to the turf while her knee twisted and popped. She had to be carted off on a stretcher and then zoomed off to Irving's Baylor hospital. The violence was a momentary distraction. It was *next man up*, and Flores and Jimenez and Smalley rushed in to fill the gap. Once the referee blew the whistle and set the ball, the women braced for the next wave, and Stout head counted: Nineteen mismatched players remained.

The navy helmets kept attacking. Jimenez felt it intimately: A missile of hard polycarbonate connected with her jaw, under her face mask, knocking her senseless. She went down, punch-drunk and weak-kneed. Smalley moved over to fill her spot, holding her own by merely obeying orders. *Just hold the line*, Hamilton screamed. Smalley clashed with the lineman, staying low, her forearms taking the pressure off her bullet-lodged spinal cord, steering the ball to her teammates behind her.

Jimenez was delirious on the sidelines, on a knee, watching her teammates wear down. She heard a voice: "We need her now!" It was Stout, red-faced, helpless. Hamilton kept his eyes on the field, lips clenched. Jimenez stood up, took a lung full of cool windless air, and snapped her helmet tight. "You better put me in," she said, "before I change my mind."

A series of perfunctory possessions left the Troopers with the ball on their own 8-yard line, in the shadow of the fluorescent yellow goalposts. Hollar was furious in the huddle. This wasn't Trooper football. Stout countered the Bluebonnet tendency with a misdirection, a *25-left sweep*. Hollar was to swing around and fake to Jefferson and give to Dauer running left. But Jefferson was too close, or Hollar too soon. They collided in the backfield, and the ball popped loose. Blue helmets swarmed near the end zone line, and the ball bounced at Jefferson's feet. Then it was automatic. The ball came to Jefferson, and Jefferson flew to space, like a ghost, on the outside slope. First she found the corner, then she saw the angle and was gone. Ninety-two yards into the Cowboy-blue turf of the end zone.

The broken play score gave them a precarious edge. With breathing room, on the sideline Burrows and White tried to figure out Goliath. Grant was as big as a house but also stationary like one. She was soft, and if you speared her before she gained momentum, Hollar would have time to distribute. It was a thankless but necessary duty, throwing your body into an oak tree as it fell. But the line understood that occupying her for a moment would give Jefferson and Gould a chance to go around her.

Stout plugged away, banking on the sheer odds of Jefferson or Gould or Dale finding a crease. Hollar kept house in the huddle, and the line dutifully bashed ahead. *Bobbie left* or *Bobbie right*, Hollar said, shorthand for Stout's unbending grind. The next possession, running away from Grant, Jefferson saw a seam and flew through into the clear. Forty-two yards and another precious touchdown from the blur that was number 48. The Bluebonnet sideline watched the celebration. Benat and his defense understood that the only way to stop Jefferson was to keep the ball away from her.

The blue helmets took their time, eating up the clock in a punishing drive on short runs to fullback Jody Williams. If there was a weakness in the Troopers' armor, Benat had found it with depth. The Dallas fresh legs could take the bite out of the attacking line. As the first half wound down, the Bluebonnets had driven 80 yards to the goal line. O'Brien took the snap and dove into the two-gap. When they peeled off the bodies, she lay in the end zone. The Dallas bench exploded in celebration, the outpouring familiar to the Troopers, but for the fact that they were watching it instead of living it. The momentum had swung as the teams headed to the lockers, the Bluebonnets down one score.

In the locker room, the tone was bleak. The drive had inspired the fear that the Bluebonnets couldn't be stopped. Hollar felt the dread and began to tremble. She could not get the thought out of her mind that her team couldn't do it. They were going to lose. The butterflies grew into a full-blown wave of nausea. The steely quarterback burst into the bathroom stall and vomited.

* * *

Stout fought the fear with a simple halftime declaration: the team had passed the test. They had seen the enemy and had stood up to the horde in blue. The encouragement was a small consolation to the team that had just given up an 80-yard drive. Then a voice said, *"She's just a big marshmallow!"* It was Eunice White, leveling Grant with a metaphor that swept away the fear.

In the locker room Stout also saw the future. In the Bluebonnet smashmouth drive, he saw possibility for the sport. The entire journey seemed to lead up to it: the standoff with Friedman, the turbulent flight, the endless barbecue, the NFL logo under the dizzying Texas Stadium, the hard turf, and the music of the collisions on the field that culminated in a referee's whistle. He'd sized up the Mathews brothers as men no less than himself. Not as chintzy promoters or fast-talking Friedmans, but as football men who would value football talent. If there was a future in the women's game, it must be made of teams like the one that had just rammed the ball down his throat.

* * *

In the second half, the Trooper defense locked down Williams and O'Brien by all-out blitzes from linebackers like Dale and Jones flying in from safety. Jimenez, dazed, threw herself into the line again and again. On offense, Hollar broke huddle with the taste of puke in her mouth. The line performed the Landry Shift. Then they let the attacking defense through, as ordered. Hollar reeled in her prey, backpedaling, then slung. Just when Dallas thought they had broken through, the Troopers executed the mindfuck of a screen pass to Jefferson, in the clear. And just like that, the score was 19–6, and Linda Jefferson was only getting started.

In the end, she scored five touchdowns, which stood as the record for most in a game in Texas Stadium. She carried the ball ten times for 208 yards. The AP reporter sitting in the press box called her a *135-pound whippet*. She could see things that weren't there, like an open space around a corner, or a blitzing linebacker shooting a gap. She darted laterally without slowing down, sniffing weakness. Her instincts carried her away from contact, including with the unforgiving concrete. In the clear she was untouchable. Her legs kept moving. If a lineman grabbed hold, she shapeshifted into something like an eel and spun safely low before others joined in.

She should've scored six touchdowns. In the fourth quarter, the Bonnets were exhausted. They hunched low with their hands on their knees. LJ swept inside the defensive end, shook the linebacker to her knees, and trotted to the corner. But Flores was flagged for a block in the back, and LJ's layer of icing was erased. Stout followed up with a counter-21, Jefferson drawing the defense away, and Gould took the handoff and plowed 14 yards for the score.

The jumbotron that welcomed the Troopers showed the final score: 37–12.

The women shook hands and hugged their opponents. Stout and Hamilton and Wright credited the Bluebonnet coaches, savoring the moment. They took pictures, standing on the NFL logo and backdropped by the massive electric scrim announcing the Troopers as World

Champions. The players drifted from the Dallas turf looking back, like the three thousand fans who came out to behold the game and its grandiose architecture.

The delirium of pain and euphoria carried them back to the hotel and throughout the return flight the next morning. Jimenez walked through the Dallas airport in a stupor, awed by the enormity of the terminal, an indoor shopping mall of clothing stores and restaurants. She settled into a cantina, figuring the departing flight would surely wait. The plane took off without her. For years to come she would suffer the derision of her teammates, who said more than they knew when they asked her if the burrito was worth it.

"Damn right it was," Jimenez said.

A handful of news outlets ran stories of Toledo's win. The AP posted a column that got picked up by hundreds of papers around the country, and beyond. Terry Dale got a call from Italy. Her brother, whose jaw she had shattered, was stationed in Sicily and called to say he'd read the story of a new Super Bowl champion, and the photograph of her hauling in a pass from Lee Hollar.

In the cavernous locker room, the women congregated in a circle, arm in arm. They sang the Trooper song: *We are the Troopers, mighty mighty Troopers!* They sang it again and again, topping each full-throated chant. They sang for Williamson and Wolf and Miller. They sang for Texas Stadium, for Texas barbecue, for the Texas-size jumbotron. They sang for the unforgiving AstroTurf. They sang for their coaches and for the bruises from the hits, for the blood stains they wore as badges of honor, and for the license to let loose in the collective joy of victory. They had risen from the shadow of the biggest team on the biggest stage the sport could build, and when they saw their reflections in the locker room mirrors, they saw themselves, transformed.

CHAPTER 11

THE BOND

In 1967, the year Friedman began his scheme to build a national audience, a newscaster for the morning show in Dayton, Ohio, had an idea. His afternoon radio show was popular, especially with women who stayed at home or worked in offices that permitted the broadcast from a windowsill radio. Following the prevailing wind, he decided to convert his program to the medium of television and created the daytime talk show. *The Phil Donahue Show* was simple in its conception, a basic interview format, value-added by Donahue's frank and disarming style. But as much as the show thrived on A-list guests like Elton John, Muhammad Ali, and Johnny Carson, the ratings needle soared when Donahue took the show to the audience for questions. In 1970, Donahue's program earned a national syndication contract. In 1973, after the Troopers' win in Dallas, he asked the Toledo Troopers to appear on his program.

To veterans like Hollar and Brzozka, the invitation to appear on national television came as confirmation on a number of levels. They had withstood the cloud of anxiety they felt before the win in Texas— *it must be a sign,* they thought, a vague dream was materializing. Stout, too, was being pulled in: The naysayers at Tillotson were coming around to believe in their crony who gloated over break-room cigarettes that he had matched the Miami Dolphins' perfect season record.

The producers of *The Phil Donahue Show* asked the players to bring their equipment and jerseys, as well as another outfit—*wear what you would normally wear.*

Stout bought a new coat and tie for the occasion. He was twenty-nine years old but could play the part of a man in middle age. His name befit his stocky frame, as though he'd settled into his barrel shape long ago. His hair receded in the corners. He was cool in front of the camera, withholding his cut-up shenanigans in favor of a blunt, direct, coach-like frankness.

Donahue wore an unassuming light sweater over a collared shirt, brown slacks, and dress loafers. Before the show, they brought cameras to the parking lot and had the women simulate a play on the asphalt. Jefferson ran a post route, and Hollar took a snap, dropped back, and launched the ball over a row of cars and into the landscaping.

Donahue had developed an edgy style, his tone somehow provocative and deferential. His weapon was his microphone, long and thin and silver like a conductor's wand that would extend to the speaker with a mere flick of the wrist. Wading through the audience, he sometimes held it with two hands.

In front of the Troopers, Donahue played both sides of the spectacle: What in the world is *this*?

"I'm here with Bill Stout, the coach of a women's football team." Donahue exhaled in disbelief: "No kidding, a *women's* football team." His pause drew out a chuckle from the studio audience. "I'm tempted to accuse you of a gimmick, Bill, but um...these women are serious."

"Yeah, they're serious," said Stout, matter-of-factly.

The talk show host asked a series of questions that played between incredulity and caveman-like thickness: *Do you really hit? Do you have plays? Do you practice?*

Stout answered flatly, as though checking boxes on a survey. Donahue was slowly painting the picture.

"And you've been doing this for two years?"

"We've played twelve games. We're undefeated. We average thirty-four points a game. Our opponents average four."

"How many are on the team?"

"We suit up twenty-five."

"And you've played in Dallas, the new stadium with the hole in the roof?" Donahue was captivated by the romance of the road trip: "Did you take a bus or fly when you played in Dallas?"

"We flew."

"Big-time!"

The memory of the Dallas game was still fresh in his mind, the victory in the fragmented Texas sunshine. In fact, imagining future Super Bowls like the *big-time* Dallas game carried him through the day at Tillotson, and through the mirthless chaos of Westbrook. He could remake Friedman's model and build a league the right way, with legitimate owners like the Mathews brothers. The paperwork took nearly a month to process, but the confirmation from the secretary of state of Ohio arrived one day along with his *Toledo Blade*: The Toledo Troopers were incorporated. And William Stout was the owner.

All he needed was a new league.

* * *

In the studio, Stout didn't deviate from his serious tone: "We run a pro-style offense. We have assignments to block or pull or pass block."

"And do you pass?"

"We pass around thirty percent of the time. We have Linda in the backfield, so we don't throw as much as we probably should. Linda runs a forty-yard dash in under four-nine."

"*What?*" Donahue played up his disbelief. "That is *really* fast." His peripatetic inquiry stopped in front of Jefferson. "Linda, c'mon. Nice-looking person like you, in a football uniform?"

"I just like to play," Jefferson said. She sat slightly reclined, her hand grazing her cheek, a natural, even donning her jersey and shoulder pads. "It's something I've always loved to do."

* * *

Beverly Severance was not watching *The Phil Donahue Show* on daytime TV. She lived in her car. She was twenty years old. She had two children, and day by day she imagined what food she could supply them with cash in hand. She never took the route of public assistance because accepting something that didn't belong to her wasn't right. She kept her Dodge Demon clean and didn't see herself as lacking privilege. Level or not, life was a playing field, and she was on it. Reality was what it was. She'd grown up just over the state line in Lambertville to parents who split when she was young, leaving her and her five brothers and sisters to fend for themselves. Every day was a fight to get what you could, and sometimes just a plain fight. The rituals began with taunting followed by a congregating circle. The fist-throwing descended into wrestling matches that ended on gravel or pavement or linoleum. She played hard tackle football with the neighborhood boys, and one day she crossed a boy with a forearm to the face that crushed his nose. Taunting ensued, followed by the circle. Severance pummeled the boy into submission. But the ritual didn't end there. The next day Severance climbed off the bus to find a circle of spectators waiting and the older brother of the boy she'd beaten. She was hit so hard, she was knocked unconscious. Best to avoid fists, she learned, and always remain on your feet, unless you're pummeling the other fellow on the ground.

As a freshman at Waite High School, Severance was targeted for her rough look, her disheveled hair. Her classmates waited at the front entrance. They made a chain with locked arms, preventing her from getting in and shouting at her to go back home. She fought her way through and absorbed a fist or two in breaking free. One morning, she let the bus that took her to the fights at Waite go by. *Why bother*, she thought. Severance was on her own. By sixteen she was pregnant, by seventeen married, and by eighteen a single mother of two. She took a job stocking shelves and scooping ice cream at the UDF (United Dairy Farmers) parlor beyond the circle of her neighborhood. She preferred the fluorescent-lit order and regimentation. She could see everything coming. She also met little Dorothy Parma, who announced one day she was heading to practice for the city's football team. Parma was barely five feet tall. Severance thought, *If Parma can do it...*

The job of a football player confirmed in Severance certain instincts, instincts tempered by physical fights and how to survive them. The tag *tomboy* was the available signifier for the trait in her that welcomed a forearm to the side of the head or a tumble to the dried yellow grass of Colony Field. Her first practice she lined up across from Hamilton, and she threw her 130 pounds into his gut and kept charging. She knocked the poppa bear clean off his feet.

While her tendency to hit found a home in the abandon of a football play, she learned something else. She was not the toughest kid on the field, nor did being the toughest matter in the larger scheme of the team. Jackie Allen hit her so hard, Severance lay on the ground stunned. There was no ego in it. Only getting back in line and bracing for the next smackdown. She learned vicariously as well. Fellow rookie Cheryl Martin broke Hamilton's cardinal rule: *Never stand still on a football field!* Martin stood there watching Jefferson return the kickoff. Then a Detroit Demon smashed into her running full speed and shattered Martin's femur. Severance had taken pride in her east-side toughness. Now she was seeing something bigger, and tougher, in the collective reverence for the game's brutal justice.

* * *

It drew them all like a muse, and when they were forced out of the game, they wept for what they were leaving behind. Wolf gave it up for motherhood. Farrell and Dauer both transferred to jobs out of town that made attending practice impossible. At thirty-five and as the president of her children's parent-teacher association (PTA), Lora Smalley could not commit to six days a week of punishment.

Debbie Skiles would later say playing football was the greatest time in her life. But in the off-season, she got pregnant. If she had a time machine, she said, she would go back.

Williamson never saw the field again after Dallas. Connie Miller's tackle in which she sustained a spiral fracture to her leg was her last. The doctors who repaired Iris Smith's shredded rotator cuff recommended she give up on any notions of stepping on a football field again.

When Olivia Flores was accepted to a graduate nursing program in Steubenville, she had to make the most difficult decision of her life. She knelt before her parents seeking their blessing. It was the first time anyone in her family had considered graduate school. Her mother let her go. Her father shook his head and told her that seeking a career instead of starting a family was nothing short of tearing up her birth certificate stating she was his daughter. She packed up her car anyway, then headed east on the turnpike. Knowing that the Troopers at that moment were at Colony Field, running, hitting, sweating, Flores was overcome. She pulled over on the side of the road. She cried, remembering the bond she felt on the football field. She'd never tasted this kind of melancholy, an irrevocable loss of a precious, formative era of her life, like looking back at the stadium as the lights were shutting down. A state trooper pulled up behind her. Through her tears, she told him she was making a life-changing decision. When the trooper let her go, Flores composed herself. She looked at her own bloodshot eyes in the rearview mirror. Then she threw the car into drive and didn't look back.

* * *

Now in *The Phil Donahue Show* studio, the women onstage—like Diane Degelia dressed in a casual blouse and skirt—could be mistaken for spokespersons for the teachers' union. Their bodies did not fit the preconceived size and shape of a person who plays football. Yet there sat five-foot, four-inch, 130-pound Linda Jefferson in her pads and green jersey. It might have occurred to the women watching at home that an athlete out of uniform was still an athlete, that the urge to line up and hit stirred inside. The camera cut away to show two pairs of legs: Degelia's high heels and delicate calves wrapped in soft nylons next to Jefferson's white, coarse, game-worn tube socks and chipped black cleats. A closeup of one wary audience member told viewers what to think: a mild shaking-of-the-head bemusement.

"Do people come to your games? Do you actually get crowds?"

Stout kept his matter-of-fact, this-is-for-real voice: "We average about two thousand fans. They come out to laugh, but after they see these women play, they leave as fans."

"You practice two and a half hours a night—are you a mean coach?"

A nervous wave of laughter ran through the players, including Jefferson. "Yeah, he's mean."

* * *

Not long after the team's appearance on *Donahue*, Stout awoke from a nap to find his son engulfed in flames. It was a startling vision—the room flickering in torchlight, the smell of burning flesh—that took a moment to understand. It was no dream. Guy had found a box of matches left on the coffee table. The strike-anywhere blue tip matches made of wood. The kind that tempt you to hold them as the flame drips down to your fingertips and then on to your pajamas that no one had thought to make fireproof.

The pajamas had gone up like tissue paper, and running for help only fanned the flames. By the time Guy made it across the house, up the stairs, and into the bedroom, he was a human torch. Stout whipped the blankets from the bed and tackled his son to the floor. In a moment he'd called a rescue squad and was holding Guy in smoldering blankets on the front porch. Guy's face was white. He responded to questions. "It doesn't hurt, Daddy," he said. The boy said he felt fine, he didn't want a ride in the ambulance. Stout knew Guy was in shock because the pajamas were welded to the skin on his leg like a blackened crust.

By the time the ambulance arrived, Stout was sobbing. He had seen the damage. He was not a religious person, but in the moment, he groveled before the Almighty, seeking some stroke of good fortune, for surely he was not deserving of this. Then he handed over his son to the paramedics as though performing some dark primitive sacrifice. They wrapped Guy in a tinfoil-like shock blanket. He screamed that he felt fine, that he wanted to stay home, but then he lost consciousness as the doors slammed shut and the sirens split the quiet street.

Guy was admitted to the St. Vincent's child burn unit, a grim first-floor corner of the hospital, as dismal as its name would indicate. He would awake to the stench of his burned body, mixed with antiseptic.

Sue appeared in stony disbelief. On the inside, she raged against the man who was to blame, but at the moment Guy's life hung in the balance. They both avoided the hurricane brewing between them, pacing in the fluorescent-lit cinder-block dungeon, imagining Guy teetering one way or the other, finding reassurance in the sound of the machines stabilizing their son's life.

Guy was placed in a room with another young boy who'd been burned when a can of lighter fluid he was holding exploded. The two boys became friends, playing War and Go Fish. The other boy's condition worsened, until one day his lungs collapsed, and he died. When Guy was carted off for surgery, he thought he would be next. The doctors removed skin from his stomach and buttocks and grafted it onto his legs. The procedures closed the wounds in safer-than-sorry sleepless increments. In all, Guy went under for nine surgeries to patch together skin they'd removed from other parts of his body, and skin harvested from a special species of pig. For three months, Guy lived at the hospital while Stout and Sue traded off visiting hours.

But the relief they felt when Guy was permitted to spend a night at home was temporary. It was as though the family was returning to a stranger's house. Confined to Westbrook, Stout and Sue targeted their anger toward each other. Sue blamed Stout for the accident. Fair or not, her resentment was an add-on to his burden that he was unwilling to bear. He had suffered, had prostrated himself in the eyes of God, and could not descend any lower. To Sue, he never showed any remorse or accountability. Sue's bitterness grew in turn. They could barely stand to be in the same room with each other, but their wrists were handcuffed together by rage and by duty. Guy's bandages needed to soak and be changed three times a day. In their tiny bathroom, Guy cried in the bathtub while Stout and Sue removed the putrid pus-filled gauze. Stout told him to look at a spider on the wall to get his guard down. Then he yanked off a bandage. In her son's screams, Sue found the breaking point.

The telephone's shrill metallic ring punctuated their arguments, like a boxing match. It became the score of their sad movie: Now the telephone's unpredictable but constant troll meant more than the dread of a bill collector. It could mean St. Vincent's Hospital, delivering hopeful results or scheduling the next phase of recovery. It could mean a call from an investor interested in bridging the financial gap for the upcoming season. It could be a prospective owner of the team cropping up regionally in Columbus or Middletown seeking consultation with the league founder. It could be a friend or neighbor or acquaintance who knew a prospective player seeking inside dope on the Troopers.

Thousands had seen Phil Donahue pace the stage before Stout and the Troopers. By the number of calls received seeking information about his team and the league, Stout believed at the least he would live to see another day of coaching, and that among the things in his life that held promise—his marriage, his career—it was football that drove him.

* * *

Phil Donahue stood in the audience, welcoming his viewers back from the commercial break. He announced the most volatile part of the program: "Let's go to the phones. Go ahead, sir. You're on the air."

Donahue had discussed hitting, practicing, conditioning. He'd shown the players in the parking lot running plays. They had talked about winning and playing in the greatest football stadium built by humankind. The first caller squeezed his voice through the speaker system.

"Yeah, I'm just calling to say I think the only thing these women should be trying to tackle is someone's diaper."

"I see," Donahue said. "You think they should be home with the kids."

"Right."

"And the gridiron is no place for a woman."

"Right."

The players shifted in their seats. They had all heard it before, the chirp from afar. *Get back in the kitchen!* It was a strange language, moving by at high speeds. They could shrug it off, the lunatic on the fringe barking incoherently. Now they were bathed in it, raining down from the lights in studio sound. If they were ever bruised by the tone of the talk of women's football, Stout and the women did not dwell. They were flattered by lights and cameras, and they could sense the explicit challenge before them: how to get the world to take the game they loved seriously. They'd tuned in to the signals of change, women's rights marches, Equal Rights Amendment debates, and the passage of Title IX, but those waves ebbed before eroding the football barrier. They were less advocates for change than livers of it. The women did not snap on their helmets and pads to make a statement, but by doing so, they were making one. And when asked about their statement, they responded as athletes. They credited their teammates and coaches and fans and stressed that the only movement they were a part of was the football movement.

Linda Jefferson's modesty attracted the cameras: "Look, we're not part of any movement. We just want to play. We've always just wanted to play. And now we're doing it. That's all."

Another caller chimed in: "Yeah, Linda Jefferson, what's a nice young lady like you doing playing football?"

A cringe ran through the audience.

Jefferson stood her ground: "I like it. I want to do it, so I do it."

* * *

Nobody at Tillotson Carburetor on Berdan Avenue had been a guest on *The Phil Donahue Show*, or had ever known anyone to be a guest on it. When Stout returned to work, he held court like a celebrity. The publicity felt like vindication for his vision that many thought outlandish. That afternoon in the break room, he was better than the degenerate who lost his paycheck on a bad bluff. In fact, his status and his cool performance, as well as the sound of the show's studio audience's applause, gave him the credibility he needed. He had made national news with his victory in Dallas. The *Toledo Blade* had run a few notices of the team's success to go along with Friedman's orchestrated press releases. But of all the angles of Stout's new league pitch, the most compelling was the fact that he had won every game. He himself was a solid bet. And while the notion of a viable league of women's football wasn't viral, it could be contagious by contact.

Frank Wallace was the materials manager at Tillotson. He worked close to the floor where Stout and his friend Jerry Davis assembled the carburetors that moved unendingly up the line. On cigarette breaks, Wallace and Davis became a captive audience to Stout's bluster, standing at the source of the story they read in the paper and watched on TV. At every chapter of Stout's epic—becoming a head coach, winning at Texas Stadium, booking the full-hour segment on *The Phil Donahue Show*—Wallace shook his head in disbelief. He may have been the first case of the Trooper follower who came out to laugh but left as a fan. Wallace liked hearing stories of Jefferson's exploits and of Hamilton's lockdown defense. *Tell me more*, he said to Stout.

The rock of Stout's pitch was that he, the football player, was now in charge. He held legal title to the Toledo Troopers. He'd sent his copyright application to the US Patent and Trademark Office to notarize his divorce from Friedman and to make his aim official. He was forming his own league.

The NFL, with a W.

For his National Women's Football League, he recruited one of his players to lead. Deb Brzozka was a disciple, a talented player since the tryout in '71. She had helped design advertisements and had herself struck deals with the local printer and stadium vendors. Stout came to her with a proposition. "How would you like to be commissioner of the National Women's Football League?"

Brzozka was smitten. She agreed it was a woman's place to be atop a women's league, and like Stout, she believed she was getting in at the right time.

It was the icing on his proposal to Wallace, who was not above a friendly wager. With Wallace's backing, as well as a handshake agreement with Bob Krasula, a friend of Lee Hollar who had been following the team's breakout, SKW Enterprises, the corporation that controlled the league, was born.

Jerry Davis, too, felt the fear of missing out but didn't have the ground-floor cash. He had something else Stout wanted: experience trolling the secondary and delivering hits as a safety, from his days at Scott. "We have a place for you," Stout said.

* * *

Below luring investors like Wallace and Krasula on the to-do list was creating franchises. Friedman's outfits in Cleveland, Pittsburgh, and Buffalo would be off the table. Stout had to find allies in the owners of Detroit and Dallas to help spawn other franchises. The Mathews brothers also operated a team in Fort Worth, and they had networked with West Coast teams in Los Angeles and San Diego.

On paper, the idea was sound enough. Not-for-profit sports schemes like the NFL had taken off. There was the World Hockey Association and the World Football League and the American Basketball Association (ABA). Furthermore, women were carving out a space to play: As *The Phil Donahue Show* was airing, the ink was drying on the first scholarship offer by a major athletics program. The University of Miami offered seventeen-year-old golfer Terry Williams free tuition (she had to pay room and board). In June, Billie Jean King founded a league for female athletes, the Women's Tennis Association, the unifying step for the sport nearly a century in the making. Also that spring, top-ranked women's tennis star Margaret Court faced off against self-promoter Bobby Riggs. And, later that year, Riggs and King filled the Houston Astrodome for their historic showdown, with marketing: the Battle of the Sexes. Riggs beat Court, but he was no match for King. Bills featuring women were drawing crowds, like Friedman had predicted. But even irrefutable scripture must be brought to life with the voice of a preacher. In Stout's presence, one became a believer in his vision. He had undeniably built a winner, and thus he would undeniably build a league.

Ken Dippman was an accounting clerk at Tillotson who, like Wallace and Krasula, was catching a spell of Trooper Fever. Dippman wasn't ready to pony up as an investor in the league, but he'd watched *The Phil Donahue Show* and the Battle of the Sexes and convinced Stout to orchestrate publicity of his own. The press release that ran in the *Blade* profiled the team and the NWFL, a transcontinental ascendant league featuring teams in Buffalo, Detroit, Columbus, Dallas, and Los Angeles. The story promoted an opener against Detroit as a retribution game: "The Motor City team will be looking for revenge," read the story, barely disguising Stout's leveraging. Stout attempted to paint a picture of a hard-hitting game, as though rebranding Friedman's creation: "The girls play rugged football—they go on the field with the intention of hitting someone."

* * *

Early in the program, Donahue addressed players seeking clarification. "Your opponents, do they really hit?" he asked.

"Yeah, they hit," Jefferson said. "And it hurts."

"Then what would motivate a woman to play pro football?"

* * *

Mitchi Collette could finally make friends. Her father was a colonel in the army and moved from base to base, never staying long enough for Collette to bond with the mismatched military daughters. She'd been to twenty-six states by the time she was fourteen, and her family settled down in north Toledo. The first connection she made was in high school, at Woodward, when a spoonful of mustard flew between the racially segregated tables in the lunchroom. Collette walked up to the table by herself and asked who the offending punk was. Debbie Haynes stood up and challenged Collette to meet after school by the polar bear statue in front of the school. Haynes never showed up. But they met again on the basketball hardwood. They found a bond in competition, and through this pilot program of girls' sports they shared a common enemy. Collette found honor in being on a team. In one of the school's first city-league games, against Libbey, Collette broke free for a wide-open layup, but she could sense a defender closing in. As she went up for the shot, she felt a knock to the side of her head. The Libbey guard had punched her, a sweeping blow that sent her to the floor. Collette was dazed, but the flood of camaraderie she felt when Haynes rallied to her defense moved her to tears. The referees stepped in to separate the teams, as Haynes stared down the pistol from Libbey, a hotshot with a reputation as the best athlete in the league, whose viciousness was belied by a shy, unassuming smile.

Haynes was the first Black person Collette had ever met, certainly the first she'd ever befriended. The reverse could be said for Haynes. The two became best friends. The two bonded through sports in every season throughout high school. Sports gave meaning to school for Collette, not the other way around. She bought in like an officer in training. Throughout her career at Woodward, she was an obedient, disciplined player, a captain year-round. Softball. Basketball. Track and field.

After graduation, Haynes discovered she was pregnant. To her rigidly religious family, it was an unforgivable sin. Her despair bottomless, Haynes closed the garage door, started the car, and went to sleep.

Her suicide sent a shock wave through the north side. For Collette, Haynes's death cut like a battlefield wound. It would always be there, the hole inside, the loss of a best friendship that was forged through a team. After graduation, there were few opportunities to fill it, and her will to play ebbed the more hours she picked up at the Goodyear factory down in Luckey assembling seat cushions, and the more she followed the instructions for what a woman her age should do: get married.

She became engaged to a firefighter that summer. Perhaps she would never have had a chance to come up with her own answer to Phil Donahue's question if it weren't for a stranger who approached her in the break room at Goodyear one day during lunch. Collette had seen her before, that cover girl smile, her Jackson Five–style Afro. It was the hotshot from Libbey who'd punched her in the face on the basketball court years before. She introduced herself to Collette. Her name was Linda Jefferson.

Collette told her fiancé about the offer to play football. Roger said, *Why not?* He had heard about the team, their perfect record. Plus, earlier that year a woman became the first to join the ranks of the Toledo Fire Department. If she could carry a man up a flight of stairs and handle a fire hose, why couldn't a woman play tackle football? Collette brought home her equipment, and they laughed as he could barely squeeze the helmet onto his head.

On the Fourth of July, the department pulled fireworks duty at Walbridge Park on the river. Roger was loading equipment off the back of a pickup truck, and for a split second, he lost his balance, and that was all it took. He fell backward, headfirst, onto pavement. He never woke up. The doctors said his brain was like an egg inside a ball spiked to the ground.

Collette herself fell, into a fog of grief and confusion. Her life's course was knocked off its bearings. Getting married was an all-or-nothing arrangement, and no backup plan existed. The hole left by losing her best friend Haynes opened up again. She was drawn to football practice in the swampy late-July afternoons, for there she found order. Space and time were divided up by chalk and whistles, and organized into unambiguous gridlike sections. She knew her place as a rookie, a private first class, to learn to hit and absorb the blow and welcome the heat and the sweat of a summer football practice. The men coaching her spoke in flat, matter-of-fact terms. The game was pain, and mistakes had consequences. At practice, the world became bearable, witnessed through a face mask.

* * *

At least forty women had come up with their own answer to Donahue's question in the late summer of 1973: The word was getting out. The image of a woman in football pads was capturing imaginations while Dippman's publicity was making a dent. Stout continued to receive calls. Many women had watched from the outside waiting for the will to step forward. Some had seen *The Phil Donahue Show* and sided against the callers who ridiculed the idea of women playing football. *I'm playing because you told me I couldn't*, Pam Schwartz imagined telling the hecklers driving by. Some women said they liked the workout, which in 1973 was a politic answer. Keeping your body in shape was an acceptable reason to compete. Some were drawn to play for a winner. And there were the twice-champion veterans who'd tasted victory and couldn't let it go.

For Teri Macias, the choice came down to playing football or going to prison. Macias had been busted for pulling a starter's pistol on a teacher at school. The arrest capped a long list of scrapes with the law, and the judge sentenced her to probation, telling the court she'd go to jail unless she found a way to stay off the streets. Then Macias heard about the Troopers. She'd never been accountable to anyone or anything. Now she had to answer to Davelyn Burrows and Sunday Jones. Like an initiation rite, the six-foot, two-inch Burrows administered a hellacious blow to Macias during the tryout; Macias would remember the feeling, like getting hit by a bus. As she got up off the ground, dazed, the feeling was not shame but a kind of pride, that this woman took the effort to lay her out like it was her job. Macias made the team, and six months after her arrest, the probation officer found Macias on the streets again, this time at an abandoned city park, with twenty-three other women in helmets and shoulder pads, knocking sense into her.

Aldah Wilhelms also faced a fork in the road. But it wasn't prison to which the alternative led but to a convent. She'd already spent six years cloistered in Tiffin, interacting only with women. But in her six-year search for God, the constant that remained was her desire to play sports. She'd grown up in South Bend, Indiana, where the neighbors couldn't keep her from playing ball with boys. They told her parents that sports would "injure her woman parts." Her six-year absence from sports didn't kill the desire but sharpened it. Her father believed in her. He drove his daughter from the convent to Bowling Green, where a football game was going on. It was the Troopers, dishing out a shellacking of Friedman's Daredevils. "I want that," said Wilhelms.

When she showed up to play, Stout found something familiar about her square jaw dotted with a dimple. He couldn't quite place her. Wilhelms was fast, and she could hit. She had a sideways stride that kept defenders off rhythm. When he couldn't decide on her position, it came to him: "You're Bronko," he said. "Bronko Nagurski," referring to the inaugural-class Hall of Famer who played both defense and offense.

"Who in God's name is Bronko Nagurski?" Wilhelms said.

"Don't worry," Stout said. "You can play anywhere." And the nickname stuck.

* * *

As Guy's scars hardened, Stout sought any excuse to get out of the house. He left for practice early, thinking of Lombardi: If you're on time, you're fifteen minutes late. It became his undying habit to be the first to arrive and the last to leave. The open field divided by pylons and chalk was the place he thrived, in contrast to the other facets of his existence, namely his luckless gambling record, his dead-end factory job, and his train wreck of a marriage. Like a battlefield general, he devised plans for his lieutenants. Hamilton oversaw the defense. Jerry Davis coached the ball carriers and defensive backs. Mike Stout supervised the offensive line. It was no accident that Colony Field resembled a basic training camp. On the field, Stout was the immersed choreographer, observing, correcting, dispatching with a dissatisfied shake of his head. All the work that the enterprise required—recruiting, managing, planning, building, executing, analyzing, and instructing—the progress steadied him, for the other side of his life drew him like a black hole. His quick wit and rough tongue among his players and coaches found a home here, on the hot, hard, weed-infested pasture of Colony Field. He rode the tackling sled and opened up on his players: *"This sorry-ass line couldn't move a dandelion!"* And then the next wave would charge into the rusted steel at the whistle. *"This line is even worse!"* The women groaned in agony, and then they hit the sled harder. As much as Stout tormented his players, they could sense the love in his tirades, and the brutality their record required bonded them all.

One day in August, after practice, Stout returned to Westbrook to find the house empty. He pulled back the curtains to reveal missing furniture: Sue's plaid swivel chair and floor lamp. Guy and Stefanie were gone. Standing alone in his house, Stout was true to his character. He did not give an inch: If Sue wanted to break the family apart, power to her. He accepted her request for divorce and the terms for custody, the spite burning away happier moments at the bowling alley or at the kitchen table playing Foto-Electric football. In the basement, Stout looked over the boxes Sue had picked over. He began digging through them. He found his all-city medal and his team picture from DeVilbiss. The black-and-white pose in full pads without a helmet, his seventeen-year-old shit-eating grin. He could sense his own picture mocking him. He dug farther and found an old playbook, and Super 8 reels of the championship in '61. Later, he brought home a projector and showed the film against an empty wall in his family room. He sat there with pen and paper, designing plays that his Troopers would use to inflict pain on whoever tried to stop him.

* * *

Dippman cut deals with the PR suits for the Mud Hens, Toledo's minor league baseball operation, and the Toledo Hornets, a smashmouth collection of itinerants that lived perennially atop the standings of the International Hockey League. The Hornets had a home, a 5,200-seat indoor sports arena on Main Street, a block of cityscape that looked like a brick-built German bunker. It was called the Sports Arena. Once, during a Rush concert, the temperature inside the hotbox measured 126 degrees.

As the season opener approached, Dippman noticed a conflict: The Troopers were opening against Columbus the same night the Hornets were playing at home.

Dippman used a barter system to promote the team on the cheap. He exchanged ad space in game programs for print costs, and radio advertisements for in-game commercials delivered by PA announcer Claus Helfer, the voice of Toledo city-league playoff games. The sport was gaining in production value, reflected in the box office pull. By his estimation, the Troopers were outdrawing the Hornets.

* * *

One night, before the first game in September, Stout returned home to find a present from Guy, an art project he had made at his new school. It was an ashtray made of clay.

The next four games, the Troopers put up 157 points and gave up

0, the most lopsided stretch at any time in their existence. At the start of every game, Stout struck a tone: *"It doesn't matter who you are. Every team can be beaten."* The veterans, now in their third year, went to work like grunts, relying on technique, hitting with abandon. If Schwartz, or Filthy McNasty as she was known, sensed timidity in an opponent, she attacked it, like a shark to blood. She ran, blocked, and lowered her shoulders with the benefit of experience. Jefferson became an unstoppable force, a weapon who could blow a game open at any moment. Jones, Hollar, and Allen outclassed every opponent. Led by Burrows, and triggered by Hollar's cadence, the line exploded with time-bomb precision. The defensive line, seasoned at the tackling sled, blew up the first sign of organization, and the attacking linebackers Collette and Macias descended like vultures to carrion.

Collette tasted the transcendent experience the others couldn't put into words. When the whistle blew, the weight of grief fell away, and all that mattered was the play in front of her. It didn't matter if they were ahead by 6 or 56.

Against Columbus, the halftime score was 30–0. Stout was furious. In the locker room, he ripped into his team. They were sloppy, they were not shooting off the line, they were not playing through the whistle. Collette had yet to learn that the score didn't matter. "But Coach," she said. "We're winning by five touchdowns."

"But you look like shit doing it!" Stout shot back.

In the second half, the women played through every down, like a tackler hitting clear through the ball carrier. Garbage time did not exist. The scoreboard didn't matter, except to indicate time left on the clock, time to set aside the fiction of courtesy. The women in green hit harder as the game went on.

Final: Toledo 64, Columbus 16.

It was the troll on the sidelines who attacked at every chance, not like he was ahead seven touchdowns, but like he was a trapped animal, like the game was the only thing left for which to fight.

CHAPTER 12

THE WORLD'S GREATEST FOOTBALL PLAYER

Verna Henderson felt like she'd won the lottery.

She had graduated in the spring of 1974 from Woodward, where she'd banged her way through the available sports. Basketball and softball had left her wanting, for the culture tended against physical contact or the stiff-lipped toughness she'd learned playing football with four brothers. When they played football in the streets, Verna was not the girl nobody wanted. She picked her own team. Her instincts were physical: Think Pete Rose slamming into Ray Fosse. An opponent was a thing to be knocked and hit and smacked, whatever the sport. Rose won the nickname "Charlie Hustle" for his hell-bent style. At Woodward, Henderson was ridiculed for taking competition too seriously.

After high school, she imagined a career in the military would satisfy her craving for toughness. Her father was against it. The army was no place for a woman, he said. So Henderson went out for football instead. She was following the buzz that was growing from an outfit of female football players from the west side who boasted a hard-hitting perfect record. She was following Mitchi Collette, a fellow Polar Bear, to the tryouts on Colony Field, where Carl Hamilton handed Henderson a set of pads and a helmet.

That was when she felt like the luckiest woman in the world.

Henderson was joining a crop of rookies drawn by the team's reputation, and by the hope for the validation it portended. *Get on board* was the message in the air, confirmed by the growing ranks of supporters from administrators to fans and the number of women like Henderson taking their chances. The disruption on a national scale suggested a fertile climate for an enterprise challenging the status quo. In the span of nine days, for example, the House Judiciary Committee adopted articles of impeachment, the president of the United States resigned, and his successor, a former football star at the University of Michigan, granted him absolute pardon. In the NFL, players like first-round draft pick John Matuszak were jumping ship to play in the World Football League, and the NFL was responding by seeking restraining orders against them. *Fighting sexism with new tactics* read the September cover of *People* magazine, featuring Toledo Waite graduate Gloria Steinem. Billie Jean King's tactic, following her triumph over Bobby Riggs, was to publish a magazine of her own to disseminate stories of women's achievements in sports. Along with the Women's Sports Foundation, King launched *womenSports* magazine, a *Sports Illustrated*–style glossy. The magazine's editorial board announced a contest inspired by *Time* magazine's best seller: Female Athlete of the Year. In 1974, United Press International announced their recognitions for both best male and female athletes.

At the end of the summer, Stout bought a plane ticket and flew to Los Angeles. Like Lamar Hunt the decade before, he held a meeting in a hotel conference room of ownership groups from around the country. Bob and Joe Mathews owned the Dallas and Fort Worth teams. Judith Cook spoke for the Detroit franchise. Jerry Patterson represented the Los Angeles Dandelions as well as the Pasadena Roses. John Mulkey Jr. and Helen Moore headed the prospective San Diego Lobos. The owners agreed that a $10,000 investment per club would get the league off the ground as well as lend credibility to the enterprise. The owners agreed to play games regionally to determine the division winners and then hold an east-west Super Bowl. On September 15, 1974, the National Women's Football League was officially born.

In Los Angeles, Patterson released a statement seeking investors, referring to a growth of sports leagues like the WFL. He suggested that the West Coast was fertile ground for the league, for it was a place where "unusual things often materialize."

A *Blade* story listed an address on Wilshire Boulevard in Los Angeles as the league's home office, and that a woman would be announced as the league commissioner. The story mentioned the Toledo standouts Hollar, Jefferson, and Schwartz and predicted that the Troopers and the Dandelions would meet in a "championship affair."

Equating high-profile NFL franchise cities like Los Angeles, San Diego, Detroit, and Dallas with the Glass Capital piqued the city's imagination. Stout and his SKW owners Wallace and Krasula, and PR man Dippman, soon expanded their circle of supporters to include Tom Loomis, the sports editor at the *Blade*, and Orris Tabner, the folksy sportscaster on WTOL Channel 11, two members of the Mount Rushmore of sports media in Toledo. Dispatches from around the country about the growing league inspired their imaginations. Loomis had covered the upheaval of football in the '60s and the passage of Title IX. The convergence of sport and legislation was playing out within the confines of his readership, he believed. Loomis had also watched opportunities appear for another female star athlete: his daughter, who would later win a scholarship to play basketball.

The next *Blade* story touted the twenty-one-game winning streak as well as a championship to be held in the Rose Bowl in November.

In 1971, Orris Tabner had reported on the thirty-five straight wins by the University of Toledo football team. Now he was covering another hometown team on a streak. Tabner envisioned his city's name on scoreboards across the country and agreed to sit on the board of SKW Enterprises to promote the team that couldn't be beat.

The press releases that the board began choreographing became the brand. There were a number of angles: The team's perfect record stemmed from their all-for-one and one-for-all, team-first mentality. The bond created by teammates having one another's backs was an essential story of sports. The sublimation of ego for team created an equilibrium that held the team together and that no one dared disrupt.

And then there was the superstar. The name that players and coaches would remember. The name that appeared in the newspapers. The name that writers began to fancy.

"*Toledo Gridders Feature Linda Jefferson*" read the *Blade* headline in the season preview before the game against Detroit. The 60-point font spanned the page. Scores of outlets around the Midwest picked it up, boasting LJ's 1973 statistics in black and white: 1,289 yards on eighty-four carries, "an amazing fifteen yards per carry." The *New York Times* ran an article after Jefferson had amassed over 500 yards in the first three games of the season. The story's hook asked who was the greatest running back: Larry Csonka, O.J. Simpson, or Walter Payton? The answer was a five-foot, four-inch cyclone from Toledo, Ohio. The story mentioned Stout's creation, the National Women's Football League, and its pan-continental cities: New York, Dallas, Detroit, Toledo, Fort Worth, and Los Angeles.

In November, Jefferson's disarming smile graced the cover of the *Blade*'s *Sunday Magazine*, the paper's full-color weekly pull-out. The headline read, "*Without Linda Jefferson, the Troopers Would Only Be Terrific.*"

The profile of the unbeaten Troopers by *Blade* writer Tom Lorenz praised the team's work ethic, their dedication, and the bonds the sport created. It also heralded Jefferson as the undisputed star of the team. She was the most incredible female football player in the country, Lorenz wrote. By which he meant *the world*.

Despite the story and Jefferson's double-take numbers, Stout began to be careful with his weapon. Fearful of the devastating consequences of an injury, he forbade her to enter the game on the defensive side to reduce wear and tear. Most of all, he loved nothing more than outsmarting

The Toledo Troopers, August 1971, at practice prior to their first game, against the Cleveland Daredevils.

Quarterback Lee Hollar, pregame warm-up, 1974.

Nose guard Jackie Allen (83) in pursuit against Columbus Pacesetters, 1974. *(Don Strayer,* Toledo Blade*)*

Running back Linda Jefferson weaves in traffic against Detroit Demons, 1974. *(Don Strayer,* Toledo Blade*)*

Lee Hollar hands off vs. Ft. Worth Shamrocks, 1975. *(Herral Long,* Toledo Blade*)*

Defensive coordinator Carl Hamilton gives instructions on tackling through the runner, Colony Field, 1975. *(Ron Jacomini)*

Defensive tackle Gloria Jimenez tapes up. *(Penny Gentieu)*

Troopers superstar Linda Jefferson takes a breather against Oklahoma City, 1976. *(Ron Jacomini)*

Game-planning for battle: Left to right: Sue Crawford, Mitchi Collette, Joey Opfer, Verna Henderson, and Pam Hardy, 1977. *(Penny Gentieu)*

Trooper sidelines against Detroit, 1976. *(Ron Jacomini)*

Offensive tackle Vicki Seel leaves it all on the field against Detroit, 1976. *(Ron Jacomini)*

Defensive end Eunice White and the Troopers stand for the National Anthem, 1977. *(Penny Gentieu)*

"We Are the Champions": Left to right: Linda Jefferson, Verna Henderson, Carla Miller, Pam Hardy, Joey Opfer, and Sunday Jones with the National Women's Football League championship trophy, 1977. *(Toledo Blade)*

Quarterback Pam Hardy (11) exorcizing pregame jitters against Oklahoma City, 1976. *(Ron Jacomini)*

Troopers rush the field after the final gun against Oklahoma City, 1976. *(Ron Jacomini)*

Defensive end Eunice White and the Troopers stand for the National Anthem, 1978. *(Penny Gentieu)*

Center/linebacker Joey Opfer walks off against Detroit, 1976. *(Ron Jacomini)*

Head coach Bill Stout watches his team warm up against Oklahoma City, 1976. *(Ron Jacomini)*

Running back Kathy Sanders and Joey Opfer sit one out, 1976. *(Ron Jacomini)*

Left to right: Carl Hamilton, Vickie Seel, Bill Stout, and Mitchi Collette administer a pummeling vs. Detroit, 1976. *(Ron Jacomini)*

his opponent, eschewing predictability. He often ran decoys to Jefferson, leaving a battering ram like Henderson in the clear, or Sunday Jones wide open on a reverse. He was most pleased when he won with guile. After all, the Troopers presented opponents with an embarrassment of weapons that limited double- and triple-teaming Jefferson.

Ramella Smith, for instance, ran toe to toe with Olympic hopeful Brenda Morehead. Flying around Colony Field in mismatched baseball cleats, Smith inspired a friendly wager among the coaches. One day at the end of practice, Hamilton set up cones 40 yards apart and told Jefferson and the new recruit that they would settle the issue right there. Smith got off the block quick and held Jefferson off. The last 10 yards were tug-of-war in the late-summer dust. Both Smith and Jefferson claimed to have won, and Hamilton was smart enough to stay out of trouble: "Too close to call," he said.

Smith admitted that Jefferson's greatness wasn't merely on account of speed. Jefferson could run off both feet, as writers described her contemporary Walter Payton, and later Barry Sanders, who many hold to be the greatest running back of all time for his ability to pivot in any direction without decelerating. In the open field, a single defender had zero chance to touch LJ, let alone bring her to the ground. A *Blade* reporter noted that "Linda Jefferson sprinting with a football is a thing of beauty. . . . She has this change of pace that confuses defenders who think they have her cut off."

No matter how carefully Stout tried to hide a tendency, it was going to be Jefferson to break a game open. On one October night against Columbus, Jefferson scored six touchdowns. One was a 7-yard dash for the corner. One was a 77-yard zigzag into the clear. Another was particularly memorable for Jefferson. She'd made her trademark cutback and found daylight over the middle. She saw two defenders closing in from the left and the right like elevator doors. In that instant, she made a decision to accelerate between them. As she shot through, she heard the collision of the defenders behind her. *That was pretty cool*, she thought, amazed at the superhero-like talent in her own body and the sheer joy it was to be a football player.

The year of Tom Lorenz's story, Jefferson ran for 1,179 yards on only seventy-four attempts, averaging almost 16 yards a carry. She scored thirty-four touchdowns and was voted MVP by her teammates, again.

It was a rare occasion for the celebration of individual performance. Unity and team governed the talking points. After the game against Columbus, Jefferson deferred praise to her offensive line. Stout was imaginative in avoiding singling out the star even after a six-touchdown clinic. He told reporters, "One thing is for sure: We have five good half-backs." He was crediting Ramella Smith, Parma, Henderson, and rookie Ruth Zuccarell, who had also scored her first touchdown, as though every number was the equivalent to number 48.

The team-first message spoke loud and clear on the defensive side. Over the eight-game stretch that ended the 1974 season, the Troopers scored 361 points while giving up only 14. They often won the psychological battle early. In the rematch against Dallas, the Bluebonnets attempted their ball control game with runs up the middle, where linemen Burrows, Allen, and Nasty were waiting. "We'll be here all night," Schwartz taunted after a series of runs up the middle went nowhere. In the huddle, Macias found an unbreakable bond and felt the obligation toward her teammates to do her job, which was beating her block. And when the ball carrier inevitably tried to peel to the outside, a worse fate awaited at the hands of Sunday Jones. The poor back would attempt to avoid the direct hit, dodging outward still, and that's when Jones, sensing fear, tore in with pit bull abandon, using the runner's own momentum to complete a thrashing. *Just where do you think you're going?* Dr. Death tormented. Meanwhile, Hamilton and Davis fumed about the 14 points they'd surrendered. Columbus's best player, Lisa Perez, managed to score twice, albeit late in the game, when the outcome was certain, when players like Jimenez and Collette succumbed to a combination of fatigue and undisciplined fun. Perez burst around the corner and fought through a tackle to the end zone. Davis took it personally. *"Ladies,"* he screamed, barely tethered to the sidelines, *"that's not how you've been trained!"*

With each game, with each season, suiting up in the green and gold for the dynastic Troopers became more than a hobby or a weight loss program. In pushing their bodies to the limits of tolerance, they found collective transcendence in the taste of dirt and sweat, and they obeyed its power. At practice, Henderson lined up across from Burrows. The offense was choreographing the *slot left slant*, in which Hollar took the snap and dumped the ball short over the middle to a crossing Jones. Henderson at guard dove at Burrows's knees. Burrows collapsed to protect herself, then shot back onto her feet. She reached down and lifted Henderson off the ground by her shoulder pads. *"Don't ever do that again!"* she said, then threw the rookie back to the ground. Henderson understood: One doesn't mess with the momma bear.

But it was Collette who won the name *Bear*. She met ball carriers face mask first, engulfing them inside a wide wingspan and taking them down, always on top.

Hitting was addictive. One of Jimenez's clients at the boutique was the slasher Zuccarell. Zukie attempted to juke her hairdresser on the pop-up drill, but Jimenez was ready. She drove through the rookie so hard that she was knocked unconscious before hitting the ground. Smelling salts brought Zuccarell back to planet Earth. Like a junkie coming down, she wanted her next fix. "At least I didn't fumble," she said.

When an early-fall rainstorm canceled practice, the team found another venue to be together and prepare as a team. All the coaches and players crammed into Lee Hollar's basement to review the game plan, like criminals orchestrating a heist. Having lost a practice, Stout spoke grimly about the team's chances. *Any team can be beat*, he reminded them. Hamilton was more specific, concerned about his defense against the swing pass. He drew up the play on notebook paper: "If you see the running back sneak into the flank for the swing pass, you've got to pop that girl, and she'll be thinking about it the rest of the game."

On a weekend without their scheduled game film study, the team gathered to watch a different film. Stout had seen Burt Reynolds portray football in its most brutal, cheap-shot terms in *The Longest Yard*. The team of women took up three rows of the Colony Theater to watch Reynolds paint a picture of devil-may-care, honor-bound masculinity. Stout instructed his team to pay close attention. "This is how the game is played," he told them, only half joking. The other half, the women did not need lecturing: In the film, the men who were faint of heart were knocked silly and carried off the field on stretchers, like Trooper opponents or teammates who'd lost their resolve on the field, even for an instant. Hamilton adopted Reynolds's nickname for his "Mean Machine" prisoners to fit his relentless band of headhunters. He christened the Trooper D *The Green Machine*.

* * *

As coverage grew, so did Stout's imaginings of prime-time glory. Since the Dallas game, he longed for a field for his team to call home. The Troopers had played their home games in several locations around the city, from Rossford to Sylvania, but Stout coveted northwest Ohio's finest venue. Waite High School, constructed in 1914 of brick and stone, stood like a cathedral overlooking the city from across the river to the east, the towering turrets and arches and parapets of stonework recalling Jesup Scott's vision of a great city. The football stadium to the north extended the grandeur, an all-brick façade that encircled the field horseshoe-like, opening to the north, the bleachers tiered, carved out of the concrete like the Roman Colosseum in miniature and named after the school's greatest gladiator. Jack Mollenkopf Stadium was widely understood to be the most venerated venue in the city, surpassing the University of Toledo's recent Glass Bowl reconstruction. The high school celebrated its heroes like Curtis Johnson, who'd helped the Miami Dolphins to their perfect season.

But ever since Stout had suited up in the orange and white, football was banned at night throughout the delta. The Toledo board of education cited fights and riots and vandalism as the reasons for the injunction. After 1963, all city-league games had been played on Saturday afternoons in broad daylight.

Stout and Brzozka made an official appeal to the board of education, claiming that their NWFL team was no high school operation and thus should be allowed to play under the lights. The board would hear none of it, until the next board meeting was invaded by a contingent of Toledo's professional football players. The players spoke about the importance of women's sports and of women's football. The sport needed a prime-time football capital to flourish. Jefferson's poise and her yes-ma'am/no-ma'am humility inspired another poll. This time, the vote was three to two, in favor of the NWFL. Chalk up another win for the Troopers: Now the Green Machine had a home field and prime time. Footnote: Two years later, a coalition of city-league teams complained of sexism. Boys were the victims of blatant discrimination, being subjected to playing in daylight when women enjoyed the privilege of playing under the lights. The board ruled that Friday night football would return everywhere throughout Toledo, where it has remained.

Procuring the jewel of Toledo's football venues was another victory, one that inspired confidence in the board of directors and the sports journalism community. Along with the rights to the stadium came a detail that seemed divine to the former high school star. Claus Helfer was the legendary PA announcer of high school football games, and his voice animating the action in Mollenkopf Stadium inspired a gravitas Stout had felt as a player. The optimism could be felt at the team banquet in December. The football traditionalist Stout stuck with the private room at Cousino's, and Brzozka oversaw the committee to provide centerpieces, trophies, and the evening's program. A lectern stood in the center, flanked by coaches and notable boosters. As emcee of the evening, Orris Tabner wore a forest-green blazer and striped tie.

The women wore evening gowns. Hamilton and Davis gave speeches lauding the Green Machine before doling out awards for best defensive player, best offensive player, most improved, rookie of the year, and most valuable player. Stout took the mic and gave an update on the growth of the NWFL and read a passage from the minutes of a recent meeting of owners: "The National Women's Football League, now comprised of twelve teams with an east vs. west Super Bowl to determine the champion." In closing, Stout thanked all who participated in the movement. "Trooper pride is growing and spreading throughout Toledo," he said. "Next year looks to be the biggest and best in the long hard struggle in women's football."

And then: "Remember, the Troopers will jive in '75!"

* * *

As Sonny Werblin had discovered a decade earlier, Dippman noticed that headlines for superstars took up more space. In the spring of 1975, he discovered the contest in King's *womenSports* magazine, in which readers would submit nominations for female athlete of the year. If surveyed, the average person could cite but a few female athletes currently competing. Two were tennis stars: of course, Billie Jean King, who appeared on the magazine's first issue, and the young sensation Chris Evert. Olga Korbut, another favorite, had also been the subject of a cover story. Dippman ran advertisements on the radio in Ohio and Michigan, imploring listeners to vote for their hometown hero Linda Jefferson. He printed nomination forms from the magazine using the Tillotson photocopier and had the players submit multiple ballots before the deadline in April. Mayor Harry Kessler promoted the drive at the city council meeting, where all in attendance submitted ballots.

The women savored what little limelight there was. Any story, local or national, gave them a flicker of validating pride. It was also motivation and lift for someone like Jefferson, whose day began at midnight. She worked the night shift at UPS washing the dead bugs off the windows of the delivery trucks. Then she caught a nap before her morning classes and another in the afternoon. Practice—for either football or basketball in the off-season—ran until dark. And that was when she went to bed, dreaming that there was a future for the most incredible football player in the country.

One afternoon in April, Sally Jefferson was watching *General Hospital* when the phone rang. She couldn't be bothered, so she told Linda to pick it up. It was Barbara Moran, the editor of *womenSports*. She informed Jefferson that she would be the magazine's first Female Athlete of the Year. Jefferson, overcome, shouted to her mother that she was the best athlete in the world. Sally shouted back—whatever the news, it could wait until her soap opera finished. Jefferson couldn't contain herself. She was twenty-one years old, and she would appear on the cover of the magazine that had recently featured world-renowned athletes like Billie Jean King and Olga Korbut. She felt like she was floating, buoyed by both pride in her superpowers and the possibilities that seemed to open before her.

The photographer had Jefferson pose with pads and jersey, holding a football diving toward the camera as though into the line of scrimmage. Her smile was as bright as the sunshine and blue sky framing her. Her expression, pure triumph: It revealed her vindication of her choice to play a game she loved as well as a glint of hope for the future of the sport. It also seemed to say *"I told you, Momma. They can't catch me!"* Here was an irrepressible spirit no one could keep down or tackle. Here was quite possibly the female version of the greatest athlete in the world. In the issue's foreword, Billie Jean King called Jefferson "probably the world's greatest football player." Since there was no video evidence of her greatness, the article depicted Jefferson in her own words, discussing her love of sports, pointing out the fact that throughout her life she never received the support or attention as an athlete that boys and men received. Or the equipment. As a track athlete, she knew she could shave a sliver off her 100-meter and break the 10-second mark, with training afforded to others. She wasn't complaining, merely mentioning that hers was a tougher road to travel. Maybe that was why she was first and foremost a football player. Her humble and hopeful voice beat between the lines. *Who is Linda Jefferson?* She repeated the question. *Just write that I'm a run-of-the-mill Black girl. You can also say that first I'm a football player, and I play for the Toledo Troopers. And even though I only work part time, I'm thinking about becoming a millionaire.*

To those in the media for whom women's football was merely a curiosity, Jefferson's ascendant celebrity legitimized more coverage. The *Blade* ran a feature that quoted King and her story while news services like Knight Ridder, UPI, and Reuters all ran versions of the story about the Female Athlete of the Year, the run-of-the-mill inner-city girl from the heartland who was the best football player anyone had ever seen.

Jefferson's name crossed the desks of television producers in New York. CBS's *The NFL Today* ran a spot on her, and so did *Monday Night Football*. ABC footed the bill for a plane ticket and a hotel in Midtown, then gave her a four-in-the-morning wake-up call for her interview with David Hartman on *Good Morning America*.

In front of a camera, or a microphone, Jefferson hit another gear: poised, unflinching, polite. As natural a speaker as she was a football player. The story lines were the same: How did an unknown from Toledo beat out the great names of sports in a sport no one knew existed? Then they showed footage of Jefferson lighting up a football field, and the Hartmans of the world got the picture. "I just do what I do," Jefferson said. She oozed confidence. "It's an honor," she said. "But I wouldn't be here without my teammates."

After the interview with ABC, she crossed the street to Rockefeller Center to spend a morning shooting the syndicated game show *To Tell the Truth*. Under the blinding lights she bluffed flatly, betraying a knowing smile, as the contestants attempted to determine the identity of the real Linda Jefferson, *the greatest football player in the world*. When host Garry Moore asked the real Linda Jefferson to stand up, she feinted once, twice, then stood up for America, smiling.

* * *

The producers of *The Dinah Shore Show* noticed. The national morning talk show in Hollywood invited Jefferson to appear with an array of popular stars including Kris Kristofferson, Tony Orlando, and Rita Coolidge.

Shore also invited Jefferson's male football counterpart, University of Southern California superstar Anthony Davis. In the studio, Shore's producers set up a rope course through which the athletes would dance, lined them both up at a starting line, and shot a starter's pistol.

Jefferson and Davis were mirror images. They were both young, preternaturally talented multisport sensations who'd won fame on the football field. Davis was heir to O.J. Simpson at USC. Like Jefferson, Davis had scored six touchdowns in a game as a running back and kick returner, in a high-profile comeback against rival Notre Dame. He was runner-up for the Heisman Trophy. He'd also led USC to a College World Series title. All told he'd led four teams to various championships. For his accomplishments, Davis had just signed a contract for $1.7 million to play for the Southern California Sun of the World Football League, which included a $200,000 cash signing bonus and a Rolls-Royce.

For being called the greatest football player in the world, as well as the master of an array of sports including basketball, bowling, and softball, Jefferson took home nothing, besides the occasional $25 a game that didn't dent the cost of playing. Jefferson wasn't even allowed to have the automobile she was awarded by the magazine. It was not a Rolls-Royce but a 1974 Volkswagen Rabbit. With her sights set on the Olympics, Jefferson asked the Amateur Athletic Union if she had permission to accept the car. It took two days for the union to find someone who could answer. They had never been asked a question about female athletes winning cash and prizes. No one could say for sure whether accepting the two-door hatchback with a base price of $2,900 would make her ineligible for international competition because nothing like this had ever happened. But the tone of their answer suggested a gray area. After consulting her mother, Jefferson decided not to risk her status by accepting the car. Besides, to the speed lover in Jefferson, a four-cylinder two-door teacup was a slap in the face. Her idea of a car was power and speed. She dreamed of one day getting behind the wheel of a machine that would obey her command, like a Dodge Charger, a muscle car statement she could take on the open road and fly. *They can have their Rabbit*, she told her mother.

Yet Jefferson was not disgruntled, even though she grasped the gross unfairness of it all. She'd been born into a universe that was skewed, and her charge was to live the change that would tilt the world toward kilter. At twenty-one, she felt privileged to win international recognition from her obscure origins on Buckingham Street in Toledo. To Jefferson, the journey was humbling, and she looked not to absorb the limelight but to redirect it onto those who might be inspired by her story. Furthermore, Jefferson never lamented what she did not have, but lived her message to the cameras—"If you believe it, you can achieve it"—by continuing to dominate her sport and tasting the supreme joy of flying into the clear, where no one could catch her. Perhaps even more valuable than the honor of the media recognition, or the VW Rabbit she turned down, perhaps even more valuable than Davis's life-changing paycheck, for that matter, was the love and pride she felt from her mother, who would miss a few episodes of *General Hospital* to accompany her daughter to promotional events throughout the country. No one could catch Jefferson, but Sally stayed right with her, keeping an eye on her from the bleachers in every gymnasium or stadium her daughter lit up.

At the obstacle course on *The Dinah Shore Show*, Jefferson and Davis ran neck and neck. Then Jefferson exploded past him and through the yellow ribbon. The man who made a million dollars with a signature trotted to the finish with a smirk, and then the two embraced for the cameras, laughing. In the interview, Jefferson said she hoped she could be a role model for young girls who wanted to play sports. Just like Althea Gibson was to her. She also thanked her teammates back home, who, Jefferson claimed, deserved all the credit. "They make the holes. I just run through them," she said. She also suggested another reason for her success: She ran against the best defense every day, during practice at Colony Field. "When you go against the best," she told the country, "you become the best."

CHAPTER 13

MIRACLE

The 1970 Plymouth Fury was eight cylinders and 350 horsepower simmering under a wide flat hood with square angles framing the chrome latticework of the grille, as though the 4,300 pounds of steel and glass was gritting its teeth. If a nose guard could be a car, she would be a Plymouth Fury. The two-door behemoth, its glass and carburetors manufactured downtown, bespoke the city's character: It was the first full-size muscle car, suitable for tough guys and family guys alike. Along with Stout's city-league championship trophy, the Fury had been his defining possession. He would coast it slowly in front of Sue's apartment on Brint Road as Guy and Stefanie ran alongside waving goodbye to their father.

On August 29, 1975, Mitchi Collette noticed that the Fury was not ensconced in its territory on the Colony Field grass. Soon other cars pulled up. Sunday, Jefferson, Jimenez, and Hollar. They anticipated another grueling workout under the swampy evening sun. Coach Hamilton parked his Lincoln, and Jerry Davis followed. By five o'clock, as the team was stretching out, they knew something was wrong. The Plymouth Fury was nowhere in sight.

The car sat askew in Stout's driveway, along with an ambulance, paramedics, and a shaken committee of witnesses of a ghastly accident. Moments before, on his way to football practice, Stout had backed his cherished Fury over his daughter. It all had happened in a blink of an eye.

He'd been in a blithe mood. It was the weekend, one of the two per month he spent with Guy and Stefanie. Since the divorce, he had grown to cherish these times, when he could teach his children to swim, play putt-putt, or hit a baseball. They doted on each other, and Stout as the weekend warrior parent could do no wrong. That afternoon, five-year-old Stefanie helped her father choose an outfit for practice. He helped Stefanie change from her swimsuit to a summer dress. He carried her down the steps and intended to carry her all the way to the car. But Stefanie wanted to say goodbye to a neighbor boy playing next door. So he let her go and decided to back the car out. Like Lombardi, if he was on time, he was fifteen minutes late.

He felt a thump underneath the carriage. What he did next would haunt him for the rest of his life. He put the car in drive and inched forward, thinking he would undo whatever it was that had made the noise. It was Stefanie. She had tripped on the railroad tie embankment wall and fallen into the driveway directly beneath the wide tail end of the Plymouth as it backed out. She lay on her side, motionless, her bright blond head a mess of red.

The injuries she sustained told the story. The rear of her skull had broken open, exposing her brain. Her clavicle was crushed, her scapula broken, and her neck fractured to a hair of her life, the doctors said. The neighbor boy Stefanie had said goodbye to watched the whole thing and called for help. In a moment, Stout was kneeling over Stefanie, covering her mangled head with a bag of ice. He was certain she would soon bleed to death, if she was alive at all. "Stefanie, don't leave me," he uttered. At some point during the eternity before the paramedics arrived, Stefanie's hand gave a gentle squeeze back.

At the hospital Stout teetered in a state of shock. He had trouble remembering information, such as where he lived. In his mind he was making the funeral arrangements, attempting to outwit the oncoming torrents of grief and guilt. But an unending parade of characters were introduced into the chaos, whirling him back to reality each time. His father and brother helped him answer basic questions. Doctors and nurses of various sorts rushed in and out, yet none could offer a definitive prognosis. A reporter from the *Blade* who was investigating another story began covering Stout's accident instead. Reverend Musgrove from Stout's family's Episcopal church held Stout's arm as he was informed that he had only a minute to look at Stefanie before surgery, and this might be the last time he would see her alive.

At some point, Stout looked up and saw a tall, striking Black woman in a T-shirt and football pants. It was Sunday Jones. And then Linda Jefferson. And giant Carl Hamilton lumbering into the ER waiting room. And the rest of the Toledo Troopers. Word had reached Colony Field, and so the team had left practice and headed over to Toledo Hospital to console their coach. Stout tried to pull together his persona: *Do anything to get out of practice.* But they knew. He was trembling. Then he began to cry. He fell into big Carl Hamilton's embrace, and for a moment Hamilton held him.

For Sue, it was the continuation of a nightmare that featured Stout as the main character. She was three hours away in the Dayton airport accompanying a man she was dating when her name was called over the intercom. The details were scant. There had been an accident. She was to drop everything and catch the next flight back to Toledo. But there were no flights to Toledo. Driving back was out of the question. So she chartered a private jet, and when she arrived she was met by a state trooper who was to escort her to Toledo Hospital. By then Sue assumed the worst possible scenario. But she was wrong. More horrific news awaited her at the hospital chapel, when her father told her that her degenerate-gambler-football-coach ex-husband was behind the wheel of the Plymouth Fury that had crushed her daughter.

In the subdued Toledo Hospital waiting room, Stout found no hope. He looked around at the sad gathering: his brothers and sisters, his ex-in-laws, his players dressed for practice. No one could help him. He refused the Valium administered to traumatized parents. The very reality in which he lived was impossible to imagine. In one instant he was jovially taking his children to football practice. In the next, Stefanie was undergoing surgery to save her life. The world seemed to be coming apart, his life story breaking into two parts, one before and one after the accident that had just happened. He drifted around the hospital not knowing where to go, except to avoid Sue and her family. The only thing anyone could do was pray. He asked Reverend Musgrove to accompany him to the chapel, where he spent most of the night groveling like a sinner come to the light, seeking divine intervention. "Jesus, save Stefanie," the reverend chanted, and the man who hadn't set foot in a church in years repeated the chorus.

* * *

Miraculously, a neurosurgeon happened to be on duty at the hospital. After performing a five-hour surgery in which Stefanie's head was stapled back together, the surgeon couldn't say for sure what would happen. Her second vertebra was broken but somehow the spinal cord had not snapped under the pressure. As for the brain injury, it was a mystery, he said. How Stefanie could recover was anyone's guess. Would she have a memory? Would the brain continue to regulate the body's functions? Would she continue to breathe when removed from the respirator? Would she have a normal life?

No one had the answers, and Sue would never forget what she saw: her five-year-old daughter bandaged from head to toe with a thousand tubes forking out of her. The only consolation came from the notion that Stefanie felt no pain. Doctors assured Sue that the brain doesn't feel, and that she lay in complete traction, held frozen by a full-body cast and Crutchfield tongs, which to Sue looked like ice picks piercing her head.

At the same time, it was a miracle she was alive. Based on what Stout had seen with his own eyes, Stefanie should be dead. In the coming days, as doctors could not offer any prognosis, divine intervention was a reasonable conclusion. Despite what Stout had done, God wanted her to live. On the night after the accident, Stout snapped, and inspiration came over him. He sat down at his kitchen table and began writing. In pencil, he relived the ordeal, the audience for his story only himself and the Almighty. He went back to feeling happy about having his children for the weekend. He narrated the moment he turned the key in the ignition and threw the Fury into reverse. There was blood, and paramedics, and the gloomy hospital waiting room and Reverend Musgrove praying in the chapel. Imagining some holy ordinance at work, Stout conflated divine intervention and cosmic justice he was owed. He titled his diary entry "An Early Christmas Present."

The new reality was like a twisted déjà vu, with Stout and Sue falling into the regimen of hospital visitation they'd established for Guy two years before. They agreed on separate duty hours to avoid seeing each other. As a kind of triage measure, Sue packed up Guy's things and sent him to live at her sister's house in Sandusky. As for Stout, he withdrew. Predictably, confusion gave way to despair. He had been the gamer. The system beater. The iconoclast who could dick the world with his inside dope, or his moxie. Now he'd become one of those sad people who live in hospitals. He had only himself to blame.

He now fully entered the next chapter of his life, initiated by the divorce the previous year. The components of his existence to which he felt little connection he altogether jettisoned. He quit his job at Tillotson Carburetor and found work across the state line in Ypsilanti repairing vacuum cleaners. The house on Westbrook seemed to belong to someone else, the married family man he used to be. The embankment wall and the crumbling driveway remained a monument to the accident. He could not come or go from his house without reliving it.

Then he received a letter from the mayor of Toledo congratulating him on the team's "spectacular achievements." "The Troopers have focused national attention on Toledo," Mayor Harry Kessler wrote. "And you have made the entire community proud."

If there was a light that drew Stout from his misery, it was the momentum that his team of women had created and the obligation to follow through what he had begun. The upcoming season boasted a schedule of eleven games. His team had a following of thousands, a roster of tested veterans, a bona fide superstar, and a record of perfection. Sponsors national and local filled the program. Champion Spark Plug, the Dana corporation, Quickprint, car dealerships, restaurants, beauty salons, banks, insurance companies, laundromats, car rentals, and radio stations paid for advertising space. The board of directors, thirteen strong, held connections to Toledo media outlets as well as promotional ties with Toledo's professional hockey team. Tom Loomis wrote of the upcoming season that the Troopers were widely publicized nationally but "largely ignored hereabouts."

It may not have been an answer from God, but the mayor's office would do. He doubled down on his dream and held faith that the value of his product was plain to see. Like the innovators who'd attracted hordes to stadiums throughout history, and the pantheon of coaches hailing from his homeland, he believed in the game of football. His was the same commodity that lifted other leagues: four quarters of hard-hitting football showcasing supremely talented and conditioned athletes. The game would sell if led by coaches like himself who envisioned women playing it.

He vowed to tighten the ship, to not tolerate lackadaisical play or disobedience.

In circling the wagons, he enlisted his family: His mom and dad and two younger sisters pitched in at home games, selling tickets and programs and serving as ushers. Guy would run the sidelines as the ball boy. At practice he became less tolerant of weakness. Laziness was a contagion, an attack on the character necessary for a thriving sport.

Jimenez became the target of his frustration. In her incessant talking he saw weakness, and he hounded her like a drill sergeant.

Other than the impatience he began to show his players, he kept his emotions to himself. He had revealed abject contrition in his letter to the Almighty, but he showed no outward remorse. Especially not to Sue. And that was all she wanted, an admission that he was accountable. But that would mean giving in, and Stout would rather die than do that.

At Colony Field, he pulled his Fury onto the grass, grabbed his whistle, and went to work. He would keep pushing his team and its star up the mountain, longing for the day he could let go and coast down the other side. But how far ahead lay the continental divide he never knew. He only had to keep pushing, or else the entire kit and kaboodle and everyone riding it would come tumbling down.

CHAPTER 14

THE BRAWL

Two stories ran in the August 31, 1975, issue of the *Toledo Blade*. One featured the headline *Girl, 5, Struck by Father's Car*. The other: *Trooper Foes Getting Tougher*.

The first story named Stout, his Westbrook Drive neighborhood, and Stefanie's status in critical condition.

The second story also named Stout, not as the father of the injured child but as the head coach of the undefeated Toledo Troopers. The article heralded the list of organizations lining up to take out the invincible team from the Glass Capital. Teams in Columbus and Detroit and Dallas boasted deeper benches, upgrades at the skill positions, and renewed resolve to stop Linda Jefferson. Rosters were stabilizing with veterans seasoned in the subtleties of the game. "Detroit hit better than us," Stout said of the previous clash with Detroit. "We just out-executed." The article introduced teams joining the NWFL the next year, including the Los Angeles Dandelions, the San Diego Lobos, and the Oklahoma City Dolls, and announced the upcoming home-and-away series with San Diego. In the story, Dippman said that while better competition might threaten the Trooper position atop the mantle, parity would create a tide that would lift all teams.

* * *

After reading the second story, Barb Church had a decision to make. She'd grown up in Trenton, Michigan, in the shadow of the smokestacks of the Chrysler plant that belched white clouds of exhaust over the Detroit River. In high school, she thrived in water, leading the group of girls who amounted to a team. Girls weren't allowed at the Trenton High School league meets, but Church's times in the backstroke would've placed third at the boys' district finals. At Central Michigan University, women were permitted to swim but had to pay their way to fly to the national competition in Arizona, where Church led the Chippewas to place in the top ten in the country. Now she was hungry for competition. She wanted to get in shape, to prime her body into its finest form. And then there was the longing, the dream of the thrill of the meet, the crowd, the PA announcer, the whistle, and the drive to perform at her best. Another factor drove Church: She'd heard the backhanded complaints about the grind of the sport of football. She'd seen the boys get everything handed to them: equipment, travel, coaching, facilities, warm-ups. Then they whined about neglect and depravity. *How hard could it be,* she thought, when the boys enjoyed sports in every season, had the best equipment, the manicured stadiums, and specialized trainers and coaches?

It became not a question of if, but which. Two teams existed, equidistant on I-75 from Trenton. And so, at the fork in the road, Church headed south.

Had she taken a right toward Kimball Stadium in Royal Oak, she would have seen Tom Brown hang a boxing heavy bag from the crossbar of the goalpost. For four years, Brown had himself been a punching bag. Linda Jefferson and the Troopers had delivered the hits and the smack talk while their relentless coach attacked without mercy. At the start of the season, Brown circled the late-September Saturday on his calendar and prepared a new game plan. He had no idea of the tragedy that had befallen the Troopers' coach, or the pall that gripped his opponent. He'd found an old canvas heavy bag at a garage sale, thrown one end of a nylon rope over the crossbar, and strung the bag up like a nineteenth-century execution. Then he dressed the tattered canvas bag in a green jersey, uncapped a can of yellow spray paint, and tagged it with number 48.

The dangling target bleeding gold was the centerpiece of the team's practice: tackling, punching, pummeling the effigy of the greatest football player in the world. Jefferson's celebrity inspired a primal savagery in the Demons. Each woman took her turn, running full speed and driving her shoulder pads between the 4 and the 8. Soon, the jersey was crumpled on the ground. So Brown painted a new directive on the punching bag: *Kill me.* The Demons lined up again and took their shots, working themselves into a frenzy. They circled the dangling corpse and shouted in unison, *"Kill Toledo! Kill Toledo!"*

Church, instead, witnessed the actual number 48, flying across Colony Field. Around the woman no one could catch ran a sisterhood, with a shared history, unbreakable rituals, and even secret handshakes in the form of a backhand high five or an elbow pump or helmet knock. As a rookie, Church understood her place on the outside of the circle, one she would enter with due experience.

* * *

At the season's outset, like the missing Fury at Colony Field, the bad news came in the form of absence. The mountain in the middle was gone. Over the summer, Momma Bear Burrows had lost the argument with her right knee. Hanging by stitched-together ligaments, her bones wobbled when she pushed off. If hoisting planters or sinking a shovel tested the limits of strength and movement, what chance had she of holding off a charging lineman?

The new year also meant the end of a sentence. Terry Macias's probation expired, and with Stout's recommendation, the state let her go. Football had wised her up, had been the penance she suffered and survived through humility, discipline, and sweat. She was allowed to return to her mother in Cleveland, but that meant leaving behind the other thing she loved.

The Troopers also lost a weapon in Ramella Smith. Smith was the first female football player to win a scholarship—to run hurdles at Texas Southern. The previous May, Smith had come within a tenth of a second of breaking the record for the 80-meter low hurdles at the state championships in Columbus. Three years earlier, when Jefferson had hung up her track shoes, athletic ability was worth a pat on the back and a certificate. Now speed was worth college tuition, and a ticket south, where Toledo winter misery didn't exist.

But another Smith returned. Iris's rotator cuff repair held. The year off whetted her appetite for the hit and gave her full range of movement to swim by linemen or bring a ball carrier down with an outstretched right arm. Women like Burrows or Lora Jean Smalley stepped away from the game on account of debilitating injury, or fear of it. At Colony Field, Iris Smith grabbed a helmet but first wrapped a green bandanna around her head to announce that she was back.

* * *

Before their first game of the 1975 season, Stout gave in to a whim: He tried Jimenez at kicker. If there was an inconsistency to their brilliance, it was the points-after-touchdown attempt. Jimenez could put a charge into the ball, but her line drives hooked left or smacked a tackle in the back. The next day, Stout brought a chain from a dog leash. He clipped one end to Jimenez's belt and the other to her face mask. "Now try to lift your head," he told her. They rehearsed again and again, Jimenez's chin fastened by steel to her chest, and the ball rising higher and higher over the cast-iron crossbar.

* * *

On a clear crisp night at Kimball Stadium under the lights, Detroit Demon safety Katie Graves was a ghost.

On Brown's orders, Graves was to hawk number 48 everywhere, to terrorize her, to torment her, to haunt her like some *Exorcist* she-demon spirit. Graves roamed the line of scrimmage, expecting Jefferson to take the handoff around Schwartz's left side. At the snap, she ran kamikaze missions to steer Jefferson into a mass of Honolulu-blue uniforms charging in. If Hollar made the exchange, Graves and a band of Demons piled on 48 in the flesh, diving in after the whistle. Following strict orders, Demon defenders attacked Jefferson every play. If she drifted into the flat, Graves was waiting for her. The Demons didn't fall for the screen. If Hollar dropped back to pass, Jefferson was engulfed in blue jerseys, forcing an incompletion or a sack. On one broken play, Graves came down with a tipped pass for an interception.

Spit woke Jefferson to the new reality. Teams from Dallas to Buffalo had tried to game plan around her, but when she went down under a mass of Detroit blue, she felt a blast of Demon drool fly from a face mask at point-blank range. "I just got spit in the face," she told her sister in the huddle. Hollar didn't console or complain. "Guess that's how it's gonna be," said the quarterback.

In the second quarter, Jefferson was trotting back to the sidelines after a stalled drive. The play was dead, but Graves was a ghost. Like the women who attempted to kill the president of the United States on two separate occasions in the weeks leading up to the game, Graves was an assassin. She attacked Jefferson, taking her down on the Trooper sidelines. Linebacker Stacy Vance joined the mugging for good measure. Graves was flagged for roughness, but that was Brown's whole point. He was sending a message. Jefferson had to be helped to her feet, and when she put weight on her left leg, she felt in her knee a needle-sharp pain.

In the huddle, emotion took over. Iris Smith sought an ally: "They're trying to take LJ out," she said.

"Ain't gonna happen," said Eunice White.

The next possession, Hollar called a *22* to Dorothy Parma, all of five feet with the help of cleats, who disappeared in the trees of the clashing lines. The Troopers never announced their intentions, which did not involve gaining yardage. They saw Graves hiding on the edge. Off the block, the line gave up their assignments and targeted the threat. Church bit hard into her mouth guard and watched as a gang of teammates threw themselves at the defensive end, sacrificing the play to articulate their reply. There was emotion in the attack, a desire to inflict pain. The blue jersey went down in a pile of green. She did not get up. She was assisted off the field by her teammates, clutching her arm close. She never returned. "We broke that bitch's hand," Browne said.

Church nodded along, then clapped her hands at the call of the play. She trotted to her position at tight end and thanked God that she had chosen this team and not the other.

* * *

In the locker room at halftime, the Troopers experienced a first: They were losing. Brown's all-or-nothing game plan had knocked the Troopers out of sync. Hollar had managed one sputtering drive in the second quarter. At the goal line she took the snap and held the ball for Jefferson but pulled it away at the last moment, then ran a footrace to the corner for a bootleg score.

The sight of Jefferson on the trainer's table for a round of tightening tape was another first, a contagion of doubt that might've attached itself to any wayward worry.

But in the locker room there was no doubt. This was a street fight. Hamilton and Davis led the town hall–style pep talk. *"We are not losing!"* they repeated. Allen commanded the rookies like Barb Church to wise up, learn on the fly. *Tape up* was the primary solution. Mike Stout and Davis worked like army medics, cutting away divots and slabs of blood-stained shells, or simply glommed on, transforming hands and wrists into pristine caveman clubs.

In Davis they saw a man on the verge of tears, as though all that mattered was the moment rising before them. Football was a gang fight, after all. If Detroit had thrown the manners of civilization out the window, then so could Toledo.

"If you get punched," Allen said, "then you punch back harder, girl. And keep punching."

For Stout, there was nothing else but the game. It was a place without guilt, grief, or shame. Less than a month before, he'd been praying in a hospital chapel for his daughter's life. Now he was driven by the charge of winning a football game back and bringing it home to the city that honored him with parades. Mercy was a fantasy.

In the second half, the Troopers punched back. Stout shelved his misdirections and reverses in favor of simple counters that chewed up yardage in bites. Jefferson, testing her knee, lined up as a flanker, and Hollar, Zuccarell, and Parma ran opposite. Hollar found the rhythm to the offense. Progress became a matter of hats. With Jefferson set wide, the gold hats tilted the field. When they reached the Demon 15-yard line, Hollar called a simple *35*, a pitch to Jefferson, who could smell pay dirt. She played a game of tag, cutting back once on a tender taped-up knee, then twice, dancing deep into the backfield, then discovering the opening among a maze of scattered Demons to the end zone.

In the fourth quarter, the Troopers kept punching. Deep into Demon territory, the Troopers showed *33*. Jefferson broke right. So did the charging Demon defense. But it was Parma who had the ball, little Dorothy Parma, scampering into the left corner like a Bowery street thief.

With seconds left on the clock, Jimenez squibbed the kickoff, and the game died under a pile of green jerseys at midfield.

Final: Toledo 20, Detroit 18.

The Troopers detached themselves from the pile, tasting a different kind of victory. On the scoreboard they had triumphed by a razor-thin margin, by far the closest win in five years. The *Blade*'s season preview was validated—foes *were* getting tougher. Tom Brown's Demons staggered off the field feeling the sting, looking back at the torn-up turf and at the vulnerability they had exposed in the unbeatable champion.

The bitter finish of the win lingered, like the swelling of Jefferson's left knee.

She took Monday off and by Tuesday felt no improvement. A soft purple bulge persisted around the side of the joint. She could feel loose tissue and hardened tendons, a clear message to avoid testing it. The next game was against Fort Worth, a Texas-size horde that had beaten the likes of Dallas and Los Angeles. The Troopers would need her. That was when she made the decision to visit the hospital and file a claim.

* * *

For the NWFL, the observable expense was the iceberg you could see: The uniform. The equipment. The referees. The venue. Claus Helfer's echoing baritone. Then came transporting players to a city and putting them up for a night. These costs did not factor in the practice time required to organize the violence, to achieve precision timing, choreography, and toughness. And then there was the cost of the violence itself.

When Bronko Wilhelms suspected a separated shoulder, the X-ray cost $14.89. When Sheila Browne sprained her knee, the out-of-pocket cost was $61.25. Barb Church paid $15.00 for treatment for a tailbone injury. Verna Henderson was charged $57.50 for the diagnosis of a bruised left hand. All told for the 1975 season, the individual visits for medical attention totaled $2,544, the price of a new car.

In a game against Columbus, Bronko was the first to put a hit on the Pacesetters running back. A wave of green jerseys followed her. Crushed under the weight of her own teammates, Bronko felt something inside her give. She couldn't breathe. Stout and Hamilton carried her off the field cradle-style, like battlefield soldiers. Their prescription of a spell on the bench did nothing to diminish the pain. At the hospital the doctor showed her an X-ray. One of her ribs broken in two. "How on earth did you sever a rib?" the doctor asked. She told him she was a football player. "Not anymore," he told her. At practice on Monday, Bronko showed up in street clothes. "The doctor said my season is over," she told her coach.

Stout shook his head. "Then find another doctor."

Two weeks later, Bronko was in the Waite stadium locker room, suiting up for the game against Fort Worth, wrapping up her body in a cocoon of Ace bandages.

* * *

Frank Wallace had worked with the Bureau of Workman's Compensation and had filed claims on behalf of Tillotson workers or contractors injured on the job, even for the most hangnail of offenses. Managing the paperwork for its employees when it came to compensation was good business, and Wallace saw the connection. Now that SKW Enterprises was incorporated, its employees could seek compensation from the state if they were injured in the line of duty. The claim was a three-page application requesting information, including addresses, dates, witnesses to the injury, allergies, and preexisting conditions. When Verna Henderson filled out her workers' comp claim, she wrote for the company's name *SKW*. For department, she wrote in script, *football*. In the Addendum Employer's Report, a prompt asked, *Nature of business*. Stout wrote, *Women's Football*. For each player, the time it took to fill out the paperwork was barely worth the reimbursement for treatment, which usually took months to process, sometimes longer. Still, the scheme took the edge off, should anyone sustain a broken bone or an attempt to diagnose one.

Like Bronko, Jefferson paid for her X-rays, which showed only mild damage to the knee but a chipped bone in her left foot. Her doctor had never treated a female football player but had seen his share of ruptured anterior cruciate ligaments (ACLs). He sent her on her way with an Ace bandage, some aspirin, and a bill for $40.

At home Jefferson sat down with the stapled packet from the Ohio Bureau of Workman's Compensation. Item number seven prompted the claimant to describe the accident. Jefferson, still seething from the low blow, wrote, *A girl tackled me out of bounds and another girl hit my knee and foot with her helmet.*

On her second visit, the doctor erred on caution's side. He told Jefferson that the knee and foot would heal themselves, given the chance, but cutting back against the grain on a tender tendon might weaken or tear it altogether. Jefferson nodded. The showdown with the Fort Worth Shamrocks was Saturday. Should she do the thing she loved more than anything? Should she use the knee that made her the greatest at the risk of destroying it? She was the greatest football player because she knew what her body could do. She was twenty-one years old. She wasn't just playing a pickup game on Buckingham Street. Her knee, taped up in an Ace bandage, would take her to the Olympics perhaps, or win her a contract like Anthony Davis. At practice, she told her coach she wasn't ready to carry the load.

Reading the *Blade* on the morning of the game did little to ease her mind. In a preview, the Shamrocks reportedly averaged 170 pounds per player and boasted of four linemen weighing over 200. The story mentioned the Troopers' streak, at twenty-four games. The weather page offered no solace: A stubborn swamp rain throughout the day and swirling winds would hobble both teams.

In the locker room, the women assembled their armor in a charged quiet. Jefferson understood that mortality is right over your shoulder. *Any given day*, her coach confirmed, *a champion falls.* Acknowledging doubt was a method of rising over it.

"Not today!" Hollar led the chorus, and the locker room lit up into its prebattle frenzy.

Outside, Waite's torn-up turf looked like a glistening bog. Stout told Hollar to play it close to the vest. She listened to his game plan to pound away between the gaps. Nothing fancy. Hollar nodded along, feeling the hiccups coming on.

The stadium felt empty; the drizzle kept fans away except for the core

families, such as Allen's sons and nephews, and Jimenez's corps of brothers. On the field, their sister was sizing up the Shamrocks, yet another
army of invaders whose massive size and numbers sent fear through the
home team. Jimenez saw no Bobbie Grant among the blue and gold
but concluded from the sheen on the white helmet that the Texas team
would be every bit the brick wall as Dallas.

At the outset, their fears were confirmed. Fort Worth shot off their
lines in unison, moving with the force of a collective unit. They did not
fly to podunk Toledo from the home of America's Team to suffer a lesson
in America's game. The Shamrocks found a clearing when Jones blitzed
and got lost in the mud. Around the corner a footrace broke out that
Parma ended inside the red zone. The other shoe fell three plays later on
a quarterback sneak, and the Shamrocks had drawn first blood.

Hollar knew that execution would be the difference. She made decisions in the huddle, alternating between Henderson, Zuccarell, and
Parma, up the middle into an explosion of mud. Jefferson, dressed for
show, played her supporting role as decoy, leading her disciples opposite
the play. Meanwhile, Hollar gathered information on the speed and
whereabouts of safeties and linebackers, as rain turned the game into a
soggy rugby scrum. The middle of the field was clogged with bodies.
Offensive linemen could find no purchase, and running backs couldn't
find any corners, their cleats weighed down by spiraling clods of mud,
while the defense knew they could not be checked. At right defensive
tackle, Jimenez saw the center betray a tendency: The white mud-caked
helmet was going for Allen—the play was a dive left. She charted her
course before the snap and timed her charge into the backfield, meeting
the running back at the point of exchange in a bear hug, then rode her
down into the mud.

Henderson played three ways. She never came off the field except for
halftime. On offense, she was an architect attempting to execute timing
and structure. On defense, she was a demolition squad blowing it up.
"Offense is work," Henderson said of the game. "Defense is fun."

After two quarters, the Troopers faced another first: a goose egg on the scoreboard. But panic was no match for the collective manufactured certainty. They felt a mysterious familiar vibe though no one had been here before—never had they ended a half scoreless. They could see what they were up against, the lumbering Texas army and a slush pond. Vanquishing both was a matter of execution and effort. Hollar felt confident: "Let's open it up," she told her coach. By now the hiccups were gone. The nose guard coach preferred running the ball, but Hollar could see the field, her line of sight over the mud-caked helmets. She knew there were openings in the flats.

She alternated *34s* and *35s*, quick pitches wide to Parma or Zuccarell, who found angles for modest mud-soaked gains. Conditioning began to show. Jefferson took a handful of carries, never forcing the issue on the soggy turf. She would amass a total of 90 yards, the lowest in her career.

Someone else would have to win it. Hollar baited the linebackers to tip their hands with her cadence, showing which side the slant would form into an open window through which she could loft the ball for Jones's and Church's long arms. As the commander of the offense needing scores, she went rogue. She saw the linebackers set wide; she took the snap and snuck on the strong side two-gap. There was always an opening. Moving the chains became a matter of finding it. She called the jailbreak screen to Henderson and executed, creating space for her receiver, who caught the ball in stride and followed an escort of Brown and Bronko, chugging strictly north-south through the mud. Henderson was easy to track and not flashy, like the jeeps they manufactured across town designed for off-road. Bringing her down came at a price. Near the goal Hollar called a play action; this time Henderson speared the blitzing linebacker to buy time, and Hollar floated the ball to the corner of the end zone where Church waited and hauled it in.

Church had medaled in countless swimming meets, accepting the praise for her individual achievement in polite exchanges. Now she was at the center of a mob. She'd just caught a touchdown pass, a gamebreaker, the culmination of eleven women at work. In that moment, parading back to the sidelines, she was no longer on the outside.

In the fourth quarter, two quick lateral passes to Jones created breathing room, and the Troopers were on the move again. The Shamrock line panted, holding on to their hips, steam rising off jerseys bathed in mud in the cool night air. At the Fort Worth 5-yard line, Hollar tried the play action again. But the safety didn't bite, and Church was blanketed and stuck. The last check down was to tuck the ball and find a portal out of the collapsing pocket. Hollar saw a path off right tackle and took the shortest angle, a collision course between her and the Shamrock safety at the goal line. Hollar put her helmet down and smashed into the defender and fell forward, the ball cradled in her arms resting in the end zone slick.

The pain hit Hollar everywhere and all at once. It took a moment to understand the new reality. But there she lay, the ball in the promised land. She commanded her body to move, and it obeyed, slowly. She unsnapped her helmet for air and tasted the rank Toledo earth, which tonight was the taste of victory.

Final: Toledo 12, Fort Worth 6.

The collective belief in themselves was validated, like prayer paying off. They might not have had their star at her best, or the complete roster of veterans, or the elements on their side. Walking off the field, Hollar could breathe only if she walked sideways; the hurt would carry into the days ahead. But for now, she and her teammates again bathed in the feeling that they could never be stopped.

* * *

For three weeks after the Detroit game, Hamilton had had a bad taste in his mouth. He could forgive the zealousness of a Demon's occasional late hit or a tackle out of bounds. There existed a shade of respect in their attempts to stop the Troopers at all costs. But what he'd seen in Detroit crossed the line. Brown had put a hit on Jefferson. So Hamilton adopted Brown's innovation.

From the cast-iron crossbar at Colony Field swung the heavy bag. Hamilton pulled the bag back and let it fall like a wrecking ball while the women lined up to take on the heavy pendulum. Mass and gravity became the instructors, inspiring the women to absorb the blow with their shoulders, lest they be knocked off their feet. For Dorothy Parma, her 110 pounds, pads included, were on the wrong side of physics. The bag swung down and smashed her back with lift, like a nine-iron. Parma hit the ground to the laughter of the team. She climbed back on her feet, reset her helmet, and got back in line. "Higher next time, Cuddles," she said.

* * *

Hollar had free rein. She took tentative steps in the huddle, calling inside runs, mixing in crossing routes to Jones and Church. Always on the hunt for a weakness to exploit. Back in Royal Oak, she found the spot in front of Schwartz. Whomever they lined up in front of bespectacled 73 got blown off the line, as Schwartz exploded upward with her forearms, like Godzilla emerging from the depths. Detroit complained that Schwartz was dirty. *"Cheap shot, bitch,"* they chirped. No flags were thrown. The Demons stopped lining up across from her. Hollar saw the wide-open gap on the right side. She called for the *33*, and called it again. Soon, the Demons were a cornered prizefighter taking a pummeling, and there was no bell to save them. The Troopers scored three consecutive touchdowns, Hollar distributing between Jefferson and Henderson, and Ms. Nasty leading the way. The dagger came when Kathy Sanders picked up a fumble and trotted 30 yards to the end zone.

Detroit was decimated, and Hamilton had a bad feeling. The banter in the hole was reaching fever pitch.

So the Demons took aim again, not at the enemy's heart, but its head.

Hollar dropped back, bided her time, then launched deep into the night for Jones on a post. Detroit defensive end Valerie Hartwell kept charging. To Hamilton, the intent was clear. Hartwell put her trident-emblazoned helmet through Hollar's back, then slammed her to the ground under her weight. Then came pandemonium.

Bronko and Jimenez went after Hartwell. Hamilton rushed onto the field, not toward the skirmish but toward the referee, whose flag remained nestled in his belt. That is, until he noticed 230 pounds of former lineman charging onto the field, and the rest of the Trooper bench following him. Five years of smack-soaked frustration came pouring out. Now it *was* a battle, and the women swung and kicked, protected by their armor. Jones ran from her post route like an attacking Hun, launching a haymaker at Demon assistant coach Dan Adair, who was pulling players apart. Jerry Davis in a three-piece suit pulled players off one another. In return, an enraged Demon took aim and launched her cleated foot between his legs. Sue Crawford got to her feet to witness human fury in Iris Smith swinging her taped-up clubs on some blue jersey on the ground. Stout and Demon head coach Dan Brown stood in the middle corralling their colors.

Hamilton was screaming at the referee. He called Hartwell a thug. *"That's not football,"* he screamed. *"That's assault!"*

The *Blade* reporter covering the game wrote that the teams played three sports that night: Boxing and wrestling were added to the bill.

Dippman described it as "a big pile with legs kicking and helmets swinging, and individual fights across the field." One of them: all four-foot-eleven of Dorothy Parma on top of a Demon lineman twice her size, smashing her in the face.

Hollar lay at the center of the ring. She'd felt a surge of pain like an electric shock. For a moment, she couldn't see. Then she located the source of the pain, a white-hot stabbing emanating from her shoulder. Hamilton helped her to her feet, but no part of her body would accept it. Delirious, she managed to stand and stumble, her arm dangling.

The group of six referees determined that both Hartwell and Hamilton were to be ejected. Stout and Davis were furious. "Then you're going to have to throw all of us out," Stout said. "My coach isn't going anywhere. He's the one doing his job!"

Cuddles didn't accept the gesture. "I'll take this one," he said. "Just finish and let's get the hell out."

Hamilton marched slowly alone from the stadium under a barrage of vitriol from the mob in the stands. He sat on the bus alone, seething as he waited an eternity in the dark for his brothers and sisters to return.

Finally, he saw them, their helmets shimmering in the parking lot floodlights. Stout had ordered his team to grab their belongings and head straight to the bus, in full gear.

For a time, Crawford was trapped in a stall in the bathroom. *"Anyone wearing Trooper colors here does not get out alive!"* a voice echoed. Crawford, standing on the toilet, waited for quiet. Then she dashed out.

Final: Toledo 19, Detroit 7.

* * *

Hollar writhed in her seat, fighting back the pain in her shoulder. Later at the hospital, she would be given Percocet so the nurses could rotate her bones back into place. Her shoulder would never be the same. After the season, she would visit the army recruiting office downtown. Enlisting had never been a question of if, but of when. On the bus home from Detroit, Hollar knew the time had come.

The team rode in wide-eyed silence. They had witnessed their leader going down. They had also experienced the primordial panic of a gang fight. Yet they had survived, grounded in the confidence that they had accomplished what they'd set out to do. They had won a football game.

We are the Troopers, mighty mighty Troopers! Iris Smith sang. The team joined in, relishing the lyric: *Everywhere we go, people want to know!* For

Iris Smith, it was the old feeling, and there was nothing quite like it. The euphoria of the bond.

Hollar looked at her teammates like sisters, the steam rising from their jerseys. They had proved themselves capable of rising up again. Players like Collette and Henderson ran every down, each play dishing out a hit or absorbing one. Jefferson had run for 115 yards and two touchdowns on a threadbare knee. Bronko Wilhelms played linebacker with a broken rib. They all knew that more pain was on its way. They would suffer through Sunday bathed in methyl salicylate and heavy doses of aspirin. It was a full-body, deep-tissue pain. Every muscle, every bone, every joint and sinew painted shut. But that would be tomorrow. For now, Hollar watched her teammates sing. It was a motley choir, a tattered collection of colors, shapes, and sizes. She saw them pound on the seats with taped fists and belt the song at the top of their lungs.

CHAPTER 15

OBSTACLE

In June 1975, the Department of Health, Education, and Welfare finalized the process by which Title IX would be implemented. That year, for the first time, a women's basketball game was televised, between Immaculata University and the University of Maryland. A twenty-three-year-old woman became the first woman in the United States to win a spot in the formerly all-male Golden Gloves boxing tournament, after beating a man. An eleven-year-old girl became the first female to win the Soap Box Derby. In November, actress and former Miss World USA Lynda Carter became an international sensation as Wonder Woman, flying an invisible jet, stopping bullets with her hands, and squeezing the truth out of men with a golden lasso.

Time magazine's "Man of the Year" for 1975 was awarded to *women.* American women. The story proclaimed that "women have so deliberately taken possession of their lives that the event is spiritually equivalent to the discovery of a new continent."

Many dismissed the metaphor as hyperbole. But these American women from the heartland had just laid claim to another perfect season, stretching their streak to twenty-eight games. To the women who stepped onto the field and felt the game's inimitable thrill, playing football for the Toledo Troopers meant discovering a new world.

* * *

Sally Jefferson had never flown. She'd never seen an airport, never stepped into the pressurized fuselage of a 727, and never experienced the luxury of ordering cocktails in flight. She was headed to Florida in the middle of winter so that she could watch her daughter go toe-to-toe with the greatest athletes in the world.

And she let everyone on board know it.

For the 1975 season, Sally Jefferson's daughter had rushed for 1,375 yards on 141 attempts, almost 10 yards per carry. Dominating stats, but not the seeming misprints of her previous years. The target on her back and Stout's restraint resulted in a slight statistical correction. After the final game of the season against Columbus, Jefferson and the Troopers hobbled off Waite Stadium's shredded turf, where a group of fans were waiting for autographs. Many held the sunny *womenSports* cover shot, and Jefferson took her time and signed every glossy cover.

She told her fans they'd have a chance to see her again soon, on national television.

* * *

In 1973, the producers at ABC listened to a pitch from a promoter attempting to confront Sid Friedman's challenge of creating an audience. Dick Button had competed in the Olympics, in figure skating, and understood that four years was far too long to wait for the spectacle of the Olympic games. Why not stage them every year, in a decathlon-style event? The competition would end the debate about which sport boasts the greatest athletes. The producers at ABC bought in and first staged Button's reality show in the winter during the ratings' dead time following the football season. *The Superstars* was for men only.

It would take two years for the flaw to dawn on ABC. Not only did Title IX's slow-motion shock wave create opportunities for female athletes, it also gave rise to an audience to watch them. The ascendency of celebrity athletes like Billie Jean King and others she helped promote woke ABC to the market Friedman had predicted. Furthermore, the male athletes did little to warrant exclusivity or end debate about greatness. In the show's first year, boxer Joe Frazier nearly drowned in the 50-meter freestyle while the overall champion of the competition was a pole vaulter.

Jefferson's invitation to compete in the 1976 games inspired imaginations and transformed LJ into a hometown hero. At the grocery store, she was mobbed for autographs. Reporters like local sports anchor Jim Tichy knocked on her door seeking interviews. Pedestrians on Buckingham Street recognized her driving by; police officers climbed out of their cruisers to shake hands with the celebrity. It seemed there could be no challenge in front of her she couldn't dodge or outrun, even with a squeaky knee.

While she was excited for the chance to compete against the best, her sights were set on something greater. The '76 Olympic trials were playing out in amateur leagues and in college gymnasiums across the country. After leading the Toledo All-Stars to the basketball state finals in Columbus, Jefferson was invited to try out for the Olympic team at a regional event in Detroit. To scouts, Jefferson at once passed the eye test. She was quick, she could fly across the court, she could take chances and make up for mistakes with eye-popping speed. She was not afraid of contact.

Her celebrity brought her attention, but her notoriety as a football player made basketball scouts leery: She could do everything well but wasn't a clear-cut point guard or shooting guard. She was raw. Her competition had been training exclusively in the finer points of their positions since Title IX mandated gymnasium time. The tryouts were schooled in the triple-threat position and keeping their hands up on defense. Jefferson was all Buckingham Street, playing with high-risk, high-reward abandon. At some point, Jefferson realized that she would not advance over girls who'd been doing nothing except dribbling up and down hard courts since junior high. She later heard that one of the tryouts she had bested made final cuts. The girl was still in high school, a trainer's daughter, a shooting specialist. Jefferson never enjoyed the grooming of a coach or a personal trainer or agent shepherding her through the obstacle course of the U.S. Olympic team qualifiers.

In Rotonda West, Florida, cash and prizes were on the line. The winner of *The Superstars* would take home $14,000 and a new car. The previous winner, volleyball standout Mary Jo Peppler, parlayed her fame as the first female *Superstar* champion to visit Johnny Carson on *The Tonight Show* and sign a sponsorship contract. If a volleyball star could cash in, surely Jefferson's all-around ability as a perfect football specimen made Jefferson the best bet.

The invitation to compete on national television was just another opportunity on a growing list offered by journalists, talk show hosts, or showrunners looking for novel content. Yet the girl from the south side of the swamp was humbled by the lineup of those she would be competing against: her megastar fan Billie Jean King, a young tennis talent named Martina Navratilova, and Olympic champion Keena Rothhammer, among others. And the program boasted a viewership of twenty-five million. *The Superstars* could be a stepping-stone.

Six months ago she had turned down a new car in order to keep alive her Olympic dream. Now she had no car and no Olympics. Accepting the invitation to *The Superstars* meant going pro unequivocally.

Yet the reality of entering stardom never hit her until she and her mother pulled into the Rotonda hotel parking lot.

She was unloading her suitcase out of the trunk of her car, dubious about the trainer that ABC had provided her, when a Buick pulled up. A well-dressed African American woman climbed out of the back seat, and to Jefferson it seemed like a movie. In the Florida twilight, here was the woman she had idolized all her life: the historical figure on whom she'd written high school reports, the Jackie Robinson of women's sports, the Wimbledon champion who was the first African American to win a major tennis match, as well as the first African American on the LPGA tour. As Althea Gibson stood before a stupefied Jefferson, it was Sally who broke the ice. The mother introduced her daughter to the icon as the *athlete of the year*. Gibson was gracious: "Nice to meet you," she said. "You're the next me." It was dizzying to stand before the legend, close enough to catch her floral perfume. No one had ever intimidated Jefferson except the other woman standing next to her. Sally demanded that the three sit down for dinner before the weekend was through. Before they parted, Gibson confided in her competition: "I hope you win."

"I'll do my best," said Jefferson.

In the qualifiers, Jefferson made good on her promise. The competition was a sun-drenched decathlon of events: tennis, swimming, bowling, cycling, basketball, rowing, an obstacle course, the 60-yard dash, the quarter mile, and the old softball toss from the GAA. LJ blew away the field in the sprint and the softball throw, but as she broke into the lead on the quarter mile, she felt her knee give; the injury from Detroit returned like a curse. Still, Jefferson held the overall lead heading into the final event.

Ignore it, she told herself. For four days, Jefferson lived the dream. She ruled the Rotonda Hilton like a baroness, ordered room service on her per diem, shared elevator rides with television crews. She held photo ops with Franco Harris, O.J. Simpson, and her counterpart Anthony Davis. During the press conference, sitting alongside Billie Jean King and Martina Navratilova, Jefferson sported her monogrammed forest-green-and-gold Toledo Troopers team jacket.

At the 60-yard dash, Jefferson settled into the blocks on the sun-baked asphalt. She felt the sting on her fingers and remembered her showdown with Roz Stoner. This was what she lived for: a straight lane cutting through a sea of spectators and the command to fly. At the gun, she was a seventeen-year-old kid again in the Toledo city championship, blowing away the field for all to see. When she returned to her senses, she was trotting to a stop among palm trees. Her time, a tournament best 7.58 seconds, was an afterthought to piercing the finish line, an echo that confirmed her a career as an athlete.

During the interviews after the race, she recognized the look in people's eyes upon discovering they were in the presence of a football player. Deeper than a double take, it was the head turning of the boys on Buckingham Street who first doubted, and then believed. Her appearance was striking, her smile as warm and bright as the Florida sun. In her interviews with Howard Cosell and Keith Jackson, Jefferson saw it, the head-shaking disbelief. Then she said that a woman's place is on the football field if that's where she chooses her place to be.

In the finals, it was bad luck and her bad knee that held back the next Althea Gibson. The rattle in her knee grew worse. The obstacle course stretched in front of her, the last event before her coronation. At the starter's pistol, Jefferson felt the wobble. Still, she flew upon the tires, a black honeycomb of hard rubber. Her right side sank into the depth of a hole and lost its spring, a lightning strike of shock burning through her. To gain her balance, her foot found purchase outside a tire. She followed her momentum with a slight limp, over the climbing wall, under the tunnel, through the finish tape. The penalty dropped her from second to fourth place in the event.

The event knocked her to third overall, ahead of Navratilova and her idol Gibson. For the bronze medal, Jefferson took home six thousand dollars. It would remain the largest sum ever awarded to a female football player.

* * *

Jefferson would see the look of incredulity throughout the bicentennial summer of '76. Back home, Sally called Ohio Bell to have her name unlisted from the white pages because the phone kept ringing. Still, the marketing department at Owens Corning found her. Attempting to catch the same wave as the NWFL, the multinational fiberglass giant headquartered in the swamp staged publicity events at schools and clubs across the country. After flying to New York on the Owens Corning jet, Jefferson saw the look, this time on the faces of the public-speaking coaches hired to train her. She didn't need to be taught how to comport herself in front of a camera, a journalist, or an audience, like she didn't need to be taught to hit the hole.

In Barrington, New Jersey, Jefferson held the attention of a room of hundreds of boys and girls at Avon Elementary School. A highlight reel of Jefferson's exploits played as an introduction. With the microphone in place of a football, Jefferson worked the room, alternately facing down a heckler and warming up to the girls who looked at her with awe. She spoke of the opportunities the sport had granted: "Football has allowed me to achieve my dream—being on TV and competing in *The Superstars*, and talking to you today."

"Sports has opened up doors for me," she told the audience.

Jefferson dismissed the inevitable comparisons to the men's game. Speaking alongside the Pittsburgh Steelers' Franco Harris in New York, Jefferson was introduced as *the Franco of women's football*. Jefferson called the recent Super Bowl champion *the Jefferson of the NFL*, and when, on a tour of inner-city schools in Los Angeles, she was introduced as "the O.J. Simpson of women's pro football," Jefferson performed the spin move again.

"We're not trying to show up men," she pronounced. "We just love the game." As Jefferson stood among the greatest athletes in the world, her cool, confident style bespoke her message: "Competition gives you the joy of self-respect and leads to success in other areas of your life."

On her run through the public-speaking circuit, Jefferson attempted to shake the perception of the female football player as a monster. "When people hear about me, they think I'm a mixture of Mean Joe Greene and Godzilla." A *New York Times* reporter described her as surprisingly ladylike, her red blouse, gold hoop earrings, and striking Afro showcasing her slender and graceful frame. "I'm a lady off the field," she said when prompted. "And yes, I hope to get married one day," she felt she should add, confronting the stereotype of the female athlete. "But not to O.J.— he's married."

* * *

How the world would have changed had Jefferson flown under the Title IX mandate in 1972, which she missed by an eyelash. Would she have been shepherded and groomed like athletes she was outrunning and out-toughing? To what university would she have won a scholarship? What would have been the story she would have told to legions of girls she was encouraging to get involved in sports?

Jefferson did not dwell on what-ifs. Had she benefited from Title IX, she would never have played the sport she loved. She wouldn't have been the best in the world. She wouldn't have been able to fly her mother on a jet airplane.

Lounging in the leather recliners of Owens Corning's Grumman corporate jet, Jefferson looked out into the clouds. She listened to her mother hold an audience, boasting of her daughter's greatness. In such a moment it was impossible to second-guess the opportunities she might have been given in another universe.

This time she took the car. With her *Superstars* winnings, LJ put a down payment on her dream: a pristine Dodge Charger, six cylinders and 300 horsepower of pure cherry-red swagger. The keys to her chariot signified a different kind of diploma. She lorded over the city, taking night drives downtown along the river. One night, when April finally broke winter's hold, LJ went farther. She crossed the river on I-280 heading south. On a dark stretch of highway, she opened it up, the machine responding to her deeper wish. The speedometer needle rose smoothly past 100 miles per hour, each ten-mile mark a gateway drug to the next. At 130, she felt the tremors in the wheel. At 135, the entire car shook. At 140, amid the trembling, she felt lightness, as though at any moment the car could lift off. LJ held. The rush was like nothing else, unless you count scoring a touchdown.

* * *

The night before returning from Florida, the superstar and her mother met Althea Gibson in the hotel restaurant. Gibson exuded optimism about the changing times. She told Jefferson that the fight for gender and racial equality is a lifelong battle. She predicted that more and more young athletes like Jefferson would be given opportunities, but they had to keep up the fight for rightful recognition.

As they said goodbye, Gibson was smitten by her acolyte. "When they make a movie about my life," the greatest female athlete of all time said, "I want *you* to play *me*."

CHAPTER 16

THE UNTHINKABLE

In the first game of their sixth season, the undefeated Toledo Troopers faced a third and twelve at their own 12-yard line, leading 8–6 with the clock on the south end of the stadium reading three minutes remaining in the game. They missed their veteran quarterback, as well as a few starters from the year before. They also missed a star recruit, who had opted against a football career. Facing a third and long, Stout circled the wagons and played it safe. He decided to punt.

The team had been out of sync from the start, and their sputtering performance was more than first-game jitters. The previous afternoon the women had boarded a Southwest flight and flown two and a half hours into the heart of the Great Plains, into the hot stagnant air of the lowlands that clung into the night. They had dressed in the stark, concrete locker rooms of Taft Stadium, a Depression-era, eighteen-thousand-seat cinder block, as a hungry crowd gathered. They'd fought back the butterflies and the jet lag and marched into the lights and the hard sun-scorched earth. On the field, the Oklahoma City Dolls were waiting.

The Troopers were starting anew. In Hollar's place stood Pam Hardy, all of twenty years and five feet, one inch, in cleats. In Bev Severance's and Sheila Browne's place came Joellyn Opfer and Brigitte Hartz, who had their names called by Stout after tryouts but were taping up in a locker room for the first time in their lives. Brenda Baskins wasn't new to sports, but she was new to football.

Another contingency was born of a car accident. The previous summer, a driver smashed into Jackie Allen's car, sending her to the hospital. By now she was healthy and ready to start. In fact, her conditioning had helped her back to full strength. But her lawyer recommended she remain behind for the opener. An injury would potentially complicate the pending lawsuit.

The new color scheme added to the unfamiliarity. The Packer-like green and gold were reversed: Charging onto the field were twenty-four gold jerseys with hazy green helmets and pants, opposite the scheme of the first five years.

Stout hoped his rookies could learn on the fly, like Henderson or Smalley had in the past, and his experienced women would teach them. But Hardy and Opfer were not hiding among a line of veterans who could see the play before it happened. Hardy lined up behind center. Opfer *was* the center. As a bartender at Jackie's on Adams Street downtown, Janelle Palmer had broken up fights. Now she was being asked to start them.

The coaches no longer stressed that proper technique was protection. The women who showed up to play instinctively developed tendencies to survive the meat grinder around which they constantly hovered. Their familiarity with hits accounted for their ability to bounce back from them mostly unscathed. Opfer knew without being told that a good football play meant diving headlong through an opponent. She had grown up playing tackle with her brothers in Graytown and watching football with her dad after church. Being tentative got you not only beat but hurt. Going all out was a safety measure.

Still, inexperience in the finer points of the game gnawed at their edges. On the Oklahoma City turf, they had already lost a fumble on an exchange, the most basic football transaction. Opfer's mind was reeling with a medical textbook's worth of information: the playbook, the blocking scheme, the snap count. In the first quarter, on third and two, Hardy imagined she could get lost long enough to lunge for a first down among the trees on a quarterback sneak. At the snap, Opfer froze. She saw the lights, the shredded point of the football, the team dressed in the colors of the U.S. flag across from her. Instead of snapping the ball between her legs, she picked it up, and, before sense came to her, she was blasted off the line in an explosion of whistles and flags. It was then that Opfer and her teammates knew.

Their opponents could learn on the fly, too.

* * *

In February 1973, Mike Reynolds, a civilian computer technician at Tinker Air Force Base outside Oklahoma City, saw an article from the *Oklahoman* posted on the break room bulletin board. *Troopers Thump Dallas Girls*, the headline read, and told of a women's football team from Toledo, Ohio, that lit up a team from Dallas in the Super Bowl of women's football, played in Texas Stadium. There was Terry Dale, eyes looking into the sky as she prepared to corral a pass from Lee Hollar. The story mentioned other cities with women's teams, such as Buffalo, Detroit, Los Angeles, Cleveland, and Pittsburgh.

Reynolds didn't know who had posted the article. Perhaps a man sharing a curiosity he'd discovered, like a circus freak show. Then again, the cutout may have been evidence for an argument of where women belong. The year before, Patience Latting became the first woman to be elected mayor of Oklahoma City, making it the largest municipality in U.S. history to be led by a woman.

In fact, the town bore a striking similarity to the Glass Capital, like twins separated at birth. In 1970, their populations were virtually identical, and the modest skylines could each be mistaken for the other. Oklahoma City's prosperity was also built on a substance ripening below the surface. The oil boom of the late nineteenth century put the city on the map, in the literal sense. The city didn't exist before 1889, yet by

1907 when the territory achieved statehood, the namesake became the capital. In the 1930s, the concrete giants the Ramsey Tower and the First National Bank edifice, designed by the architects of the Empire State Building, shot up out of the prairie. But just as quickly, the oil ran dry. A desperation lingered as the white demographic fled downtown to the outskirts, and to Norman to the south. The city seemed willing to entertain schemes to regain its glory, namely in revitalization projects and the other boom for which the region was known.

In 1964, the city volunteered to be the subject of a Cold War experiment to determine the effects of sonic booms. For months, Oklahoma City citizens agreed to be pounded with shock waves that were strong enough to shatter skyscraper windows and crack plaster. But the deafening supersonic flyovers from Tinker Air Force Base were grounded when an injunction against the experiment cited the rising cost of repairs as well as the psychological damage to the citizens. Most accepted the manufactured thunder, however, as a point of civic duty. After all, the nation was in the throes of a Cold War, and the conflict in Vietnam was heating up. Like many on the prairie, the Air Force computer technician Mike Reynolds, a veteran himself, tended to accept sacrifice for a greater cause.

The other greater cause in Oklahoma was football. Baseball and basketball were quaint diversions that Oklahomans entertained to pass the time during the off-season. The men and boys who suited up in Norman and Stillwater conjured the spirit of Jim Thorpe, widely believed to be the greatest football player of all time. Thorpe was born somewhere on the Oklahoma grassland before the region became a state, and followed football eastward to Ohio to lay the groundwork for the Hall of Fame in Canton.

If Toledo bore a stepchild chip on its shoulder, Oklahoma hid in the shadow of its football-loving sister to the south. Texas pulled the spotlight away from the Sooner State by way of its weight in football programs from El Paso to Houston. The Oklahoma City Plainsmen of the Continental Football League had recently packed Taft Stadium for their clashes with cities like Little Rock and Huntsville. But the COFL had collapsed, leaving only Dallas to reap the lion's share of gridiron attention. The rivalry drawn by the Red River inspired spite: If Dallas could put a team together, Oklahoma City could do better. With men, or women.

Reynolds read the article twice. The story stayed with him, just like the advertisement in the 1971 *Toledo Blade* remained with Stout. Reynolds phoned his brother Hal, who had recently returned from a tour in Vietnam. "We have to get in on this," he said.

Reynolds called the Dallas chamber of commerce to track down information on the football team from Dallas. The secretary assumed he meant the men's team and suggested he call the Cowboys front offices. He was interested in the women's team, he said, the Dallas Bluebonnets. The city put him in touch with Joe Mathews, the Bluebonnets owner, who, along with Stout, was attempting to grow franchises, and welcomed Reynolds's interest.

Mathews told Reynolds he could start a franchise in the NWFL for $10,000, an ante that financed travel and marketing and ensured that only legitimate, committed owners joined the enterprise. "We play real football," Mathews said. "This is no gimmick."

The Reynolds brothers bided their time, completing their service in the army and saving up for their investment in football, and following the progress of the NWFL. They targeted the summer of 1976 to make their move, when the ubiquity of bicentennial fever lent a sense of hope to sports. The best movie that year was about an underdog boxer, the biggest sports headline was about an American winning the decathlon, and the theme for the Super Bowl between Dallas and Pittsburgh was about the nation's two hundredth birthday. The optimism inspired Reynolds to write a check for $2,500 as a down payment, with a promissory note to close the balance by the end of the first season. He hired a law firm to notarize the paperwork, and the

Oklahoma City Dolls Football Club Inc. was born. The color scheme he chose for his team was red, white, and blue.

Like Friedman, Reynolds promulgated his dream through the newspaper, which cast the widest net in the state. The *Oklahoman* arrived on doorsteps from Tulsa to Norman to Boise City, spreading word of the National Football League, for women.

Reynolds felt vindicated when he arrived for the tryout at Moore High School in the south suburbs of Oklahoma City. The steamy parking lot was filled with pickup trucks. By the time he and Hal set up cones on the field for the speed test, dozens of women were stretching on the sidelines, and dozens more were trickling in. His excitement shifted to panic by the time the tryout began: He now stood in the presence of seventy-five women who all wanted the same thing.

Their stories echoed the plotlines of the Troopers: The women had played with their brothers in backyards, had scratched the surface of competition through pseudo sports of the GAA. Charlotte Gordon had cut her teeth playing with her brother Rod, a three-time All-American linebacker at Oklahoma. Doris Stokes dated Lucious Selmon, one of the Selmon brothers, all of whom played on the line at the University of Oklahoma (OU). Sherry Mathis had other ideas of what it meant to be the wife of an NFL football player. Her husband, Reggie, played for the New Orleans Saints and later the New Jersey Generals of the United States Football League (USFL). Why couldn't she? When the coach of the OU women's basketball team reached the front of the line, Reynolds thought she was applying for a job as an assistant. But Cathie Schweitzer wasn't interested in coaching. She had missed the tide of Title IX and wanted to play on a professional team.

At the tryout, Mike Reynolds spoke frankly about what the women stood to gain. There would be no payment for their services. In return for smashing into one another, they would receive a set of tickets for friends and family. Should the league take off as he predicted it would, more compensation awaited.

Like the rest of the seventy-five tryouts, Schweitzer was not deterred. "I just want to play," she said.

"Then start running," Reynolds told her.

Their first test was the two-mile run. Then came calisthenics, then more running, this time through a tire course. Then came the crab roll drill, a test of agility. The women rolled laterally, spinning on all fours and then on their backside from hash mark to hash mark. If anyone was still interested in playing football, they could come back tomorrow. The next day only half showed up, and fewer the next day. Practice with pads and helmets identified those without stomachs for violence, and Mike and Hal parsed what remained into thirty-five of the best football players in Oklahoma.

* * *

A belief system as viral as Christianity had taken hold on the plains, a core faith that a trinity of running backs would be impossible to stop. The revelation of the wishbone offense was preached by Sooner coach Barry Switzer, who was the biggest name in Oklahoma football, which meant the biggest name in Oklahoma. The Sooners had won the Big Eight every year of his tenure, had once gone two straight years without losing a game, and now had brought the national championship to Norman two years running. Cathie Schweitzer knew Switzer from Sooner athletics department luncheons and introduced him to Oklahoma's start-up professional football team. Switzer agreed to pay the Dolls' camp a visit. When he came out to see the Dolls practice, he liked what he saw.

He saw a military operation. He saw fundamental training and football players hitting hard. Reynolds consulted Switzer on the wishbone and used his best versions of its constitutive parts. Jan Hines took the snap, and behind her a three-woman track-and-field meet broke apart: Doris Stokes was the track side, the sprinter, while Frankie Neal was the field, a former shot put medalist who ran one direction: downhill. Cindee

Herron completed the trio with a combination of both, a bruiser who Reynolds would keep on the field at all times. Switzer told Reynolds that discipline was the key to the wishbone: When the team executes with a collective and precisely timed explosion, the scheme will knock out any defense like a boxer's power cross.

* * *

Their first two games of the season proved it. When halfback Herron took a handoff from Hines and dove over the goal line for the first official Dolls touchdown, the conclusions drawn from the experiment in discipline and conditioning were clear. They beat Dallas twice in their home-and-away series. The three-headed monster kept the ball moving. Even when the Bluebonnets and Bobbie Grant attempted to account for every option, they couldn't cover all the permutations of the wishbone.

In the locker room after the second win, Reynolds was cautious. He told the women they'd won nothing, that their victories were dress rehearsals for the real thing. The next opponent had never lost. Their guests were the undisputed champions of the sport, led by one of the greatest living female athletes. They read Jefferson's sensational headlines, announced her logic-defying statistics, showed clips of her highlights on TV, and revealed the enemy on the cover of *womenSports*.

Later, Bluebonnets coach Henry Jackson confirmed Reynolds's fears. The two Plainsmen had a common enemy in Toledo, and Jackson had been a victim of the Greatest. "Stop Jefferson, and you have a chance," Jackson told him. He described the Troopers' schemes, their tendency to get the ball to LJ in the flat. "And watch out for the bootleg," Jackson said.

* * *

Like most of her teammates, Brenda Baskins from Toledo's west side had never been inside an airplane, had never traveled west of the

Mississippi—nor, for that matter, had she ever crossed a time zone. Like all her teammates, she was on the adventure of her life, traveling like a queen, anticipating playing on the road, and sharing in the dream of the incredible barbecue they'd had in Dallas. But underneath the anticipation lingered worry. Baskins felt outside her own skin after a daybreak departure and a layover in Chicago. Disorientation arose from the sticky Oklahoma air and the extended reach of daylight. At the Holiday Inn in Oklahoma City, the team looked at their watches and killed time lounging by the pool or decompressing in their cool rooms rehearsing the playbook. When a chartered school bus arrived, they were pacing, their gear lined up in the parking lot. Outside the sunset cast a lighter hue, and the dusk fell in a different direction over the stadium that ran north and south, not east and west like the friendly confines of Mollenkopf back home.

Anxiety found a home in the rookies, like Brigitte Hartz. As she walked behind the bleachers, she could hear the crowd. She felt like a Roman Colosseum victim about to be fed to the lions. *What have I gotten myself into?*

On the field, the game fell away from familiar patterns. The Dolls' persistence slowed the machine. Oklahoma linemen Mickele Day and Kathy Scott stood like iron moorings, impossible to move. Mary Blue-Jacket and Mary Scherer obeyed orders to press in on the edges to hold contain. With every play that didn't break, the Dolls matured. Jefferson and Henderson made small dents in drives, falling forward in the maze of an eight-player box. In her first game at quarterback, Hardy, standing nearly a foot shorter than the Doll tacklers, attempted only three passes in the first half and completed none of them.

But their toughest opposition, Hardy admitted, was themselves. In the first half, the line in front of the rookie quarterback struggled to get on the same page. Four times they were flagged for motion. On third down, in Dolls territory, Opfer's exchange slipped from Hardy's hands, and middle linebacker Cindee Herron bolted through to collect the fumble.

In the second quarter, combination punches of Jefferson and Henderson gave the Troopers a first and goal at the Dolls' 10-yard line. Three consecutive running plays pushed the ball to the two. Stout didn't hesitate. This was what the game was all about. *I'm coming through you, and try to stop me.* Stout called on his old standby, the misdirection, the bootleg. At the snap, the play ran to the left, and Hardy kept the ball and spun to the right. But the surprise was on Hardy. Her nemesis Herron stayed home, protecting contain, as she was instructed, and bear-hugged the thief to the ground.

On the sideline, the realization spread that the game would be a grinder, and the veterans were reminded of the old feeling, the fear and the release of trotting out onto the battlefield. On defense, Hamilton's Green Machine held steady, the line relishing in the price they paid for it. Stopping the wishbone required focus, resolve, and guesswork. White and Jimenez and Schwartz blew up blocks for Collette and Henderson to diagnose and attack. The Green Machine moved like chess pieces, staying low to keep leverage, hemming in the backfield. If Collette got her hands on Schweitzer, she hung on, if only for a moment, before the gang tackling cavalry came tumbling in. The first half was a cantata of quarterback signals, popping pads, whistles, and scant ball movement, as the clock bled out. The score was 0–0.

For the rookies Hardy and Opfer, halftime in the concrete locker room was like waking up from dreamless sleep. They sat together and divined in the eyes of the veterans and their sweat-matted hair a charge of absolute duty. In their coach's barking they sensed threats against inexperience and cowardice. There was no Hollar and no Burrows, but there was also no going back. Only the command to execute.

Henderson opened the third quarter on a reverse, gaining the corner and tumbling for a chunk of territory. Hardy trusted her window and launched toward the sidelines, where Sunday's tall frame entered the picture and swallowed up the ball. The machine was working again. As though she could smell the end zone, Jefferson took a pitch from the

6-yard line and found just enough of a seam on a cutback to fall over the goal line. The sideline erupted in triumph. For Hardy, it was relief. She had to fill the void of the leader, as her team burned its tank inching down the field. On the conversion, Jimenez inhaled a lungful of the hot prairie night air. She waited for the count, then kept her head down and let fly. The ball shot up over the scrum like an escaped bat, fluttering end-over-end over the crossbar and falling somewhere else, it didn't matter where. The daughter of Mexican immigrants had kept her head down and drilled the exclamation point, giving the champions an 8–0 lead.

From either sideline, Dolls quarterback Jan Hines looked like a veteran. In the face of an onslaught, she held the ball close, then fired a spiral on target to the tight end in the clear. But success through the air required skill at both ends. Twice, tight end Debbie Sales, who had adopted the moniker "Tinker" after the Sooner standout Tinker Owens, couldn't secure Hines's throw as it descended from the lights, knowing Dr. Death awaited. The game progressed into predictable movements, Hines alternating between Stokes and Neal and Schweitzer, and the 3-yards-and-a-cloud-of-dust football resembled the game in its golden era.

Playing from behind, Reynolds took a chance on fourth down. He liked the battering ram he saw in Neal, and she proved up to the task of tumbling over the line of scrimmage for a razor-thin lifeline. The gamble kept the drive alive. On third and two from the Trooper 25, the Green Machine sold out to stop Neal. An invasion of yellow and green tore into the Dolls' backfield. But Hines kept the ball on a sneak, and she kept the angle, too, beating out Jones to the pylon for the Dolls' first touchdown.

Beginners' luck, Jimenez rationalized, watching the enemy celebrate. Her hope was confirmed when the Dolls attempted the tying kick: The line drive hooked wide, and the lead held 8–6.

The gambler's faith in the odds held firm. Like so many rolls of the dice, it was just a matter of time before Jefferson broke free. She'd been pinned in all game by the attacking Dolls. Still, she'd amassed 100 yards on fifteen tries, plus the touchdown. Clinging to the lead with a three-minute eon left in the game, Hardy called for a *33*, hoping Jefferson could find her way to the marker and ice the game.

Jefferson found it. She exploded through the hole before Herron could close it, then darted straight for the corner. Herron would be named the defensive player of the game for the Dolls, for her fourth-down stop and three fumble recoveries. But on this play, she discovered why number 48 was called the Greatest. With the game in the balance, Moonie was not going to be beaten. She found the corner and was gone, flying down the sideline, moving the ball out of the shadow of the goal.

But just as fast as the euphoria swept down the Trooper sidelines, it disappeared: A yellow flag lay crumpled on the empty field.

Palmer, the rookie, was called for a block in the back. The game turned and turned back on a single play in the referee's deliberate march back to the Troopers' 12-yard line. On third and long, Stout elected to drain the clock, running Henderson off tackle. The Dolls used a time-out with two minutes on the scoreboard.

That was when Stout made the call to punt the football.

* * *

Most Trooper drives ended in the end zone. The punt, like the two-point conversion, was a play at which the team that had never lost could look mortal. And if the odds would swing in the women's favor, they could also swing back.

Not even a perfect snap by the rookie could prevent the onslaught of all eleven Dolls into the backfield. Church decided to tuck the ball instead of risking a catastrophe in the face of the walls closing in. She disappeared in her own end zone in a wave of blue jerseys and white helmets and red stripes, and by the time her senses came back, the referee held his hands together above his head. The safety evened the score.

The pendulum swing brought back the delirium they had felt all day.

As she walked back to the sidelines alone, Church looked back like Lot's wife, only to see a parade of blue jerseys backdropped by a raging stadium. In the span of two plays, victory had slipped through their collective fingers. Now the team entered a new realm with a terminal ring: sudden death.

The final plays of the game unfolded in a bewildering sequence that inspired the suspicion that they'd been doomed from the start. The first: a flip of the coin. Jones, her elbow raw from four quarters of hammering, called heads. The coin landed tails up. Jimenez, Collette, and White shrugged at the line, expecting their medicine in the form of the broken wishbone. On the first play, they got it: Neal took a handoff and bashed into the line for a short gain.

Then Reynolds called the play they had rehearsed every practice but had never run: *the Sooner Special.*

Hines took the snap and rolled. The wishbone transformed into an added line of defense. Hines, with time, had one target in mind, Charlotte Gordon, who chugged from her tight end position into a gap 10 yards into the enemy. Hines lofted the ball toward the outside, delivering it as though bubble-wrapped into Gordon's lap. The tight end secured it, and in charged Henderson and Collette swarming to take her down. But before Gordon hit the ground, she heaved the ball sideways, and there was Doris Stokes running a wheel route around the corner with nothing to stop her. She gathered the pitch clean, galloping down the sideline.

Against the best defense the league had ever known, the Dolls executed the magician's final act: the hook and lateral.

Sunday Jones, too, was possessed. She had been a workhorse for forty-eight minutes, picking up the rookie slack. As Stokes burned in front of the Fourth of July parade that was the Dolls' sideline, Jones found the angle, forcing Stokes toward the sidelines. Dr. Death was not going to allow the streak to die. She dove, grabbing a handful of Stokes's face mask and ripping her down. A flurry of yellow flags and whistles ended the miracle. Jones was called for both the face mask and unnecessary roughness in the same play. After the referees walked off an additional 15 yards, the Dolls were in the shadow of the goal line.

The 3,200 heat-worn Oklahomans in Taft Stadium stood screaming. Hamilton scrambled for an answer, sending Jefferson in for Jones, who in dragging Stokes down by her face mask had both saved the game and shamed it. "Everyone in the box," he commanded.

Again the plunge up the middle, but Hines had the ball, rolling into the open. She drifted forward, near the line of scrimmage, buying time and baiting. Jefferson was caught in no-man's-land, between dropping in coverage or stopping the run. Hines felt the gates closing. She gathered her feet beneath her and fired into the expanse of black Great Plains, then tumbled to the ground under the hit.

Perhaps it was in the stars that an outfit from the Great Plains would put an end to perfection for one from the Midwest. Plainsman Lamar Hunt had the decade before staked a claim to Ohio's pastime and made it his own. And like the merger, the predominant side may have capitulated, but the league won. In the upstart Oklahoma City Dolls Football Club Incorporated, the NWFL boasted a legitimate football franchise west of the Mississippi, from their savage hitting down to their matching red- and blue-striped tube socks.

* * *

In the Trooper locker room after the game, there was no chanting. In silence the women dressed in the fluorescent-lit cinder-block cold. *"What just happened?"* Schwartz asked no one in particular. There was no answer, for there were no words for the feeling. A strange bitterness of mistiming and failure, pain from fifty minutes of beatdown, and the abiding mystery that losing had been predestined since they set foot on the Southwest flight that morning. The women had never felt this unknown species of heartbreak. There was also respect for the foe that could execute the game at a fundamental level and hit hard as a bulldozer. In the Dolls they had seen themselves. Winning had been an experience of the collective, a symphony, a celebration of totality from the practice whistle to the final horn of the scoreboard clock reading triple zeroes. Now, they were obliterated, exiled to their separate corners to suffer as individuals. There was no singing. Platitudes like the ones Stout told them were false refuge, Band-Aids for an axe wound. *We have to play all forty-eight minutes—and more*, and *It's the little things*, and *Be ready Monday*.

The man whose purpose in life was to win football games knew it, too. He stopped talking. He blamed himself for the lack of preparation and the lack of discipline. On the flight home, he would stew over the fumbles and the nine penalties that cost them an acre of field position. The league's success story failed to calm him. He had been beaten, by an opponent. Even if it meant the advancement of the league, he would rather die than give in.

They could hear the celebration. Outside the locker room, a red, white, and blue mob of thousands cut loose at the 50-yard line. The Dolls had stolen away the win on a safety, a hook and lateral, and a surgically executed 20-yard strike. Tinker Sales knew she had beaten Jefferson to space, and Hines put the ball where only Sales could get it. She reached up and hauled in Hines's work of art and tumbled into the end zone. The referee hoisted his two sweet hands in the air, and the game was over. The Dolls hesitated at first, not knowing whom to hug. Then they stormed the field like they had won the Super Bowl. At the center, Hal and Mike Reynolds preened like emperors, pounding the shoulder pads of every last Doll. For the women, no limit existed to their joy. There had never been anything like it. And there never would be again. They had beaten the team that couldn't be beaten in a game they weren't supposed to play, and it was the greatest thrill of their lives.

PART III

CHAPTER 17

SHOWDOWN

The average career for a player in the National Football League was three years. Longevity varied by position and playing time. Placekickers tended to last longer. Starting wide receivers sustained injuries that ended their careers at a much higher rate. There were outliers, like Jackie Slater, the Los Angeles Rams offensive lineman who began his career the year the Troopers lost to Oklahoma City and did not hang up his cleats for twenty years. On the other side of the ledger there were the nameless multitudes whose preseason injuries or roster attrition prevented them from entering a single regular-season game.

For players in the National Women's Football League, tenures were shorter. Many opted for jobs to pay for schooling or family. Pregnancies often ended football careers. Others, like Judy Verbosky, turned away from the game for the shame they brought to their families. Deb Brzozka quit playing to become the league's commissioner, got married, and took the name Schuster. But injuries took the greatest toll. Connie Miller never played another down after breaking her leg. Nor did Linda Williamson. Davelyn Burrows and Lee Hollar both obeyed the call of broken-down body parts. In their first year of existence, four Oklahoma City Dolls went under the knife to repair torn knee ligaments. Some women stepped down for damaged wrists or ankles. Those who kept playing often did so despite the pain. Most carried on with undiagnosed sprains, fractures, or concussions. They all heard the nag of a question that accompanied a severe bruise or jammed ligament or stinging bone, a question Tom Loomis put in black and white: *Is it worth it?*

Pam Schwartz and Jackie Allen returned for a sixth year. Jefferson, Jones, and Jimenez a fifth year. Collette, Bronko, Smith, and White a fourth. Henderson, Parma, and Zuccarell a third. They earned no money, except $25 per game, if the attendance allowed. There were no guarantees, no benefits, and no retirement. What brought them back was the love of suiting up in helmets and pads with a platoon of other women clashing on an open field lined in chalk and the bond it created.

What if I have to be carried off?

The loss to Oklahoma City in late summer 1976 hit them like a collective hip stinger. They wept for the pain of losing but also for the uncertainty of a new era. Up to this point, the women lived in a utopia, a world without loss. Now the pristine showroom model bore a dent. The injuries they suffered were no longer marks of their sacrifice but signs of their weakness. The tweaked heel and the cricked back lingered, like doubt emerging from remission.

For the coach, the heartbreak persisted. He clung to the good news of Stefanie's recovery. In the coming months, she made swift strides compared to Guy's tortuous convalescence, her brain healing quicker than grafted skin. When her body cast was removed and she stood for the first time since the accident, Stout felt a weight lifted from his shoulders. Still, the surgeon warned that the consequences of her injury might never be known.

More uncertainty blossomed in the form of dissension in the west. The owners of the California teams were going rogue. The San Diego Lobos and the Pasadena Roses had staged a game without the sanction of the league. The teams were carrying outstanding balances from the original franchise fees according to league bylaws. The West Coast commissioner, Charles Jule, suspended the teams and negated the San Diego win.

Furthermore, infighting within the San Diego front office led to the firing of coach and general partner John Mulkey Jr. Stout received a letter informing him that the Lobos were canceling the home-and-away series with the Troopers because of financial mismanagement and personality conflicts among the team and its coaches. The league was suddenly contracting. And then another cloud began forming on the horizon.

* * *

Seventeen-year-old Frani Washington was the best at whatever she played. Her bright, wide eyes sized up every opponent, then devoured them with confidence. She strode the crowded halls of Woodward High like a disguised superhero, knowing she could beat anyone. She'd won a closet full of medals for track, she could play any position on the diamond, and she became a driving force behind the Polar Bears' first organized basketball team. She'd seen the Troopers on Channel 11, read about their undefeated run in the *Blade*. She could imagine herself a football player. When she heard that her hometown champions were holding tryouts, she brought her track shoes, and the vision forged in her mind of a wide receiver. She knew she was going against the very best in icons like Jefferson and Sunday Jones. When she lined up in the overgrown grass of Colony Field she believed she could be the Lynn Swann of the women's game, a freakish acrobat who could dominate a game like never before from the receiver position.

As a final farewell before boot camp, Lee Hollar showed up at the tryout to pass the baton and the post routes. Hollar took seven step drops and launched the ball into the swamp sky, and each time Washington found the bead, soaring to meet it in stride. Against headhunters like Sunday Jones and sprinters like Parma and Zuccarell, Frani Washington found gaping space in the secondary. To Stout and Hamilton, the next Linda Jefferson had arrived: armed with two superstars, the undefeated Troopers would somehow become more unbeatable. And if first-generation

Linda Jefferson put the sport on a map, the league needed a superstar 2.0 to continue its rise.

Washington wanted football. She told her mother there was nothing better than flying through the secondary, reaching her hands into the air, and collecting the ball from the sky. She said she would fly west of the Mississippi for the team's first game against Oklahoma City. But like Sally Jefferson, Frani's mother put her foot down. Hundreds of college scholarships had been granted for girls like Washington, in a growing number of sports: swimming, golf, track. Washington's mother demanded that she stick with Woodward's inaugural basketball team, even though Ohio had yet to hold a state tournament for girls. *If basketball doesn't pan out*, her mother said, *then you can play football*.

Was the loss of talent to scholarship sports an omen? Commissioner Deb Schuster remained hopeful, buoyed by rank-and-file support of the city. It was true that SKW Enterprises, the corporation that owned the team, held on by a thread. But if there was a silver lining to the disaster in Oklahoma, the loss was nothing if not an exciting football game for the thousands who paid to watch it. The NWFL brand needed winning teams like Toledo, or Oklahoma for that matter, to attract talent. Likewise, the flagship team needed to hold its winning course. The alternative meant the death of the dream.

* * *

In the August heat, Stout kept the women running until they struggled to stand. Plank crawl, lunges, rolling burpees, and then the pop-up drill, the crab drill, and the Hamilton Special. To onlookers like the reporter from *Ebony* magazine, the event looked like a military operation. Stout added a neck-conditioning workout in which the women lay face mask down, then suspended themselves on their heads, as though burrowing into the ground. Then they flipped over and performed the drill upside down, bellies in the air. Schwartz felt her body stretched as though on a rack. *Torture*, she called it, pushed to the brink of sanity. They collapsed onto the earth, one by one.

Don't want to stand? Stout said. *Fine. Leg lifts!*

Walking among them, Stout held the workout until each woman succumbed to the pain, their faces wincing in agony. *What did we ever do to you?* Jimenez cried.

Stout rejected the grumbling like an old joke: If anything, Jimenez's insubordination inspired his wrath. In it, he saw a lack of discipline. The coach and president of the team tended not to absorb new reality but double down on the old. His team was not going to change its ways, except to embrace a harder version of themselves.

In fact, in cutting corners or half measures, Stout now saw the collapse of the entire enterprise. His tone did not lighten or bend, nor did it differentiate. Jimenez and her band of veterans had been serving the team year after year, throwing their bodies into its machine. Stout gave tenure no regard. At the point where the women were stretched to exhaustion, Stout commanded the women on the line: wind sprints.

Playbook rehearsals in the shredded field had no predetermined ending. *"Line up, line up, line up"* became his centrifugal force mantra, if the choreography of a new play dragged or rushed, if one chorus member was out of step. Stout singled out the offending lineman and broadcast a personalized harangue berating her. Hardy and Opfer replayed the miscues from the loss again and again, until Hardy's hands blistered from taking snaps.

A beleaguered feeling grew among the players. Sometimes they took out their frustrations on one another. At the end of a long session, the tyrant ordered the team to repeat a passing formation. Timing was of the essence: Church luring the safety to collapse into the line while Jones ran an out route. Hardy was hesitating, reluctant to throw the ball to dark, open space. Back from the legal red tape, Jackie Allen at nose guard blitzed every play, but the tether of Stout's whistle held her in check before she could demolish Hardy. Again, the whistle stayed Allen's attack, mocking her. With every repetition, she approached the boiling point. At last she charged through the whistle and took the quarterback by the collar. Her nails dug into Hardy's neck and drew blood. Then she flung the rookie like a hammer throw. "Get rid of it, sister," she said.

Sue Crawford took spells behind center. After Hardy's thrashing, Crawford told Stout she was opting out of the next game. She'd been invited to a softball tournament in Michigan. "Do what you want to do," Stout said. "But if you go, don't come back."

Crawford left.

* * *

They felt it again, the specter of defeat, early in the following game against Detroit. The defense had already given up a touchdown when Hamilton yanked Bronko for not administering sufficient violence on the enemy. She watched as Detroit found a soft spot bashing away against rookies Carla Miller and Hartz. Before halftime the Demons steamrolled Miller into the end zone to stretch the lead to 14–6. Miller was dazed. *"Get your ass back in there!"* Hamilton ordered Bronko, the fear of God, or of losing, in his voice. Miller understood, too, despite the separated shoulder she suffered getting pile-driven. But that diagnosis wouldn't come until the morning. In the second half, the Demons never crossed midfield. The green-and-gold team snapped back into formation at the whistle. They played to the momentum of the game, turning one sack for a loss into another. On offense, rookie Brenda Baskins was the beneficiary of Detroit's game planning for Jefferson. She bulldozed her way to two touchdowns in the second half, and the Troopers hammered down the nail 20–14, going away.

Vulnerability was apparent. "Both offense and defense had problems," Loomis wrote of their next performance against Columbus. To keep defenses honest, Stout attempted elaborate permutations, including an item stolen from Oklahoma City. At tight end, Schwartz caught a pass, then attempted to lateral back to Jefferson. But the timing lagged, and number 48 went down under a wave of red. The hook and ladder was not their lesson to learn. On the other end, Pacesetters running back Faye Howard and quarterback Lisa Perez alternated takes, driving through Hamilton's defense on a 79-yard statement of a drive that cut the Troopers' lead to 12–7.

As much as Hardy and her offense loved deception, it was conditioning that destroyed opponents and dried up the fear. In the second half, the veterans once again asserted relentless pressure, gaining momentum as the game wore on. The front seven could feel the turn, and when Columbus revealed nothing left in the tank, the Green Machine never let go the stranglehold.

Final: Toledo 30, Columbus 7.

To the reporter's eye, Jefferson was the difference, tallying 161 yards on nineteen carries. "Linda Jefferson remains a force," Loomis wrote after the win. "She's twice as quick as ninety percent of the players on the field. She knows when to put her head down and crack for extra yards when cornered." There was no mention of the second-half shutout, or any ink for the defense except that the Troopers' secondary looked confused. "The pass defense leaves much to be desired," Loomis wrote. Had Columbus receivers converted a few attempts, "the results of the game may have been different."

"I'm not impressed," the coach revealed to his team. "I'm happy, don't get me wrong..." Then he removed all signs of the compliment with a gloomy shaking of his head: *"But..."*

If softness like Bronko showed to her opponent inspired his rage, so did incompetence. He questioned how the league would earn respect if teams didn't respect the game itself. When his opponent was down, he kicked. On four consecutive plays against Philadelphia, Stout called for the same off-tackle plunge, punching like a hockey fighter, daring the Queen Bee defense to stand up to him. "Don't like it?" he said, standing firm on the sidelines. "Then stop it." The score at halftime was 56–0.

The attitude trickled down into the trenches, where the Philadelphia outfit faced a baptism by fire. The Queen Bee left tackle made the mistake of betraying fear to Eunice White. "Go easy on us," the rookie said. They were not seasoned in the fundamentals, or of competitive mentality. Attempts at choreography collapsed at the snap. White turned the pre-snap still into a game of chicken. "*You* can't move," White taunted. "But I can." Then the front seven punished the Bees for their inexperience.

For a 100-pound ninja of a quarterback, Hardy could sling a dart 40 yards, but her low line of sight forced routes to the outside. The Troopers added one more score, on a 27-yard missile from Hardy that fell into the arms of Jones in the end zone. Execution became an antidote to the fear of injury or of loss, a glorious realization of football choreography that brought to mind the game how they first played it, with boys on cool fall afternoons in backyards and vacant lots.

Under the lights, in their armor of polymer and foam snapped tight, the women lived in those moments. But following the final whistle they fell back to their earthly existence, as swelling, bruises, and sprains settled in, as well as the edge they bore against the coach who would rather die than give in. Living with reminders of their imperfections, the women at times ignored the game's practice call. As the fall daylight faded, Jefferson complained of her knee acting up. She stood on the sidelines as the women ran in full gear. Kathy Sanders missed a practice to run errands. Brenda Baskins's transportation fell through. The sporadic absences had a ripple effect. When the group lost critical mass, the women's attention strayed to their individual pain. An injury could sprout at any moment, during drills, calisthenics, or reps without contact. The lack of sharpness was contagious.

Is it worth it?

In turn, Stout fumed about individual compromises and tightened his grip. Meanwhile, precious daylight dissolved. The field was an ensemble of shadows lit by the swirl of gray and acetylene orange from the Jeep plant. Stout pulled his Fury and Hamilton his Lincoln onto the ragged grass, and they kept running by headlights.

"Games are easy," Eunice White later told a reporter. "Practices are hard."

It was the last rep of the night. Janelle Palmer shot the gap on a sweep to Baskins, diving in low and grabbing hold. Her momentum swung her like a carnival ride, launching her in the dark cauldron of bodies. One of them didn't get up. It was fellow rookie Ernestine Davis. Palmer sensed it was bad, the way Davis screamed. Just how bad, Palmer discovered later, on the eleven o'clock news. Orris Tabner was previewing the rematch against Columbus and cut to a reporter on the hospital beat. Davis had sustained an oblique fracture to her tibia. Her career was over. Palmer sank, knowing her teammate was badly hurt, and that she had done the hurting.

* * *

Schuster and the Troopers board of directors attempted to sell NWFL through neighborhood news advertisements, press releases, television interviews, radio commercials, *Blade* thumbnail notices, rotary club guest appearances, and flyers posted on kiosks and grocery store vestibules. The commissioner bartered PA announcements and program advertising. The swamp radio station WLQR gave her discounted rates if Troopers could be available for afternoon interviews. A daytime disc jockey in Detroit agreed to hold a call-in prior to the second game with the Demons. The DJ put out an all-points bulletin for "the dirtiest player in the league." The cheap-shot thug for the Troopers wore number 73: Pam Schwartz. The Demon assassin Katie Graves called in to the show and called Schwartz and her teammates *thugs*. "They play dirty," she said. She mentioned the brawl and Hamilton's ejection from the stadium. She did not mention the play that took out Hollar. Then Graves broadcast a prediction for the game that was biblical in its irony. *"We're going to make the Troopers eat dirt!"*

On Saturday afternoon, a stubborn storm front drenched the city. The rain would slow to a mist by kickoff, but the damage was done. The game would be another box office bath. Stout met Schuster at the gate, sulking at their bad luck. "At least there's one thing you can control," Schuster said.

"What's that?" asked Stout.

"Don't lose."

The churned-up Mollenkopf Stadium turf had taken a hit. Under a misty haze, reservoirs of sludge spotted the field. Whatever machinations Detroit had cooked up dissolved in the fog that seemed to thicken by kickoff. The teams fell into their tendencies, Jefferson finding room on the less swampy terrain up the middle, and Hamilton's defense unbending like an arm wrestler with leverage. The fog thickened. "I don't like it," Hamilton said, recalling the brawl bowl from the previous year. He thought the stadium looked like a ghost pirate ship. By the second half, the Troopers ahead 18–0, Stout couldn't see his opponent on the opposite sidelines. For the Green Machine, it was constant blitzing, from every position. In the third quarter, Demon quarterback Judith Cook saw hope on the edge. Collette was in pursuit and anticipated the cutback. She caught Cook from behind and dove forward. Cook sailed headlong through the fog and landed facedown into the hogsnot with a splash. Every Trooper on the sideline, grasping the poetry of the moment, erupted, as though they'd waited all night for justice to play out before them. As Cook surfaced, the mud poured from her face mask.

Collette's hit on Cook did more than stop the drive. The humiliation of the moment robbed Detroit of its will. After three quarters and the score 28–0, Brown ordered his team off the field. They were crying mercy. Some just crying. The team in mud-soaked Hawaiian blue hobbled off the field, toward the locker room. Collette and her teammates watched as Brown led his Demons out of the stadium. Their final attempt to beat the Troopers came later, when the team filed a protest, citing poor officiating and unplayable conditions. It wasn't the Troopers that had beaten them, they claimed, but bad refs and low visibility. The *Blade* headline read *Trooper Victims Quit Early*. Protest denied.

Stout saw Collette's play as the model. He wanted to hit with such force it would jettison will, like a detached mouth guard. Hard-knocks football was how the game was supposed to be played. That was the football that people paid to see no matter who was playing. But on a cool Saturday in October, he saw the team going through motions against the expansion Middletown Mavericks. The new franchise looked alive and hungry, keeping pace with the champions in the first half. In the locker room Stout sensed complacency, a softness for the enemy. The weakness broke him. His eyes became a squint. He launched his shrill voice into every corner of the room in what Opfer would later learn was a *tirade*, by definition. *"You are football players!"* he shouted. *"Not babysitters!"* More instructions came in the form of philippic: *"Get off the ball!"* and *"Crush her!"* Stout detected resistance to his rage in Vickie Seel. "You stand there with a stupid smile on your face." He grabbed her face mask. *"Annihilate her!"*

The women stared into space, the emotions surfacing. Brigitte Hartz couldn't understand everything he said, but his message was crystal clear. He wanted his team to kill, to find weakness and destroy. He wanted them to play without mercy.

In the end, the Troopers scored three unanswered touchdowns and closed out the game 32–6. But it wasn't the victory Jimenez took away, it was the hard tone of the unbending son of a bitch in the middle. She didn't leave her indignation on the field but carried it to the locker room and beyond. After the game, a cohort of players convened downtown at the 19th Floor. The consensus was clear: Stout was going too far. What had begun as resentment was now a wedge.

The story in the *Blade* the next morning pushed the team further apart. For everything they had sacrificed, the women were ignored. Instead, Loomis penned an homage to the tyrant: "It remains difficult to envision how any coach could do a better job than Stout has in teaching a bunch of mostly out-of-condition women to play a man's kind of precision football." According to the story in black and white, there was only one point of view, and it belonged to the coach.

* * *

On his way home, Dippman drove underneath the billboard above the Cherry Street Bridge by the Sports Arena and came up with an idea. He consulted a local advertising agency, who invited Jefferson to their studio for a photo shoot. They did not invite other players but a couple of champagne models and photographed them in Jefferson's jersey and shoulder pads. The next week the billboard facing the Toledo skyline across the river featured Jefferson's familiar next-door-neighbor sweetness flanked by two anonymous blondes, above the caption *PRETTY TOUGH.*

Many of the players took the billboard in stride. They understood the pun and did not go so far as to call the display false advertising. But substituting the face, or faces, of the team didn't sit well with others. The picture wasn't who they were. Evidently the women putting their bodies on the line were not commercial material, except for Jefferson, Jefferson the superstar, the player who was given a pass from wind sprints.

The preferential treatment Jefferson received drove the wedge deeper, metastasizing their rancor. Some players demanded insurance for injuries. Some sought transparency, demanding to see the books and questioning the $25 they received for putting their bodies through a demolition derby. They had done the math after playing in front of thousands of fans. They had read about outdrawing Toledo's new International Hockey League iteration the Goaldiggers in the Sports Arena. They should be getting a healthier cut, or one that didn't intermittently decrease or disappear. Each complaint added weight on the scale. With the force of momentum and solidarity, Jimenez's call for organization was fueled by resentment of the man who would rather die than give in.

* * *

Earlier in the year, a group of female athletes gathered to voice their concern about unfair treatment. The women of the crew team at Yale

University were given shoddy equipment, denied equal training time, and openly mocked by male players and coaches. The galvanizing grievance was being barred from using the showers at the boathouse after practice. The writer among them compiled a list of complaints and a statement they called "The Declaration of Accountability" and brought them to the director of physical education. *"We have come here today to make clear how unprotected we are, to show graphically what we are being exposed to."* Then they took off their clothes, revealing *TITLE IX* lipsticked on their bodies. The women won their demands, and the program transformed from a laughingstock to national champions within three years. The women were called the Rosa Parks of Title IX, films were produced about the dramatic protest, and the women became known as the Yale Nineteen.

On October 6, 1976, at the corner of Nesslewood and Detroit Avenues, twenty-four women gathered at Sunday Jones's apartment in the shadow of the Jeep plant and the Overland Smokestack. They crammed into the living room and found space on the floor. Gloria Jimenez took roll and jotted down the minutes. "We're a team," she said, setting the tone. "And everyone's voice will be heard." What followed was the validation of labor grievances as old as human organization, in emotional outpour. The women paid homage to order, speaking in turns and nodding in assent to each pronouncement. Jimenez sought transparency from the front office. She wanted to be aware of the financial health of the team and the league. She also wanted more effective promotion of the sport and demanded that Dippman be replaced. Eunice White brought up the preferential treatment some players enjoyed. Jackie Allen criticized the coach's decision to play rookies instead of honoring the women who knew the positions. Kathy Sanders demanded consistency in her positioning so that she could develop specific skills. Many repeated the chorus against Stout's dictatorial style, ignoring suggestions from his assistants. Church claimed that the harangues they endured for slight infractions undercut collective morale. Parma said Stout did not deserve respect because he gave her none. Hardy said Stout's method of singling out players amounted to public humiliation. Cathy Cupp suspected that the coach was taking out his personal problems on his players.

The most common refrain, however, was a word that struck a chord, and it was repeated by each woman crammed into Sunday Jones's apartment: *respect*.

The record Jimenez compiled read like a grievance against a world that had ignored them, a Declaration of Accountability of their own. And like the declaration, the typed, single-spaced report read like an ultimatum.

Jefferson was there, too. She knew that the complaint about preferential treatment to some extent fell on her. Certainly, the PA announcer called Jefferson's name more than any other. However, she had always credited her offensive line, knowing she would gain nothing from football without the sacrifice of her teammates. She was moved by the unanimity of the movement.

They had sacrificed much, Jimenez wrote in the introduction. From July to November, they had set aside their lives to punish their bodies six times a week. They had bitten their tongues and accepted the harness and yoke of the toil to become champions. They were the essence of the organization, the team itself, the product people paid to see. Without them, there was no story. Without them, there was no champion five years running. Without them, there was no dream. They were merely asking for fair consideration from SKW because football had become their dream, too.

"We hope that you the corporation will take into consideration that we want only what we deserve."

* * *

The gradual ripple effect of Title IX played out in public sectors in the form of scholarships and improved amenities for female athletes. But the

Troopers' declaration did not have the backing of legislation. It had only the force of solidarity and the leverage of timing.

While the Troopers gathered in Sunday's apartment, in the west Oklahoma City was stomping through their opponents. Reynolds and his wishbone had destroyed its conference teams including routs of Los Angeles, Lawton, Dallas, and Houston. All roads pointed to a culminating clash between the Troopers and the only team to beat them. The rematch would be the Super Bowl of the NWFL, a marquee matchup of the titans of a league that connected regions east and west of the Mississippi. It was agreed that Toledo would host the title, which meant that Stout and SKW would foot the bill to fly some forty Oklahoma women and coaches to Toledo, put them up for two nights at the Holiday Inn downtown, and then stage a contest of brute violence between them and its Troopers. The venture would cost the company tens of thousands of dollars, in fact every penny to its name, and more.

To finance the event, Stout launched a scheme to sell shares of stock in SKW. He manufactured notes of tender and traded them to Krasula and Mike Stout for cash that footed the bill for a Super Bowl, a championship to be played at the largest venue in northwest Ohio, the Glass Bowl, a twenty-thousand-seat home to the Toledo Rockets and their recent thirty-five-game winning streak. The university was not bound by antidiscrimination law to share the stadium, but the winds of Title IX as well as the critical mass of support in the city convinced the athletics department to do what it had never done: draw up a contract to rent the stadium for women's football.

As Stout waited for the contract to arrive from the university, he was hit with the declaration that knocked his feet out from under him.

It was fitting that Sunday Jones delivered the blow, in a manila envelope containing the typed statement the women had composed.

When pushed, the nose guard tended to push back. Perhaps the thought occurred to him to reject their demands outright and burn down the house. He may have considered the manifesto and all twenty-four signatures as another sign that the league was doomed. But the Super Bowl was in motion, checks were cashed, stocks invested, and contracts signed. The game would be played on December 12, in forty days.

He wondered, *when had he crossed the line?*

The air needed clearing. Stout met with his lieutenants Hamilton, Davis, and Mike Stout to share the grievance. Hamilton begrudged their case but was leery of claims of going too far. Preparing for battle was a constant pushing and stretching the line. One cannot know where it is without crossing it. Davis felt betrayed by the loss of unity between coaches and players. He'd seen their success as the result of every gear of the machine working together. He took issue with some of the complaints. It was the nature of the football coach to excoriate players, but it was understood that what happens on the field remains on the field. There's nothing personal in coaching up a player who has more to give, he said. The men had felt the malcontent brewing, had heard comments about preferential treatment, about not hearing their names broadcast in fair frequency from the PA announcer. About not playing positions they wished to play. About being called on the carpet in front of their teammates. *It was pettiness,* Davis thought, *gone full-blown.* Mike Stout had always put the players first, describing them to the media as some of the best athletes in the United States.

Mike's older brother couldn't sleep. He paced back and forth from the living room to his kitchen in his tiny house, smoking. As with Stefanie's accident, he wound up in the middle of the night at the kitchen table with a pencil and lined paper, like the dedicated student he never was. He wrote, attempting to distill the feelings of his coaches as well as articulate the team's course moving forward. He avoided emotion that came to him in gusts. He tore up several drafts of a response, each time steering away from trip wires that would only entrench the women in their resistance. In their declaration, he recognized the sense of accomplishment and unity created by the team and the hope of the league's growth and prosperity. In the end, they had the same dream.

Perhaps it was the persona of a buck-stopper, instilled in him by his coaches like Dave Hardy, a man who would assume accountability for failures of the team. This was the tone he never took when his family crumbled. To accept responsibility, he would own his mistake. He would give in.

Alone in his kitchen, it was a different kind of understanding that came over him. He composed a final copy free of mistakes and neatly drawn on the page.

It appears "respect" was the most common word in the grievance. I will take total blame for letting this happen. For respect has been preached into the heads of my coaches from day one. So, beginning tonight, we the coaching staff will not denigrate any members of the squad. The word "Respect" is a word that has to be earned. If respect is lacking between players and coaches, I am sorry. We the coaching staff respect each and every one of you for your abilities to play football.

At practice, under a blustery October sky, he stood before the women and read the letter. He announced that the coaches would meet with representatives of the team to discuss other demands not specifically addressed here. He set forth a new set of rules to remove punishment, or the appearance of it, during practice. To address the dissatisfaction, he prescribed discipline. Each practice was broken down into undeviating intervals of training, interceded by specific conditioning. Forty-five minutes for offense. Forty-five for defense. Thirty for special teams. He abolished awards for offensive and defensive players of the week and specified the list of duties for each coach. He had put it all in writing, so there would be no confusion, and announced that the new system would begin tonight, which meant right now.

He would talk about transparency. He told Jones that the league was costing him and his family tens of thousands of dollars. While it was true, the women put their bodies on the line for $25 a game. The box office pull wasn't enough to keep the league afloat when taking into account the cost of equipment, transportation, and the production of a football game. Still, if respect was the linchpin of their demands, they could claim a victory. Jones could hear the emotion in his voice. They had punctured the ego of the face-mask-grabbing curmudgeon. It hadn't been in their demands to knock Stout off his horse, but now Jones faced him eye to eye, and she could see vulnerability behind the hard-nosed façade.

Already it was growing dark. Saving the good news to the end, he announced that the rematch against Oklahoma City would be played next month in the Glass Bowl. The team would face the women who had showed them defeat in the region's largest stadium. According to his proclamation, they would be having practice five nights a week leading up to the game.

"And there are no individuals on this team," he said. "We win or we lose, as Toledo Troopers."

CHAPTER 18

DEADLOCK

The rematch between the Oklahoma City Dolls and the Toledo Troopers was held in the University of Toledo's Glass Bowl on a blistering cold December afternoon. The sky was clear and bright. In the morning, the grounds crew used plows to remove layers of snow and ice from the field, shaping it into small mountains along the stonework and leaving a frozen green sponge of a playing surface. At kickoff, the thermometer read twenty-two degrees. The wind chill, below zero. Stout had dragged the team through a gauntlet of preparation, adding new plays to the offense and driving the women on the sled into the night. On a day full of sunshine and bitter chill, the teams bashed away at each other, each play potentially breaking the game one way or another. As the final seconds ticked off on the massive stadium scoreboard, the Troopers counted down like New Year's Eve. At triple zeroes, they felt the incomparable joy of redemption, and they rushed the field like champions.

They thought they had won.

* * *

For weeks leading up to the rematch, the *Blade* sprinkled stories of the team's preparation. *The Champion of Champions Bowl*, the posted handbills read, recalling the clash of stallions at the turn of the century. The three local television stations paid a visit to Colony Field, as well as to Springfield High School, where Eunice White coached three sports and taught physical education. White convinced the administration to allow the Troopers to use the gymnasium for rehearsal. Now that the championship was on the line, the team saw what was in front of them: a team that had beaten them descending on the Glass Capital to repeat the humiliation. Under the purple glow of the gymnasium lights, the offensive line trotted into formation, Opfer over the ball, and Hardy's signal-calling echoed off the stacked bleachers. The women came set, frozen like a photograph, then an explosion of movement in every direction, their sneakers squeaking on the hardwood floor.

Stout, donning his forest-green Trooper jacket, told the reporter that his team had a score to settle. "We know what we're up against." The reporter asked him what he thought of the Wild Bunch, the name the Dolls had adopted in their western division champion run. "They're big, and they hit hard," Stout said. He paused, and for a moment he flashed back to the disaster at Taft Stadium. He saw the red, white, and blue mob scene after Sales caught the touchdown. "I can tell you this," he told the reporter. "Oklahoma City is not flying across the country to lose."

Tom Loomis asked a question in his headline that essentialized the dream: *A Super Bowl in Toledo: Why Not?* In a cheeky tone, he described the upcoming clash of the powerhouses of the NWFL as a first. Four years earlier, the Troopers had traveled to Dallas, yet that was the design of Sid Friedman, whose WPFL was all but forgotten. Saturday's bill brought together the best the sport had to offer, from east and west of the Mississippi. Tellingly, the game was fraught with story lines that give meaning to sport, that create an audience and hold their attention. How would the vanquished champion respond? Was the loss on the prairie back in September a fluke? Had the rookie-laden Troopers learned to close? What new wrinkles did each have for the other?

To counter the sweep, Stout revealed his strategy: "We'll depend on our corner linebackers like Verna Henderson. Then it's up to the interior linemen to provide pursuit."

"If Stout talks like the head coach of a man's team," Loomis wrote, "women's football isn't all that different."

* * *

In the locker room, Opfer pounded her fist on her thigh pad to ward off panic. As the center she and the quarterback Hardy had spent three months and eight games perfecting the exchange. But the unknown was the enemy. The Dolls promulgated the fact that they had added an equal to Jefferson in running back Sherry Mathis. "We've heard it before," said Stout, attempting to slow the anxiety. In the room's hard fluorescence they felt exposed, vulnerable. They tested their breathing and let go long escapes. The familiar echoes of snapping shoulder pads and tearing of tape became reassuring music. The long sleeves and layers felt like added armor. A debate about fashion distracted the women from the butterflies: what footwear best suited the green neoprene concrete. Schwartz was sticking with cleats; her treads were small enough to grip the plastic surface. Others opted for low-cut Ponys, or black-and-white-striped Adidas Samba shoes. Brenda Baskins laced up a pair of good old high-top Chuck Taylors.

Game-day uniform for Stout meant a coat and tie, like his heroes Lombardi and Landry and Hank Stram.

The women stood in a circle as winners of eight straight games tallying 282 points while giving up 41. And they were still standing, in part by his demands and in part in spite of them. The coach stood at the center.

The first message was duty. "We're the better team," he said flatly. "We were better then. And we're better now." He told them destiny had arranged the meeting to set things right. In September, the enemy had not won the mantle but had it given to them. It's the calling of a champion to right the wrong. Then he called on Hardy and Opfer and

Miller and Hartz. "You've led us back here," Stout said. "You are rookies no more."

Trotting through the tunnel, the Troopers felt the cold, followed by the tinny music and the PA announcer. Guy, the ball boy bundled in a parka, skipped behind. They could hear the crowd calling them into the breach. For Hamilton, it was the moment of transcendence, gathered in the shadows for a moment before bounding into the light, with revenge in their hearts. Like being born, there was nothing like it.

For the NWFL, running out of the tunnel meant another moment of truth: Like an actor measuring the house, there was the dream of the crowd that would breathe life into the league. The Dolls in their royal-blue tops and white helmets clustered on the opposite side, in front of hundreds of Dolls faithful, friends and family who'd flown with the team or made the thousand-mile road trip. On the Toledo side sat thousands bundled up in scarves and mittens and knit caps, filling up the midfield sections of the bowl.

Schwartz and Jones represented the team for the coin toss. A camera crew accompanied the ceremony, the teams and referees lining up in ritual fashion. When Jan Hines called heads and the coin rolled to a stop, luck would begin on the side of the Dolls. They chose to defer and play defense first.

Nothing, not nature's cold, not the pregame huddle, not prayer, cleared the mind like the first hit. Opfer took her spot on the ball, face-to-face with the enemy. At the snap, she was demolished by a blue wave, the Dolls stacking the box and containing on the ends. Jefferson lined up as a decoy each time while Baskins's red sneakers found only blue jerseys of blitzing linebackers. The line lost their bearings in the frigid daylight, their breath visible in intermittent bursts, like a caldron. Church was standing on her own 18-yard line when she took the long snap to punt. She put her foot into a frozen stone that elevated, dropped, and bounced backward, rocking still on the Troopers' 37.

On came the wishbone, a combination of Hines, Stokes, and Mathis, battering away between the wide hash marks. Hamilton had schemed around the wishbone, but the first drive betrayed a slight wrinkle. Frankie Neal had played mostly linebacker back at Taft Stadium. Now Hamilton saw their game plan in the way number 45 thundered onto the field. Neal carried the ball on four of the first seven plays, like a pick to a block of ice, smashing into the line for chunks of yardage. *If anyone wants to stop me*, Neal said, getting to her feet, *be my guest*. On second and goal from the six, Neal took the handoff from Hines and barreled into the frozen end zone.

Nothing fancy. Just punch-you-in-the-mouth Sooner football.

Nor was there anything special about the extra point attempt. Except that the conversion would go down as the most infamous play in the history of the league.

The Dolls assumed the kick formation, Hines the holder and Mary BlueJacket the placekicker perpendicular to the line. Hines took the snap and BlueJacket unleashed a line drive that fluttered sideways like a buckshot duck. The ball careened off the bleachers behind the goalposts. The referee waved his arms: no good.

Mike Reynolds and the Dolls couldn't believe it. They'd witnessed with their own eyes: the ball sputtering sideways through the goalposts. Reynolds screamed in protest, but the referee would not budge, and there was no such thing as instant replay.

After two possessions, the teams fell into their tendencies. The Dolls blitzed on the corners, containing Jefferson. Hamilton moved his tackles wide, a bend-don't-break approach that threw sand into the gears of the wishbone. Now Jackie Allen was blowing up the middle, as well as adding pressure when Hines dropped back to pass. Palmer, fluent in the physicality of bar fights, threw herself into the pile each play. The Trooper defensive line became a wall of bodies that was too high to climb and too wide to run around. On third and nine, Hines took the shotgun snap and launched a punt into the returnerless secondary. Reynolds, playing for position, was up to his old tricks again.

The game still in its adolescent stage, the Troopers at midfield, Hardy called for the team's first combination punch. On first down, the line surged forward for Henderson, who tumbled into the left of the line for two frozen yards. A jab, to be followed by an uppercut.

In preparation for Reynolds's containment, the Troopers had rehearsed a play said to be invented by none other than Pop Warner himself. The trap run called for Schwartz to pull back off the line and run lateral to the hole on the left side. Jefferson feinted right, then cut back, taking the handoff and following Schwartz into the breach.

Dolls middle linebacker Pam McDaniel charged in to fill the hole but was met by a surprise party of one, a gold number 73 jersey running full speed. Schwartz's collision cleared Jefferson into the daylight of the secondary, and there was nothing there but open green AstroTurf and blue sky.

It seemed the entire Dolls team lost track of the one player they couldn't afford to. By the time Jefferson crossed the goal line, she was trotting, holding the football into the sky. The closest to her was Sunday Jones, who hoisted the superstar into the air like a christening.

The explosion gave the two thousand spectators a reason to get on their feet. Cowbells and whistles accompanied the roar of the families and fans who had ignored the cold to see a game of savagery and strategy and were graced with the very thing.

On the extra point, Stout kept the surprises coming. Jefferson dove up the middle on a decoy, hoping to leave Sunday clear in the flat. Hardy lofted it toward the corner, but the ball sailed out of reach. The Troopers had missed the chance to take the lead, but they trotted back to the sideline knowing the Dolls' defense could be solved.

To his side of the equation, Hamilton shouted instructions that reduced the game to its animal sensibilities. *"See the ball, get the ball!"* he commanded. The gusty cold sky made throwing the ball near impossible, so Hamilton crowded the box and dug in.

Facing third and eight, Reynolds showed field position conservatism.

Hines grabbed the shotgun and let sail another punt. The quick kick was a sleight of hand that kept the ball away from Jefferson in the open field. Reynolds was satisfied punting to no one, even if the Troopers knew it was coming.

In the third quarter, the Dolls' ice pick offense nudged down the field inside the Troopers' 20. But after a holding penalty, Hines faced third and long. Collette sensed the rollout and forced Hines to jettison the ball out of bounds to avoid the steamrolling.

The Dolls did not score, but Reynolds's game plan was paying dividends. The Dolls took the next possession at their own 26-yard line and began pounding. On came Frankie Neal, running inside the tackles, a methodical sledgehammer swinging down into the mass of gold and green. The Dolls could withhold their intentions, right or left, until Neal or Mathis came crashing through. Reynolds instructed the women to simply fall forward through the gaps, a strategy of death by bloodletting, and as the Dolls marched with metronome certainty deep into Trooper territory, the clock relentlessly wound down. Hamilton looked for fresh bodies. "Opfer!" he called. He began swapping out his linebackers for Stout's offensive line, the freshest bodies he could find. Still, the Dolls would have their yards.

On second and goal from the Troopers' 6, on came Neal, barreling toward the goal line. Opfer at linebacker rushed to the hole and understood that the only option was suicide by subway and threw her body in front of the train and held on. When she opened her eyes, she lay on her back, empty-handed. Neal had crashed through and tumbled into the end zone.

The thirteen-play, 74-yard demonstration of toughness took nearly seven minutes of clock to play out. Mary BlueJacket's kick sailed wide, but the Dolls held a 6-point lead and a confirmation that nothing can stop Oklahoma football.

The confidence could be seen on the ensuing kick, the blue jerseys galloping down the field. But if anyone knows how to turn an opponent's momentum against them, it's the nose guard. Sunday corralled the kick at the 15 and paused a beat like a penitent about to pray, then darted across the field gaining steam. She drew the blue jerseys to her. At the moment before takedown, she showed the ball, like a handoff.

It was Jefferson, swinging back across the field, on a reverse.

But Jones had waited too long. The attack wave of Dolls surfaced suddenly, and the exchange was no handoff, but a kind of flip, the pigskin suspended in the churning air. The ball, and the game itself, careened off Jefferson's hands and kerplunked onto the turf in front of her, a championship a matter of a football's bounce. Jefferson could have smothered the ball, but desire and instinct took over. Her legs kept moving, and her hands picked the ball clean off the turf. Dolls marauder Leah Ott was fooled twice. Once by the counter, and then the fumble tempted her further. Diving toward the ball, Ott gave up on her angles, and Jefferson was gifted a bead on the corner. With no ends to hold contain, Jefferson flew down the sideline, asserting her will in speed past the last Doll, a disaster turned somehow into a miracle by design.

The 85-yard botched jailbreak tied the score. On the extra point Hardy called for the trap, predicting the Dolls' tendency to rush the ends. Opfer had taken note that missing from the Wild Bunch was the defensive MVP of the first game, Cindee Herron. She'd torn her ACL in a game against Tulsa and did not make the trip. Starting from the I-formation, Jefferson took the handoff and followed Henderson and Baskins into the gut of the defense. It was a sheer bum-rush, the green helmets pushing, and Jefferson falling forward over the goal for a 13–12 lead. An eternity of 1:45 remained.

Hamilton was raging: *"This is not over!"* He wasn't wrong. Anything could happen, as the night in Oklahoma had proved.

But the Dolls were not constructed for the quick strike. The unstoppable, time-consuming wishbone wasn't an option for Reynolds. He put the game in the hands of his captains Hines and Sales. And just like the heroic win, Hines took three snaps over center, and it was over. A Hines pass died in the cold and skipped on the turf. Dolls slotback Barbara

Mitchell was flagged for holding when she tried to stop Jimenez's rush, pushing the Dolls deeper in the hole. The third attempt was a 15-yard curl, Hines flinging the ball to the corner. But Zuccarell saw it. She jumped the route, as though she'd been waiting all season, or her entire life for that matter. In her mind two points connected—getting knocked unconscious by Jimenez at Colony Field and securing the ball and the championship in her hands. She tumbled to the ice with a baby in her arms, amid the strangers in white face masks looking down at her. A mob of green helmets invaded, lifting Zukie to her feet. They came at her, her teammates, and she could not fend them off, for she held the ball tight, nor could she hear her name echoing over the stadium.

This time it was the Dolls who endured the stun. They had outgained the Troopers from the line of scrimmage. They limped back to their lines, looking over their shoulders at the celebration. Like pepper spray on the wound, the notion that the referees had it out for them had taken hold of the Dolls' sideline. The phantom penalty on Mitchell corroborated the conspiracy.

Hardy and Opfer formalized the final, executing three clock-killing snaps, icing on a mistake-free, frozen afternoon. The shot of the starter's pistol at triple zeroes framed the moment with an exclamation point, and a dash. The teams mingled among cameramen from Tabner's Channel 11 for handshakes and cursory interviews, then ran to the sweet warmth of the locker room. Mitchi Collette did her best Joe Namath trotting off the field, signaling *We're number one!* and her teammates did their best Collette, a line of Troopers trotting into the tunnel, their frostbitten fingers pointing to the sky.

Loomis wrote that Jefferson was the difference, the most valuable player, scoring both Trooper touchdowns on breakaway plays. Loomis quoted a salty Reynolds, who knew that the superstar accounted for every single Trooper point, and spectacularly so. "Without Jefferson," he said, "that team would be different." He did not mention that the Green Machine defense held the pile driver offense to two scores.

Amid steam and sweat and heat breathing from steel radiators, Bronko unveiled the case of champagne donated by her grocery store in Bowling Green. Corks bounced from the concrete ceilings, and women showered one another with bubbly. For Bronko and Church and Palmer and Allen, the sweet burn of champagne was the final taste of football. Bronko and Palmer followed jobs out of the swamp. In the fall, Allen's son would follow in his mother's footsteps and begin his football career, one that she would follow on fall Saturday afternoons from Pop Warner all the way through four years at Ohio State. Allen wrapped her fingernails around the bottle and permitted herself a pull, as a Trooper who never lost a game.

Collette's jersey was streaked with blood. Loomis said the team looked more like they'd been in a war than a football game. "Yeah, yeah," the linebacker said. "Isn't it great!"

Jefferson stood on the outside of the circle, smiling. Next to her teammates covered in beer, blood, and bubbly, she looked brand-new. She appeared not to have broken a sweat, instead of a running back who'd run for 143 yards on twenty-one carries and scored all 13 of Toledo's points. "I'm ready for another quarter," she said. Plus she hated the taste of champagne.

Jimenez was on her feet, leading the cheers, one for each member of the sisterhood. Every woman who'd run suicides, who'd pushed the sled, who'd signed the petition. Jones lost her voice from screaming. Her six solo tackles and seven assists would leave marks. Tomorrow there would be pain, but her answer to Loomis's question was direct and clear: "This," she sang to her teammates, "makes it all worth it."

It was also worth it for the fans, those who braved the cold, and for the brass of the future great city of the world. At the next city council meeting, a motion was unanimously passed and signed by Mayor Harry Kessler to make an official resolution commemorating the Troopers' "First-ever National Women's Football Championship." The declaration listed all twenty-four players, who "*achieved a record perhaps unparalleled in local sports history…for their exploits on the football field and their dominance of the National Women's Football League as expressed by their newly won championship."*

Stout, too, declined champagne. He preferred lingering with his coaches and feeding sound bites to Loomis, steering the credit wagon toward players besides Jefferson. He said Schwartz "played a heckuva game," delivering punishing blocks that didn't show up in the scorebook. And Hamilton's spread maneuver was the key to containing the Dolls' power sweep. If he harbored doubts about his league's survival, it was temporarily buried under a backhoe load of vindication. He'd bested a mastermind in Reynolds, who understood strategy like one understands a hammer. Stout's trap blocks, the reverse, and their execution won the day while Hamilton's triage slowed the unstoppable force long enough. Above all Stout had orchestrated a culminating national championship, the centerpiece of an emergent league.

"I hope we never play them again," he said.

* * *

During the 1976 NFL season, the director of officiating, Art McNally, attempted a crude form of instant replay when he used a stopwatch to time how long it took for a play to be reviewed. In November, a month before the Troopers woke up to an ungodly cold morning of the championship, McNally saw a blown call involving O.J. Simpson that could have affected the outcome of the game. He attempted to persuade the league to implement an instant-replay policy, but his plan was rejected, and it would be another generation before the phrase *after further review* gained currency. It simply took too long to review a close call.

For the disputed extra point in the NWFL championship, the review took twenty-seven days. Back in the warmth of his Oklahoma City living room, Dolls assistant coach Mike Reynolds watched on his Super 8 projector as the Dolls and the Troopers lined up in frozen sunlight for the first-quarter extra point. Shot from behind the goalposts, the film showed the ball ascending from BlueJacket's foot, over the maelstrom of the line of scrimmage, tumbling toward the posts. Then he paused the projection. He watched the film backward and forward. He slowed the projector down to a stop-action crawl. There was no doubt about what he saw. He wrapped the film and sent the package to the commissioner, along with a formal protest.

Deb Schuster, formerly Brzozka, had watched the game from the radiator-heated press box on the Oklahoma City side. From above the field, she had not seen the play clearly, nor did she witness the Dolls' outrage at the call. When Schuster watched the film, her heart sank. She, too, could not avert her eyes. The ball flew sideways, skittering, in between the uprights of the goalposts. The kick was good.

What compelled McNally, Reynolds, and Schuster was the spellbinding power of film. Up to now discrepancy among witnesses of disputed events was chalked up to human imperfection. Super 8 film changed that. The reel revealed a secret that reshaped the past and changed reality. What Schuster held in her hands in a circular steel canister was the Zapruder film. It was unshakable, and considering the high stakes of a championship game, it was as though she held visual proof of the existence of ghosts.

For days Schuster was tormented. The blown call wouldn't let her go. It was a 2-point mistake in a game that ended 13–12. The woman who once congratulated her opponent for knocking the shit out of her knew that Oklahoma should be awarded the conversion. But because the mistake happened in the first quarter, she couldn't award the points retroactive to a moment within the game. On the other hand, there it was, ball careening through uprights, in flickering living color.

She had no one to consult. She couldn't ask her former teammates or the coaches. There was nothing in the rule book and no precedent on which to base her reasoning. It was the most difficult decision of her life, she later confided.

In the end, her conscience guided her. On January 6, she rolled a blank page of NWFL letterhead into her typewriter, and by the power vested in her as commissioner, she began typing.

After reviewing the film of the game, it was proven that the extra points kicked by the Oklahoma City Dolls after their first touchdown play were good. We cannot let this error pass. In the same respect, it would be unfair to strip the Toledo Troopers of the national championship title...if the extra points had been called good, the strategy of the game would have been different.

Due to these extenuating circumstances, the league shall rule that the Oklahoma City Dolls and the Toledo Troopers be declared co-champions of the National Women's Football League. This decision was reached after thorough consideration by this office.

Schuster added that both teams played extremely well and remain a credit to the NWFL.

Thus, both teams deserve the title bestowed upon them.

And so the victory did not happen. The win paid for in frostbite, contusions, and blood was erased from the books. The countertrap, the reverse, the interception. Never happened. By decree, the win was vacated and a tie inserted in its place.

As a caveat, Schuster added that future protests and "judgment calls" would no longer be resolved by the commissioner's office.

She signed the edict, prepared carbon copies for both teams, then bundled up before heading out into the cold to mail the announcement once and for all.

CHAPTER 19

BLIZZARD

If there existed a point at which the dream began to die, it is tempting to imagine the moment the Troopers gathered in the tunnel before taking the frozen Glass Bowl turf. Half in darkness and in light, it was the moment Carl Hamilton dreamed about. The roar of the crowd and the echo of the PA announcer's voice. A moment of supreme arrival, the transformation from civilian into savage in broad daylight.

But for Stout, in his sixth season, the moment was a walk of the plank. It was a reckoning faced by impresarios, barnstormers, and sports promoters seeking the unmistakable thrill of a packed house. The fruits of their labor evident for all to see: Would the spectacle attract the threshold of paying customers to sustain itself? Was the vortex of publicity strong enough to put butts into seats?

The estimated crowd was two thousand, less than half of what the league had hoped for. Some blamed their hometown's meteorological congenital defect, a godforsaken slot machine that turned up blue skies and sun but temperatures that would kill a person from exposure. By January, the cannon blast of triumph was dissolving, revealing the financial reality of the Champion of Champions Ice Bowl. All the pushing and pulling of the newspapers, television, radio, the city council, and the mayor couldn't overcome a surprise deep freeze. All told, the game would cost the league, and therefore SKW, over $14,000, mostly owing to the travel expenses for forty Oklahoma City Dolls and their coaches. Sponsorships and the box office covered less than half, leaving Stout's not-for-profit sunk deep in red. He was staring at a $15,000 debt for his SKW company, and outside his lonely hole on Westbrook, the forecast was colder. That was when he received the letter.

The Oklahoma City Dolls and the Toledo Troopers: Co-champions

Stout's first response was nose guard vitriol. He phoned Schuster and flat-out told her she had betrayed the office, not to mention the women, some of whom were former teammates. He had not ground out a victory by the closest of margins in the blistering cold only to have it taken away by revisionist history.

Schuster relied on what she saw with her own eyes: *"But it's the truth."*

"If they want to share the trophy," Stout said, "they can come to Toledo and try to take it."

In the swamp, the temperature hovered at zero for weeks. The deep freeze forged in Schuster a restless, barricaded mentality. She feared she might have betrayed her sisterhood in the name of integrity. Had she made a mockery of the city's resolution? Doing the right thing had not removed the cloud of the blown call but had shaded it, made it heavy. By the end of the month, Schuster grappled with doubt, as outside the Great Black Swamp had endured its coldest month in recorded history. Then the blizzard hit.

It began on Friday, the snow falling like a flood, burying houses and drifting over two-story buildings. For three days a tidal wave of snow pummeled the city, shutting down roads and stranding travelers throughout the state in a storm that became a national emergency. Dozens of people died, mostly from being buried in their cars. Amid the storm, Schuster grew detached from her decision. As the city emerged from its burial in snow, she found peace in believing that she had done the right thing, and in realizing that her decision was her final act as commissioner.

Under the blizzard lockdown, Stout, too, soul-searched his own football career: his days as an all-city champion under Coach Hardy to his Pop Warner years to his tenure as the Troopers' coach, which in his mind amounted to six championship seasons. He listed his accomplishments in bullet points, his "unparalleled record" of thirty-nine wins against one loss. He listed his fellow and former coaches who could be checked as references. Then he sent the résumé to the NFL teams in Cleveland, Detroit, and Chicago, and one to Bum Phillips, his mirror image, the buzz-cut, potbellied galoot of the Houston Oilers. Phillips wrote back. The Houston iconoclast acknowledged Stout's success, then wrote that the Houston Oilers had the previous weekend filled their coaching vacancies. Stout's hopes crumbled, not for lack of talent or drive, but timing. As the gambler attempted to parlay one fading bet with another, he felt the paralyzing contradiction of how little, yet how much, separated him from his dream.

Instead he stepped in to fill Schuster's void. He called for an emergency meeting of the league to exert pressure on the owners to get their financial houses in order and to set the course for a final attempt. He called for a winter meeting in Dallas at which the ownership groups would chart the 1977 season. The league welcomed new franchises in Houston and San Antonio but cut ties with the sinking ships in Los Angeles and San Diego done in by infighting and bankruptcy.

A personal transformation coincided with his heel-digging hibernation. He took on a new life that included a change in jobs, a new car, and a new marital status. First, he walked away from his job repairing vacuum cleaners and began driving trucks for 7 Up. Then he married the woman he'd been dating since the previous summer. Chris Delf was a secretary at the vacuum cleaner plant in Ypsilanti, and the two agreed on a small ceremony. Stout chose for his attendants the same men who stood beside him on the football field: Hamilton, Davis, Jim Wright, and Mike Stout donned light blue tuxedos for the ceremony. The newlyweds moved into a house on Willow Lane, close to the horses at Raceway Park.

Accompanying the farewell to the Tudor on Westbrook, Stout traded in the lumbering Plymouth Fury for another statement: a black Chevy van, a 350-horsepower, V-8 locomotive-size fist of a vehicle, a football practice on the move. On alternate weekends he drove it to the McDonald's on Monroe Street to take custody of Guy and Stefanie at five o'clock, not a shade of winter darkness before. Stout and Sue remained unspeaking enemies, both remaining in their corners, even during the exchange of their children.

* * *

The hopeful owners of the NWFL franchises saw advancements of women in other areas as indicators of the sport's imminent ascension to profitability. Earlier that year, the Episcopal Church had declared women eligible to be priests. The U.S. Air Force decided that flying a plane was not a gender-specific activity and graduated its first class of female pilots. The Chicago White Sox hired the first woman to be a television announcer, and a woman refereed a heavyweight boxing match for the first time. In the fall, fifteen thousand women gathered in Houston for the first National Women's Conference, an event reporters likened to the civil rights march on Washington and the moon landing. If a woman could be a priest or a fighter pilot or an announcer or a referee, surely the world would accept her as a football player. Furthermore, if a champion could be built in a forgotten corner of the heartland, in fact the birthplace of football, the major markets would surely follow. The birth of the NFL itself had been a less likely Hail Mary.

Most of all, the owners had witnessed what women were capable of on the gridiron.

What the NWFL lacked, in Stout's estimation, was a centralized force to shepherd wayward teams. What it lacked was organization. What it lacked was being on time. During the freeze the imperative gradually dawned on Stout to assume control of the entire operation. But by grabbing hold of the league, he would have to let go of his team.

At the winter meeting in Dallas, Stout arrived as the de facto commissioner. At precisely ten a.m., Stout put an end to the small talk among the owners and began. Item number one on the agenda was the double-edged sword of expansion. On one hand, the media, the lifeblood of industrialized sport, flocked to the transcontinental matchups. The *New York Times* ran a story about Linda Jefferson after the Troopers' win in Dallas, and news of the Texas Stadium matchup inspired the Reynolds brothers to establish their own team in Oklahoma City. ABC Sports televised the contest between the Los Angeles Dandelions and the Detroit Demons in 1973. However, staging a game that necessitated air travel and hotels came with a staggering price tag. Plus, the lack of organization of the California teams was evident when no West Coast owners showed up. The franchises in Pasadena, Los Angeles, and San Diego had attracted players and a modicum of investors, but there had been no Lamar Hunt to unite the teams on the same page.

The owners agreed to two regional divisions. The transcontinental dream of Sid Friedman, carried out by Bill Stout, featured ten teams and two divisions: the southern division, made up by the Tulsa Babes, the San Antonio Flames, the Dallas/Fort Worth Shamrocks, the Houston Herricanes, and the Oklahoma City Dolls; and the eastern division, comprising the Middletown Mavericks, the Philadelphia Queen Bees, the Detroit Demons, the Columbus Pacesetters, and the Toledo Troopers. Like a television pilot on its final shot, the sport's ratings in the form of revenue would decide whether the program would get picked up.

Above all, Stout expressed the need that the women had spelled out: respect. He had seen the legitimacy of the sport and believed that demand for it would overcome the myth of its gender specifications, as long as the league carried out its business with the utmost professionalism. All phases of the league operations, from practice to gameplay to administration, must be impeccable.

Stout was the unanimous choice for commissioner of the league. With Schuster out, the owners set a timeline for Stout assuming full duties as commissioner. It was decided that Stout would take over the office, but only after one final season on the sidelines.

He had one more score to settle.

CHAPTER 20

ANGELS IN THE BACKFIELD

In 1977, tens of millions of people tuned in to a television program featuring three female police officers saved from domestic chores in favor of more intrepid crime-stopping as private detectives. The conceit of *Charlie's Angels*—supermodels playing a man's game—was at once a celebration of the women's rights movement as well as a Friedman-esque perversion of it. Some praised the program for showing women boldly collaborating in a man's milieu, while others dismissed the show as salacious exploitation.

In episode 19, "Angels in the Backfield," shot in the fall of 1977, the three leads pulled on football pants, laced up shoulder pads, and snapped their helmets tight. They went undercover as members of a women's football team that tried to create a "genuine, big-time women's football league." The main character of the episode was a running back named Pokey Jefferson, and the plot hinged on the turnout of the championship game. When ticket sales lagged, an angel lamented the future of the sport. "She may have had a nice dream," said the angel Kelly Garrett, played by Jaclyn Smith. "But it wasn't big enough to fill many seats."

At the same time the program was being shot in sun-drenched Southern California, the women and men who shared the dream of such a league lived out the episode in the fading Rust Belt corner of the Midwest.

In their final year under Coach Stout, the Troopers tore through the eastern division of the NWFL, putting up lopsided scores for dwindling crowds. Their execution of the sport was unmatched. In the 1977 season, the Troopers faced an eight-game schedule against their regional sisters. For both offense and defense, the play began in the crucible of the line of scrimmage. The defensive front of Schwartz, Jimenez, Smith, and White bullied their opponents, allowing linebackers Henderson and Collette to attack with animal abandon.

On offense, experience at every skill position translated into execution. Hardy with a disputed championship under her belt worked behind an exploding line of Opfer, Schwartz, Vickie Seel, and rookie Carla Miller. Two game-changing options were added to the attack. The first was *pro set right 20*. Hardy, catlike quick and confident, betrayed nothing at the line except cool. A speedster like Baskins or Hartz lined up in the slot. Hardy could identify the isolation on Sunday set wide, and at the snap Hardy saw a glorious open window through which to launch. If the outside backers or safety bit to double Sunday, the middle became an open pasture lined in chalk for the flanker. For the season, Sunday hit career-high marks in yards and touchdowns.

When the Troopers took the field, duty was the driving force. As the women sought respect, they respected the game. Each woman became a perfectionist of her position. If they were ahead 70–0, it didn't matter. As Opfer at center nestled up to the football, there was no score. There was only the choreography internalized, and an opponent standing in their way. And at the snap, savagery. Collette executed the uppercut of the block, hitting low and driving toward the lights, standing up the woman across from her.

After the stand of solidarity the year before, Stout and Hamilton tended toward gut-check assurances and teamspeak. "Don't let me turn!" shouted Hamilton as he rode on the tackling sled, and the five women drove in unison through the crabgrass.

The stands at Mollenkopf Stadium were barren but for a speckling you could quickly count. The emptiness, especially on the road, inspired Stout's vindictiveness. If only his opponents played the game as it should be played, the box office would bloom, and the women could get paid. Unremarkable play was a cancer, and the only cure was a beatdown.

The season-long wrecking ball began with a 26–6 conquest of their rival Detroit on the road, then lopsided thumpings against Columbus and Middletown. They beat Philadelphia 78–0. They squashed Detroit at Mollenkopf Stadium 59–0. For the entire regular season, they gave up two touchdowns while notching fifty-five. At home they outscored their opponents 301–0.

After a 62–0 thrashing of Middletown, a reporter asked Stout if he'd ever thought to let up on his opponent. He shot back a confused look. "We train to win. We play to win. We don't train to let up." As though letting up on the field meant letting up on the dream.

Another ray of hope stood five feet, three inches, and weighed 140 pounds. A country girl, Tina Pirtle had broken track records at Woodmore High for speed and strength. But universities new to the process of scouting tended not to bother with girls of her dimensions. Plus the village of Elmore was cut off from recruiting trails since the Ohio turnpike passed it by.

Pirtle's appearance on the football field sparked optimism for the next generation. The promotion of the team and by extension the league historically followed the story of its superstar, the real-life Linda Jefferson. It had been two years and hundreds of hits for the running back since LJ's nationwide splash. Moonie showed no signs of slowing, but the next generation needed its Jefferson. When the stranger from Elmore showed up to the tryout, the coaches thought they had captured lightning for the second time. At the 40-yard sprint, Pirtle exploded at the whistle as though without accelerating, superhero-like. Pirtle had size and spring, a dangerous bounding quickness that yanked her away from anyone trying to catch her. And if a defender pinned her in, no arm tackle could bring her down.

Against Detroit, the Troopers' offense lined up for their first offensive play at their own 20-yard line. Jefferson deeked to the left, and Hardy handed off to Pirtle right. The rookie burst into the crease, blowing through the linebacker. She carried bodies, chugging toward daylight, until she emerged running into the clear: an 80-yard touchdown on her first play.

Blade reporter John Bergener, watching from the press box, was struck by her resemblance to another player. He thought of Texas A&M's George Woodard, the Heisman candidate, whose tackle-shredding runs stole the highlight shows. In the rookie, some veterans saw a renewed chance that the sport could win respect.

By the fourth game, Pirtle was living in the end zone, taking the *27 right*, a straight handoff from Hardy around the end, like a game of tag. She tallied six touchdowns in the first six games. The only rookie to score more had been LJ.

The new weapon forced defenses to be honest, giving Jefferson free rein against single coverage. If Jones or Pirtle scored a touchdown, Jefferson hugged them like a proud parent, but on the inside her ego grew hungry. She made sure she got hers. In the two games against Middletown, Jefferson, running on a confident knee, scored eleven touchdowns, leaving no doubt of her supremacy. In her sixth season, Jefferson ran the only way she knew how, like she was on Buckingham Street, and the boys were trying to catch her.

* * *

After the ice bowl, Stout had told reporters that he never wanted to play Oklahoma City again. Now it was his mission. The Dolls held up their end of the bargain, completing an eleven-game season undefeated in the southern division, their wishbone offense racking up 40 points per game.

The final game of his career, the 1977 NWFL championship, would be played on the last Saturday in October, at Taft Stadium, the site of the team's only loss in seven years.

The clouds hung low over the Great Plains on the cool evening before kickoff, and the night revealed itself behind the glow of stadium lights. Inside the locker room, time itself was a palpable thing. Jefferson could feel the moments tick away, like air being sucked from the room. The women used routine to calm them. Sunday hung her tan leather jacket on the same hook as she had fifteen months before, suiting up in the corner of the concrete WPA-built bunker. In order, the women taped up, Mike Stout and Davis kneeling before them, wrapping ankles and wrists. The PA announcer's muffled voice triggered déjà vu. Pam Hardy could feel the presence of thousands in the house, no rain or snow or cold to keep them home. When the women gathered in the dark tunnel, the lights revealed a parabola of screaming Oklahomans, and the red lights of the scoreboard glowing in the mist like the eyes of a demon. Standing in the belly of the beast, they all felt it, the electricity in their veins as well as its only antidote: the bond of the pack.

The opening kickoff suggested disaster. The ball sailed toward Sunday at the goal line, then sank, skidding off the hard turf. Sunday butchered it, the ball bobbling loose into the maelstrom. She took an angle, scooping up the ball before collapsing under a wave of Dolls in blue. It was a stumble out of the gate, and a recovery. The Troopers were setting up shop inside their own 20-yard line. And the Dolls were here to hit.

In the huddle, Hardy called the *straight 34* to open the proceedings. The gold and green broke into a standard set with two backs, Jefferson and Parma, Sunday and Pirtle, flanking either side. Hardy stormed to the line with the confidence born of two years of seasoning since the debacle. In Opfer's hands the ball felt good in the autumn chill.

Hardy took the snap and spun, catching Jefferson in full sprint left for the exchange. Henderson at left guard pulled, heading off Dolls defensive end Mary Scherer, who'd shot in for contain. The only thing between charging defensive tackle Kathy Scott and LJ was the halfback Parma, who took on the 160-pound guard like a heavy bag. The choreography required millisecond timing, the explosions launching Parma into the backfield and Jefferson into the clear. Dolls safety Skip Corder, trained on human speed to read angles, fell away, and Sunday's downfield escort extended space. LJ found a lane down the left sideline, in front of Hal and Mike Reynolds and a battalion of Dolls, their faces shocked with eye black. She found separation, and the closest to her as she crossed the goal was Zukie, who'd knocked her woman off the line and watched the rest at full sprint, howling unrestrained.

A quick strike against the aggressive enemy allowed the women to breathe, to settle in, and to brace for the onslaught.

The Dolls sprang to formation, in lockstep. Three setbacks in a line, like the knuckles of a fist. Doris Stokes and Pebble Myers flanking Frankie Neal. In rhythm, Hines over center alternated left and right, ramming down Carla Miller's throat at nose guard. Gathering the ball at full speed, Neal powered in one direction, carrying bodies and always falling forward. After two first downs, Hamilton ordered Sunday and Henderson and Opfer into the box. On second down, the Dolls shifted. Myers took the ball right on a sweep, then cut back to avoid McNasty. Then she experienced something she'd never seen: a green torpedo in the form of Miller's helmet. The nose guard had fought one battle with the center, then churned up the line like a wayward skyrocket and blew through the ball.

On third down, Hines pivoted to Stokes looking for a seam outside left. Henderson at linebacker stayed home, saw the gap widen as though from memory, shot, and buried her helmet between the 3 and the 3. Stokes fell back for no gain. The Dolls had attempted to vary the attack, but Trooper discipline won out.

On first down, Pirtle attempted a charge up the middle, but the attacking Dolls closed the gaps before she snuck into the crease. Jersey grabbing slowed her, and with no momentum after 2 yards the Dolls piled on. Then it was Baskins's turn for the *pro set 27 left*. Baskins shot to square one, but cornerback Jamye Beaty forced Baskins to the center of the Wild Bunch, a hurricane of royal blue. Her helmet slammed on the dry Oklahoma turf, and she was underwater, the sound of thousands cheering muted by a deadening ting. She tried to stand, but her legs didn't obey. Her arms went numb. She stumbled to an oasis on the Trooper bench, plummeting inside her head.

All week long, Mike Reynolds had been telling his team and the media that the only way to win a championship was to stop Jefferson. The *Oklahoman* noted her eighteen carries and 137 yards from the ice bowl tie. "It boils down to us holding down Jefferson." He did not mention Parma, or Carla Miller, or Iris Smith, or Zukie.

The 37 called for a quick pitch right, Hardy spinning and hitting Jefferson with a fling at full sprint. At fullback Parma stood up the on-charging tackle, using the Dolls' own abandon for leverage to steer. "Just hold that block for a second," the rookie guard would say, "and then sit back and watch." Parma took the hit, holding up the defensive end for the blink of an eye and a flash of daylight. In the clear no one came close. If you turned away for a moment you missed it, Jefferson burning untouched down the right side, this time in front of her teammates and coaches. She teased Corder at safety, lulling her to close, then with a final burst of speed left her diving into the dirt.

Jefferson trotted into the end zone, turned toward the carnage and the five thousand fans watching, and lifted her arms and held them, like a preacher blessing her congregation worshipping speed.

Two possessions, two touches, two touchdowns. Like Reggie Jackson in the World Series nine days earlier, Jefferson went yard, on consecutive first pitches. It was a devastating and lasting statement of supremacy on the sport's most illustrious stage. The Troopers matched the scoring output of the first two Doll games on their first two possessions, as though the fates were righting the wrong of the overturned call.

But Reynolds held his team for a beat before they took the field again. "Who's ready to play now?" he charged. "As long as time remains, we have a job."

On the extra point Melissa Barr took advantage of Opfer, blind from the snap. She barreled through the crease and swatted away the kick. The Dolls would be nobody's fool.

On second and seven from the Troopers' 32, Hines rolled right, her phalanx of runners lining up for protection. She fired into the flat for Sales, and the tight end hauled it in for a first down, tumbling into the Dolls' sidelines. A wave of life lifted the women. They were off the mat, swinging with a counter to the Troopers' packed box.

In her career at quarterback, Jan Hines threw one interception, the game-ender to Zuccarell in the ice bowl. Reynolds called her the best quarterback he'd ever seen. She could make any throw, but her favorites were the ones to Tinker Sales. With time winding down in the first half, Hines lofted the ball into the flat over the head of end Eunice White. Sales caught the ball over her shoulder, in stride, and barreled downfield until Henderson blasted her out of bounds. After Schwartz batted down an attempt to the right flat, Hines looked left again. The play action gave Sales space toward the pylon, and Hines floated the ball to the corner before going down. Sales hauled it in and spun once, standing in Great Plains paydirt. When she turned and spiked the ball, her message was clear. The night was young. To corroborate the message, Mary BlueJacket drilled the conversion for two.

The machine kept charging to start the second half. Three backs in a line behind a two-tight-end fortress. Hines handed off right and left behind six-foot, 220-pound right tackle Melissa Barr. To adjust, Henderson, Opfer, and Sunday ghosted Neal's number 45, which gave Myers a seam on switchbacks to fall forward for just enough. The primary intention was to hurt, to out-tough the toughest. Giving up chunks of dirt was collateral. Then Stokes beat Schwartz to the corner for another combination. Hamilton threw everyone in the box. It didn't matter. The Troopers' defensive front took a beating for sixteen relentless rushes. Finally, it was the déjà vu of Neal punching the ball over the goal line for a 2-yard score, the culmination of a six-minute, 76-yard pile driving, and the dread was back.

The front line of White, Jimenez, Collette, and Miller stumbled back to the sidelines, gassed. Stout brought the twenty women around him. The red glow of the scoreboard above them read 14–12 in favor of the home team, a tally that echoed the ice bowl. The game, the season, and by extension the legend of the team hung in the balance.

It wasn't right, Zukie later said, from a moral standpoint. The sweat, the pain, the hits, the torn muscles, the bruises, the broken bones. Only to find themselves facing a deficit on the scoreboard. Reality needed correcting.

The potbelly marched in front of everyone, shouting at no one: "You're better than this team! You're faster! You're tougher!"

"Play Trooper football," he said, "and you'll be champions the rest of your lives."

* * *

In the climax of "Angels in the Backfield," Pokey Jefferson scored the winning touchdown as the clock expired. Her teammates hoisted her on their shoulders and carried her off the Los Angeles Coliseum field into thousands of screaming fans, fans who believed in the sport of women's football and were held captive by its story.

But that was Hollywood.

CHAPTER 21

THE RETURN

The fourth-quarter comeback in football is rare, according to a statistical study of the sport: 80 percent of teams ahead in the last frame close out the win. After three quarters of bashing into one another, each side is blessed with full knowledge of the other. Gone is the romance of the matchup. There are no secrets. The linemen have internalized the limits of their counterparts and employ tactics to fully exploit their weaknesses or minimize their strengths. Each knows the other's tendencies, their tricks, knows where they are and when and for how long.

The feeling would remain in their memory, in their bodies, their blood. Facing a second-half 14–12 deficit in the rubber match championship in Oklahoma City, the Troopers circled around their coaches. Baskins remained on the bench, unable to see straight. Pirtle bounced on the sidelines, working through her nerves and the blow to her solar plexus. The line had just endured another fourteen-play, eighty-six-yard bludgeoning.

As a collective unit, the Troopers knew. Stout ordered an imperceptible spread in the line. Brace for the attack, he told them, and hold.

"Stay in the fight!" Hamilton told the brooding faces looking back at him. They knew what he meant. Both previous matches swung on a gamebreaker, and the moment would fall to whoever struck and held.

The next drive began with the new weapon. Hardy feinted to Jefferson, then launched 30 yards toward the Trooper sideline, where Sunday, running an out route, gathered it, spun, and charged ahead for breathing room. A reverse spun the Dolls' heads again, the ball switching directions in the backfield, Jefferson to Jones, a long-stride gallop around the corner for another first down. The field was opening up, and the Trooper line was holding on long enough.

In rhythm, Hardy stepped behind center. She could hear the hissing of the crowd, a cowbell rasping. At the snap, she spun 270 and fired a pitch into Jefferson's gut. Collette at guard pivoted, forcing the tackle to the inside, then braced for the shift. When the linebacker McDaniel turned outside to catch Jefferson, Collette stood her up, leveraging her drive. Jefferson read the gap and shot through into Oklahoma pasture. Even if they knew Jefferson was coming, they couldn't stop her: The Dolls could scheme, they could position, and they could press. But they ran in slow motion. The moment middle linebacker Pam McDaniel lifted her shoulders to look for number 48, Iris Smith was sinking a shoulder into her chest. Troopers flying in low occupying the Dolls' lineman was enough. Jefferson ran wild in the middle, scorching the Dolls for 26 yards inside the hash marks, then added 19 more, exploding into a seam and darting right. Henderson took a dive and administered a punishing run to the Dolls' 9-yard line. On second and goal, the Troopers showed reverse. But Jefferson held it. She froze Schweitzer with a hesitation, creating a sprinter's inside lane to the corner pylon.

The mob in the end zone bled to the sidelines, the women lifted by collective witness: The drive was a dismantling, a six-step touchdown instruction manual, executed by all eleven women working in sync.

For the conversion, Stout opted for the devil she knew. Jefferson lined up behind Hardy and charged up the gap. Hardy hid the ball behind her thigh as Jefferson dove into the mosh pit of bodies. The quarterback took another step back to view her target and flung the ball to the end zone flat where no one but Sunday Jones waited, the entire Dolls defense biting on the bait. Sunday held the ball for a moment, and like Zeus chucking a thunderbolt, she hurled the ball into the earth in a mammoth spiking, a gesture of exclamation as clear as any touchdown they would score. The Troopers had taken back the lead, corrected reality's wrongs.

Hamilton, watchful of complacency and slack: "Stay. In. The. Fight!"

When the Dolls took the field with nine minutes left on the clock, their scuffed white helmets betrayed no panic. All-out hitting was what they, too, had dressed for, and their drive began with more punishment. They kept between the tackles, avoiding the potential disaster of a loss on the flank. Hines spun left and right, alternating gives to Neal. Jimenez, Smith, Miller, White, and Schwartz up front, backed by Henderson, Collette, and Opfer, began decoding the formations. On third and four from the Dolls' 39, the give went to Stokes running lateral. To Schwartz it was a drill. Hold contain and wait for the cavalry. Sure enough, Sunday and Henderson led the thrashing, as Stokes disappeared under a wave of gold. It seemed the entire eleven-woman unit raged into the backfield.

Reynolds called time-out to reset for the fourth and five. Taft Stadium could breathe for a minute, but bracing for the finale only pushed it to the edge. The crowd of five thousand stood and began a low-pitched anticipation. They had waited for this moment, had both wanted it and feared it, the play that would turn the outcome one way or the other. Hamilton served up a pull of water for his defense. "This is it, ladies," Cuddles barked. "Show me fight!"

It was another dimension of the Trooper superpower: fight. The Dolls came set in the same power formation. "Here she comes," Collette taunted. From the respite of the time-out, the linebackers gathered a modicum of strength. Collette danced, feinted a charge before the snap, as though announcing her intentions. Barr lost her concentration, distracted by the math of getting to her spot. The mountain flinched. She tried to pull back. But the whistles and flags broke the strain. The Green Machine forced a critical loss without making a tackle.

"Let's end this," Sunday said in the huddle, knowing fourth and long was not in the Dolls' playbook. The Dolls broke huddle and showed a two-back formation, Sales at tight end standing in the slot.

Now Hines, rolling out, was jettisoning backfield bluffs and counters. All eyes followed Neal breaking to the right flat as though trying to keep a secret. Schwartz and Jimenez closed as Hines checked down, stood in the shrinking pocket. Hines disappeared; at the moment of her burial, she found a foothold and launched, not toward Neal, but deep, a moonshot over the middle, where Tinker Sales ran free. The ball hung in the night sky before falling into the hands of the Dolls' tight end. For an unfathomable moment history repeated, the ball was secured, the first down was secured, the championship secured, the ball moving across the planes in a galloping blue jersey. Breathless, Sunday and Pirtle closed on Sales, ripped her to the ground. The three lay at the Troopers' 9-yard line in the shadow of the red-eyed clock ticking down.

The Dolls broke huddle at the end zone doorstep, like a SWAT team mobilizing for a raid, the battering ram in the hands of number 45. Pirtle saw the imperceptible pep as Frankie Neal came set in the backfield. It would be her, an inside dive. Pirtle stood up to the block, timed her swim, and when she slid free her helmet met Neal charging into the breach. The collision sent an electric jolt through the fullback, knocking her fourth-quarter arms past the limit of her control. Like a bad dream, the football fell away. Neal couldn't fall fast enough to find it. Then came the screams, primordial voices from a swarm of gold jerseys and green helmets, the revelation of the greatest prize tumbling naked on the turf. The fumble-drill-tested Troopers dove in, and at the bottom of the pile lay Eunice White, her arms crossed over the ball as though suffocating it.

Pirtle leapt and punched the sky. She led the rush home to the sidelines. The wheel had spun from certainty to doubt and back to certainty again. Uplifted by the miracle, Hardy and Jefferson sprang the offense on the field. The next series of plays were academic, the worn-out and one-legged Dolls defense doomed to the fool's errand of catching Jefferson running as though every royal blue jersey was her rival Roz Stoner on a city championship track. Jefferson's legs kept their spring as the Dolls lost theirs. In four plays, Jefferson led the golden horde across midfield, into the red zone, and to the goal line's doorstep. The final dagger was the same as the first, a *33* that Jefferson deeked inside to create a lane outside. The offensive line knew their enemy, had only to distract and occupy a tanked blue jersey for the magic to work. Jefferson cutting back left McDaniel on her knees, then followed a Jones clearing to the angle. She blew past Schweitzer, then danced to the corner pylon. It was her fourth score of the night, icing on 309 yards of cake.

The women skipped back to the sidelines holding on to a new kind of joy. Jefferson's final statement of supremacy rang within every Trooper as a conclusion of an argument. Up to this moment, there had been room to question who they were. Now the hometown scoreboard and red glow spelled out their identity, measured against a team that averaged 40 points per game, and had given up three scores the entire season. There would be no replay this time, except for memory.

Final: Toledo 25, Oklahoma City 14.

As the scoreboard bled to zeroes, the Troopers took to the field. Jones leapt into the arms of Cuddles, who held her for a moment, her arms outstretched into the cool night like a preacher's. The twenty-four women basked in revelation. A circle formed, and Iris Smith led them in their trademark song: *"We are the Troopers, mighty mighty Troopers!"* The curmudgeon was right: The song would remain with them for the rest of their lives. He led his coaches in handshakes with the Reynolds brothers and made his way toward the tunnel. Stout looked back one more time, seeking any remnant of joy to devour.

If anything could slow them down, it was the strange feeling that overtook them as they walked back into the Taft Stadium locker room, a wave of triumph and tragedy, a foreign emotion possibly called humility, for there were no more worlds left to conquer.

CHAPTER 22

BROKEN BAND

On Wednesday, January 11, 1978, just after ten p.m., Tina Pirtle was riding with a group of friends in the back of Sunday Jones's Cadillac, heading west on Dorr Street near the Richards Road intersection. The nineteen-year-old who had found herself on the football field had been partying with Jones and three others. They had visited the Peppermint Club, then made their way to Jackie's bar on a blistering cold winter night. The women belted out Diana Ross and carried on about Tina Pirtle's flashy red boho hat. The night was young. As a prank, one of the women rolled down the window and flung the cap into the roaring night. Pirtle demanded Jones pull over. "Let me out" was the last thing she said. She whipped open the door and stepped into the street. The first car that hit her knocked her tumbling back, across the double line into oncoming traffic. She was struck by two more cars and run over by a fourth. She was pronounced dead at the hospital, but Sunday, who saw a blur of lights and shrieking tires, knew she had died in an instant.

On Saturday, her funeral was held at a church near her home in Woodville. The unbending swamp winter reflected the dread inside the church. Pirtle had no surviving family besides her mother. Dozens of her Troopers teammates attended the service. A herd of champion football players including Opfer, Collette, and Smith hoisted the casket, carrying Pirtle like they carried Hamilton on the tackling sled, one last time.

The grief was an opponent they couldn't defeat. Some directed their blame toward Sunday, who'd been careless. As the driver, she was the responsible party and shouldn't have pulled over, or somehow should have stopped Pirtle from exiting the vehicle. Now Pirtle and her indomitable smile were gone. Her death was as unnecessary as it was violent, and the shock strained the bonds that held the team together.

Coinciding with the changing of the guard at head coach, Pirtle's death was more writing on the wall. Without the nose guard Stout, the moorings were strained. No longer stalked the taskmaster who demanded punctuality, no longer raged the tyrant who ordered the women to run as punishment for shoddy effort, no longer schemed the field general diagnosing weaknesses and designing formations to exploit them.

Instead, Stout's official capacity was limited to administration. For the last two years of its existence, Stout held the National Women's Football League together with his Black Widow Chevy van and Galaxie deluxe typewriter. He attempted to mend bridges with his nemesis Sid Friedman, who still held title to the Cleveland franchise. He drove to games throughout the region like a scout, arriving early, taking notes on the fan experience, the quality of play, and the body language of players. When he arrived back at home, he composed letters. He demanded professionalism in all aspects of the game. He wrote to Middletown and Columbus, admonishing them for kicking off a game seven minutes late. He demanded that the players stand in a prearranged line for the national anthem, and that concession stands remain open, clean, and welcoming until the final gun sounded. He adjudicated disputes and imposed suspensions on players who broke rules. He wrote a book with the help of the Columbus office called *The National Women's Football League Public Relations Manual*, eighty-four pages of optimism for the future of women's football. The eleven chapters and two appendixes covered aspects of media relations from game program design to radio and TV advertising to press box best practices. He itemized every aspect of a football game from the opening of the stadium's gates to the removal of trash after the stadium cleared out.

He saw hope in the ways that women were upending the conventions of their place in other sports. In September, a New York judge ruled that Major League Baseball's ban of women in locker rooms after games violated the Fourteenth Amendment. Women could now access spaces once legally restricted to men. The NWFL adopted a reciprocal policy. In a regression to Friedman's carnival come-on, the league announced that male reporters would be allowed into the women's locker room.

Yet without a city of believers behind it, other franchises were fated to die. Philadelphia folded, followed by Toledo's big stepsister Detroit, who could never in thirteen tries beat their rival in the Glass Capital. In the end, the league was reduced to a regional trio of teams that included Columbus and Middletown. The southern division crumbled in step. Facing bankruptcy, Houston and the long-standing Fort Worth Shamrocks closed down. The dream in Oklahoma City dissolved when a coach defected to the Lawton franchise, taking a few players including Frankie Neal with him.

The promise inspired by the lightning rod of Title IX and its inexorable implementation proved to be false positives for the sport of women's football. On the one hand, Title IX mandated that colleges build women's sports programs, which in turn transformed high school sports for girls. Gone were GAA tetherball and jump rope clubs, and in their place year-round specialized training and conditioning. Female athletes like Frani Washington were now competing for the real skin of college scholarships. But the sports they were playing did not involve helmets and shoulder pads and tackling sleds. In 1982, the NCAA held its first national championships for women in the sports of basketball, volleyball, softball, and track. But not for football.

The movement for equality evidenced in Title IX advancements, marches for equal rights, and national women's coalitions hit the ceiling. The Equal Rights Amendment never passed. About the National Women's Conference the year before, Gloria Steinem said, "It was the most important event that nobody knows about." The momentum of the tumultuous decade regressed to equilibrium. For women's football, the other shoe failed to drop.

Over two seasons, the Toledo Troopers and the NWFL ended with a whimper. Realizing the team was not the same, Hamilton and Davis followed Stout into the sunset. Subsequently the absence of the grizzly bear known as Cuddles, who'd inspired the women to *get up!*, and of Davis, who'd wept openly at demonstrations of team unity, left a gaping hole.

At their first practice of the 1979 season, several players were no-shows. Some cited injuries as the excuse. Jefferson's ankle, for example, grew worse. The ligaments were so torn, the bones so chipped and ground down that doctors prescribed an operation that would replace her ankle with a plastic one. Schwartz pulled herself off the team after being diagnosed with mononucleosis. Hardy took on a second shift at the Jeep plant. By the third meeting under the shadow of the cast-iron goalpost at Colony Field, only twelve women showed up to practice.

"These are difficult times for the perennial champions," wrote the *Port Clinton Times*. The thrill that had brought scores of women to play the game was buried along with Pirtle, and when the Troopers took the field, the thick black band encircling the sleeve of their jersey represented more than the death of a teammate.

The new head coach, Mike Stout, tended not to raise his voice but goaded the women along with small affirmations. The good cop shook his head at lackluster play and sprinkled ominous sound bites in the *Blade*'s waning coverage of the team. Mike Stout cited player absences and lack of commitment. In his second game, he benched Sunday and Pam Nagel for missing practice.

In their final two years the Troopers finished with a record of 13–4, tallying losses to Columbus, who turned the tables on the seven-time champions.

In their final game, on the sunset of the 1970s, Jefferson limped away from her teammates to take refuge on the benches built into the stonework of Mollenkopf Stadium. She couldn't afford surgery, so she wore bandages and a cast made of tape. She remained in the shadows for the rest of the game, watching her sisters fail to score. Even Sally chose to stay away, for the Troopers were not the same. Jefferson sat alone in the stone alcove. After the game, no fans remained for her autograph. No company sought her endorsement. She looked beyond the stadium lights and imagined the audiences that had gathered, not to see her play but to hear her speak—boys and girls of inner-city schools and YMCA clubs. She belonged there, in front of a crowd of schoolchildren, teaching them about the experience of competition that can be found nowhere else.

The loss was not publicly documented. No *Blade* reporter covered the story, no Channel 11 News produced a spot. The referee's whistle rang into oblivion at the final play. The hundreds of spectators dispersed quietly. Some of the women shook hands. Some made plans to meet up at the 19th Floor. Stout waited in the press box looking down on the concrete coliseum, an indifferent echoing bowl under the lights. Then he closed the windows and locked the doors. He walked the stadium grounds for a final clearing. The turning of the decade was upon him, a clock was timing out, a candle flickering. His dream was a distant echo of the past. He could imagine the sound of the hit just over his shoulder, the roar of Page Stadium for the championship on Thanksgiving Day. He could imagine meeting a traveling huckster, stashing the box office cash into a manila envelope, and the stiff dusty grass of Colony Field. A quarterback heaving the ball into the sun, and the fastest woman he'd ever seen running to catch it. A football fluttering sideways around the goalpost into the stands lined with snowbanks. A long fearsome stride of a football player running full speed in an Oklahoma sunset, lowering her head into the belly of a receiver, a tackle textbook in its perfection. A casket carried by a group of women down the stone steps of a church on the east side, backdropped by the eternal flame of the Sun Oil refinery. He could sense it all, right there over his shoulder. But he refused to look. There was only the bright empty stadium under an orange night sky, and the steel switch that shut down the lights.

CHAPTER 23

THE WOMEN OF TOMORROW

For Gloria Jimenez, toughness is a drug. In the years to come she gets her fix playing and coaching for the Toledo Furies, the next iteration of women's football in the swamp. The Furies, also coached by Hamilton and Davis, last for five years, bringing along Troopers like Jimenez who love the sport, as well as her fan base of five brothers. She leaves her career cutting hair to take on management jobs in restaurants, and credits her experience on the football field that instilled in her toughness. She always hears Hamilton shouting, *"Get up, Gloria!,"* and Gloria finds the will to get up. She keeps her faded Troopers jersey in her closet. "I played for the Troopers," Gloria Jimenez says. "And it was the greatest thing I've ever done."

* * *

Eunice White remains a high school physical education teacher for thirty-five years. Coaching volleyball, basketball, and softball, White sees the transformation of high school sports for the next generation of girls. In her heart, she knows that the joy and the pain she experienced on the football field are part of the metamorphosis of women's sports. "We were no women's libbers," she says. "But we were a part of the change."

* * *

When she returns to Cleveland after leaving the Troopers, Teri Macias stays clear of the police, until ten years later, when she joins them. For a decade, Macias patrols the Fourth District on the southeast side and once bursts into a burning building and carries out six survivors while her male partner watches. Then she tries out for CPD's motorcycle unit, a position never held by a woman. During training, a supervisor attempts to sabotage her test because women don't belong on the motorcycle force. On a turn, he pushes her off balance with his billy club. Macias does not stand down. She tells him, in her own words, that if he touches her again, it will be the last thing he ever does. Backed by the thought of what her Troopers teammates accomplished, Macias passes the test. She becomes the first female motorcycle cop of the CPD.

* * *

In basic training, the army attempts to strip away your individual identity in favor of that of the team. Verna Henderson understands what it means to put team first, not to mention what it means to push herself to the brink of physical exhaustion. The Army National Guard becomes Henderson's second team, the one she will serve the rest of her life. She becomes the first female command sergeant major in the Army National Guard. Being a Trooper has taught her to take charge, to sacrifice, and how to block. During her two tours in Iraq, she oversees a security detail that includes route clearance. Her company navigates graders and bulldozers on the outskirts of Baghdad, knocking out IEDs, clearing a path for infantry. On the battlefield, surveying the bombed-out road-side for deadly homemade explosives, Henderson is vigilant. She carries toughness and responsibility for the lives of the soldiers under her command, leadership qualities baked into her in the swamp heat of Colony Field.

* * *

When Nancy Erickson discovers that the Arcadia, Florida, school district does not offer softball, she files a suit on behalf of girls who were denied the chance to play. Softball has been her life, dating back to her years with the Kalamazoo Lassies, the team enshrined in Cooperstown after the film *A League of Their Own* told its story. The Lassies are the first Hall of Fame team Erickson suited up for. The second is the Troopers. As a result of her lawsuit, backed by Title IX, Arcadia redesigns the school district's facilities, adding softball and girls' track.

* * *

After playing for the champion Troopers, Judy Verbosky finds another means of kicking ass. She becomes a Song Moo Kwan tae kwon do world champion. During her travels, she joins a mission trip to a remote village outside Isiolo, Kenya. She spends weeks digging holes, hauling concrete, and constructing fences to protect orphans from predators from the bush. Then she discovers that the real threat comes from within. The water the children are drinking is giving them cholera, dysentery, diarrhea. What they need is a solution for clean water, and when the idea of constructing a well comes to her, she thinks the same thing she had thought before playing football for the Troopers: Why would I *not* do that?

* * *

Beverly Severance refuses to take free money. She lives in her car, working two jobs and playing football when she can. She gets a job at the Doehler-Jarvis plant, die-casting iron, steel, and aluminum parts for transmissions. When she walks into the shop, she is the first woman to do so since World War II. She's also the best. She wins an apprenticeship, beating out dozens of male candidates. They harass her, build a wall around her, and sabotage her work. One night she finds a bullet hole in her car. Another night, a co-worker attempts to close her off inside a casting machine and kill her. She becomes the first female journeyman to work for General Motors, accepting lower salary than the men she's better than. She makes enough to pay for college, earning a degree in business and women's studies. At General Motors, she invents a new system to improve the maintenance of the factory floor. The company adopts her plan; in fact, her brainstorm becomes the standard for General Motors factory floor operations around the globe. "I was just doing my job," says the former linebacker. "Like playing for the Troopers. We didn't care what other people thought. We just went out there and played the right way."

* * *

Carl Hamilton and his wife, Judy, remain in Toledo, a safe distance between their parents in Cleveland and Kentucky. Judy works nights at Lakepark Hospital, and Carl works days as a deputy sheriff in the courthouse. Over the years, as they raise a family and cover their living room wall from floor to ceiling with family photographs, many of their children and then grandchildren play sports. It doesn't matter the season or the sport, Carl and Judy travel to watch their sons and their daughter compete. Looking back on his days when he donned a gold polo shirt embroidered with *Toledo Troopers Coaching Staff*, Hamilton gets misty. "People can say what they want," Cuddles says. "But that was the greatest era of our lives."

* * *

One day waiting for the bus, Linda Jefferson feels the gaze of a young woman sizing her up. She recognizes the feeling, the darting look from strangers, Toledoans who lock on to her unmistakable smile, tripped up by the presence of greatness. "Excuse me," the woman says. "Are you Ms. Jefferson?"

LJ hesitates, cornered by a name no one calls her.

"I want to thank you," she says. "Because you saved my life."

She is not a fan after all, not of football, or of sports of any kind. She'd been a student at the Cummings-Zucker school on the west end, the last depot for at-risk students before prison. She'd been at the end of her rope, expelled out of one school to the next. Then she met a counselor at Cummings-Zucker named Ms. Jefferson, a woman who speaks the truth with her eyes. Ms. Jefferson is the greatest football player in the world, after all.

"You were my teacher," the woman says.

Jefferson remembers. Her experience speaking to athletes across the country gives her confidence to blaze a career, working with children. For twenty years, LJ works the front lines of education, teaching and counseling teens with the greatest needs. "If you believe it," Ms. Jefferson tells captive audiences and classrooms and troubled teens, "you can achieve it."

* * *

Do they love the game that much? Loomis asks in his column.

"It's an addiction," Ruth Zuccarell says. Putting on pads, living on the limits of what her body will give her, and hitting hard. Like many of her teammates, she cuts ties with the Great Black Swamp when the league can no longer provide her fix. She follows her job to warmer climes in Florida, bringing her helmet and jersey with her, just in case.

* * *

Mitchi Collette shakes her head to the question Loomis once posed: *Is it worth it?* To her, taking a field in football armor is freedom found nowhere else.

After the championship in Oklahoma, Collette thinks of hanging up her cleats, tempted by the sunset of a perfect season. But to athletes like Bear, life without the game is unimaginable. "I tried to quit, but I can't." She has been an athlete all her life, one who found football at her most formative moment. She remembers the shock of losing her first friend and teammate Debbie Haynes. "If I didn't have football, I'd be all through."

Collette never quits, even after the league folds. She plays for future iterations of women's football, the Toledo Furies, the Mustangs. She becomes the matriarch of the sport as the founder, general manager, and coach of the Toledo Reign. When she looks back at her life story intertwined with football, she wipes away a tear. Her voice softens, as though in reverence for what the sport has given her. "What we women did, what our coaches did, will never be forgotten."

* * *

Pam Schwartz wakes up in a hospital in Fort Wayne, Indiana. The last thing she remembers is flying in a Cessna twin-engine 337, before a raging ice storm knocked it out of the sky, the same winter system that took down Air Florida Flight 90 over Washington, D.C. The plane clipped a tree, then nosedived into a field a mile from the runway, killing the pilot and Schwartz's friend seated in front of her.

The doctors are astonished that Schwartz's neck could withstand the impact, as though she'd been wearing a protective brace. But Schwartz knows, as sure as she knows she's alive. The torture she endured at Colony Field conditioned her body to survive a plane crash.

Forty years later, Schwartz still wakes up with sore bones and occasional back trouble. She also carries with her the lessons of football: playing with heart, how to take a hit, and sisterhood. She tells her grandchildren she wouldn't trade the hard knocks on the football field for the world.

* * *

Carla Miller knows she can do anything. She inherits a vision from her father and grandfather, who operated an independent lumber mill in eastern Indiana. One day she buys twenty acres of forest west of the city and begins building. She uses hundreds of custom-cut timbers and some she found on her own to construct a log cabin timber frame home with her bare hands. Through all four Black Swamp seasons Miller carves every mortise, burrows every tenon, and hoists each timber. Having lived the metamorphosis of college dropout to NWFL Super Bowl champion, she has lived the transformative power of belief. "There's nothing I can't do," she says, an abiding truth she discovered in helmet and pads. Her vision is complete, a design inspired by her DNA, constructed where she'd always dreamed, in the shade of trees.

* * *

Joey Opfer can't talk about the Troopers without welling up. She thinks about the time she took off work as a nurse's aide to play in Oklahoma City. The staff at Toledo Hospital decorated the ward in green and gold. *Good luck, Champion*, the banner read. Thinking back, she feels the love and the support of the city that believed. As an anesthesiologist, she has seen everything, but nothing like a locker room full of women raging after a championship.

She also carries something else: the site of Tina Pirtle's unmarked grave. Pirtle's mother did not have money to buy a headstone, at the same cemetery as Opfer's grandparents. The lack of closure burns in her, and forty years later, with the help of social media, Opfer tracks down Pirtle's mother, living in Georgia. They discuss plans for a proper gravesite. Opfer reaches out to her teammates, and together they raise $2,000: a contribution to Woodmore High School's girls' athletics boosters in Elmore, and a donation to the Woodmore School District's charity for families in need. Today, Pirtle has no gravestone, but her name is engraved on the brick entrance to the new stadium.

* * *

Olivia Flores works the front lines. Against her father's wishes she earns a nursing degree instead of one in cosmetology. After playing football she understands with stone certainty that her life's work is not simply getting married and having babies. She works for the Midwest Migrant Health Information Office, holding the line between migrant workers and their health care. She drives hundreds of miles a day throughout the swamp to makeshift health clinics, diagnosing illnesses and treating injuries. She sees how migrants work and live in the asparagus fields, families making just a few dollars a day. Children sharing a piece of bologna for dinner. Flores is drawn to the work, as an offensive guard is drawn to the line of scrimmage, where the game is decided. "These families are the foundation of the whole system," she says. "I prefer to fight in the trenches. That's where I've always belonged."

* * *

After her mother forbids her from playing for the Troopers, Frani Washington tries basketball. She leads Woodward's first girls' varsity basketball team to the state championship in Columbus. Ohio State coach Mary Wilson sees Washington play and offers her a scholarship on the spot. As a Buckeye, the Great Black Swamp native sets scoring records that would last for decades. In 1979, the year the Troopers fold, Washington becomes Ohio State's first female All-American. "But if they had football scholarships for girls," she says, "you would've seen me catching touchdown passes."

* * *

Before Sue Guy marries Bill Stout, her mother warns her. Stout is trouble. He is not an abuser, he is not a slacker, he is not a drinker. But he fails out of school twice and blows their money at Raceway Park. He is brash when he had no right to be. Sue's mother sees a smart-ass ne'er-do-well whose reckless chip would ultimately be his undoing. The horrific accidents to her grandchildren are nightmarish told-you-sos: She thinks his negligence was criminal. To his partners in SKW, Dippman, Wallace, and Krasula, Stout is a sharp talker who they believe can convert a love for the game into a league like the NFL. Nobody knows the game better, and knows it top to bottom, from the way a team should stand for the national anthem down to the proper technique of taping a mangled ankle. To his children, he is by turns a local celebrity and absent father, a sports legend and restless schemer of the system. To his players, he is an unbending trainer and strategist. He and his coaches lay down the gauntlet, and the women respond by becoming champions. He's been a willing pupil and teacher of a new sport, and the women show him that they can play the game in its most brutal and beautiful form.

As a coach, he has won forty-six football games and lost one. Most of the contests are not close. Each season they face teams hoping to knock off the jewel of women's football only to get blown out of the stadium again. His practices instill toughness, discipline, and heart, the essential qualities of football players. He has chauffeured Linda Jefferson to national superstardom, in the hopes of creating a coast-to-coast league for the women's game. His team has captured the imagination of his hometown, garnering appearances on TV, the radio, and countless newspaper features. He has bet his life that the league would fly.

One summer afternoon, he is teaching twelve-year-old Guy how to hit, in his front yard on Willow Lane. Stout holds the tackling pad as he'd held it against his players, as Guy musters every shred of his strength to take him on. In full view of cars driving by, Stout knocks Guy to the ground. "Get back up and hit me!" the football coach says. But the boy is in tears. The lesson in toughness has gone too far.

Still, Guy holds his father on a pedestal, a champion for his years as a coach. So does Stefanie. Both children bear a reverence for their father as a local hero, a champion whose greatness is unsung.

Bill Stout returns to his second love. On the thirteen-acre plot behind his ranch house along US 23, he envisions a dream within reach. He carves out a circular path through the overgrowth and constructs a stable in which to raise standardbreds. His Dundee ranch becomes a stop-over for trainers throughout the area before heading off to compete at Raceway Park. Stout also spends the next twenty years as transportation superintendent for Dundee schools. On fall afternoons, he heads over to the high school practice field to volunteer his services. He doesn't wear a whistle, or carry a clipboard, or wear a coach's shorts, but he is known to the men and boys as *Coach*. He lines up in a three-point stance, waits for the whistle, then explodes, showing the boys how it's done.

EPILOGUE

At the end of their decade-long run, Bill Stout and Linda Jefferson take one last trip. They load up Stout's van with a collection of history, including team photographs, game-day programs, newspaper clippings, ticket stubs, game-worn jerseys, cleats, shoulder pads, helmets. Stout drives east on the turnpike three hours to the Pro Football Hall of Fame in Canton, where the VP of public affairs, Donald Smith, and a group of curators collect the items for a display. Then Smith gives the winningest coach and the greatest player a private tour. Stout sees the 1922 Toledo Maroons, one of the NFL's first teams; he sees the busts of Paul Brown, George Halas, Vince Lombardi. He can't help but compare his seven championships and .978 winning percentage.

As for Jefferson, there is no one among the greats in the hall to compare. Her place seems beyond even the reach of her untouchable numbers: 150 career touchdowns; 9,250 yards in seven seasons; 12.1 yards per carry.

Smith invites the two champions back to be the featured speakers at the upcoming Hall of Fame Club meeting. Then the conversation turns, as it always does, to the subject of the future for women and football. Stout shakes his head like he knows a secret. "It's bound to happen," he says. "Women can play."

"It took decades for the NFL to grow," Jefferson says. "Someday, there'll be a football hall of fame for us."

For now, Canton will have to do.

THE TOLEDO TROOPERS
1971–1979

Jackie Allen '71, '72, '73, '74, '75, '76, '77, '78, '79

Delores Anderson '71

Brenda Baskins '76, '77, '78, '79

Sharon Browne '71

Sheila Browne '71, '72, '73

Deb Brzozka (Deb Wright, Deb Schuster) '71, '72, '73

Davelyn Burrows '71, '72, '73, '74

Barbara Church '75, '76, '77

Mitchi Collette '73, '74, '75, '76, '77, '78, '79

Sharon Cool '72, '73, '74

Sue Crawford '74, '75, '78

Patricia Crider '79

Cathy Cupp '76

Terry Dale '72, '73

Peggy Dauer '71, '72

Ernestine Davis '76

Diane Degelia '72

Charlotte DeVincent '79

Kay Dickey '72

Sherry Dotson '79

Sheila Ellison '73, '74

Nancy (Erick) Erickson '74

Patsy Farrell '71, '72, '73

Carol Finn '71

Olivia Flores '72, '73, '74

Jen Francis '78, '79

Karen Gould '72

Anne Grote '74

Jayne Haley '78, '79

Pam Hardy '76, '77, '78, '79

Brigitte Hartz '76, '77, '78, '79

Verna Henderson '74, '75, '76, '77, '78, '79

Lee Hollar '71, '72, '73, '74, '75

Judie Janquart '79

Linda Jefferson '72, '73, '74, '75, '76, '77, '78, '79

Gloria Jimenez '72, '73, '74, '75, '76, '77, '78, '79

Jennie Jimenez '77

Sunday Jones '72, '73, '74, '75, '76, '77, '78, '79

Lynn Juress '71

Karen Kelly '71, '72

Kathy Keough '75

Carol Kurtz '71

Joy Langendorfer '79

Lynn Losek '78, '79

Teri Macias (Teri May) '73

Sharon Marienfield '71

Cheryl Martin '73, '74

Karen Mayer '79

Carla Miller '77, '78, '79

Connie Miller (Constance D'Angelis) '71, '72

Keely Miller '78

Pam Nagel '75, '76

Joellyn "Joey" Opfer '76, '77, '78, '79

Janelle Palmer '76

Dorothy Parma '74, '75, '76, '77, '78, '79

Melody Pieper '79

Tina Pirtle '77

Becky Redmond '79

Marilyn Robinson '71

Peggy Rough '74

Kathy Sanders '77

Pam Schwartz '71, '72, '73, '74, '75, '76, '77, '78, '79

Sandra Scott '79

Vickie Seel '75, '76, '77

Bev Severance '74

Deborah Skiles '71

Diane Skiles '71, '72

Lora Jean Smalley (Lora White) '72, '73

Diane Smith '79

Iris Smith '73, '75, '76, '77, '78, '79

Ramella Smith '73, '74, '77, '78, '79

Eula Streeter '75, '76

Virginia Van Hook '77

Denise Vance '71

Judy Verbosky '71

Pat Westwood '71

Eunice White '73, '74, '75, '76, '77, '78, '79

Aldah Wilhelms (Bronko Moonwater) '73, '74, '75, '76

Linda Williamson '71

Laurel Wolf '79

Nanette Wolf '71

Ruth Zuccarell '74, '75, '76, '77, '78

THE COACHES

Jerry Davis '73, '74, '75, '76, '77, '78, '79
Carl Hamilton '71, '72, '73, '74, '75, '76, '77, '78, '79
John Henderson '78
Larry Layton '78
Bill Mosley '79
Bill Stout '71, '72, '73, '74, '75, '76, '77
Mike Stout '73, '74, '75, '76, '77, '78, '79
Jim Wright '71, '72, '73

IN MEMORIAM

Davelyn Burrows
Ernestine Davis
Jerry Davis
Carl Hamilton
Sunday Jones
Dorothy Parma
Tina Pirtle
Bill Stout
Lora White
Jim Wright

ACKNOWLEDGMENTS

I have so many to thank. As this is very much a book of memories, I am indebted to the players, coaches, their family members, National Women's Football League officials, and referees who have shared theirs with me: Jackie Allen, Sheila Browne, Barbara Church, Mitchi Collette, Judith Cook, Sue Crawford, Terry Dale, Constance D'Angelis (Connie Miller), Peggy Dauer, Jerry Davis, Danise Dinardo, Ken Dippman, Erick (Nancy) Erickson, Patsy Farrell, Olivia Flores, Jen Francis, Katie Graves, Felissa Green, Karen Gould, Carl Hamilton, Judy Hamilton, Pam Hardy, Brigitte Hartz, Verna Henderson, Cindee Herron, Lee Hollar, Jim Intagliata, Linda Jefferson, Gloria Jimenez, Karen Kelly, Gaye Lattimore (Anne Grote), Bob Krasula, Dr. Ted Ligabel, Teri May (Teri Macias), Mary Meserole, Carla Miller, Keely Miller, Bronko Moonwater (Aldah Wihelms), Pam Nagel, Joey Opfer, Janelle Palmer, David Parker, Becky Redmond, Hal Reynolds, Mike Reynolds, Denise Risin, Pam Schwartz, Cathie Schweitzer, Bev Severance, Debbie Skiles, Diane Skiles, Iris Smith, Ramella Smith, Doris Stokes, Becky Stout, Bill Stout, Stefanie Stout, Sue Stout, Vicky Stout, Nancy Taggart, Judy Verbosky, Frani Washington, Eunice White, Lora White (Lora Jean Smalley), Deb Wright (Deb Schuster), Nanette Wolf, and Ruth Zuccarell.

I have relied heavily on the work of Sheila Browne, the former center for the Troopers and unofficial scorekeeper of the team who kept detailed game records throughout the nine seasons. The statistics and game story lines were corroborated by many news publications such as those from the *Akron Beacon Journal*, the Associated Press, the *Cleveland Plain Dealer*, the *Detroit Free Press*, the *Detroit News*, the *Dallas Morning News*, the *Oklahoman*, the *New York Times*, the *Port Clinton Times*, the *Sandusky Register*, the *Bryan Times*, and others.

Special recognition must be paid to Tom Loomis and John Bergener of the *Toledo Blade*, as well as Orris Tabner at WTOL Channel 11. Their reporting of the Troopers throughout the 1970s gave legitimacy to the sport of women's football and became the spark of inspiration for this book.

I'm grateful to the *Blade* sports photographers Don Strayer, Herral Long, Luke Black, and Don Simmons, who shot game footage throughout the decade. As well, thank you to photographers like Penny Gentieu and Ron Jacomini who used good old-fashioned 35mm film to capture genuine Trooper moments of camaraderie, anticipation, and triumph. Speaking of the *Blade*, thanks to Tom Henry for his continued support of all things Toledo, especially the Troopers.

I would also like to thank family and friends for their support and belief in the Troopers' story. Thanks to Bob Eckhart for his feedback on early drafts of the manuscript and his enthusiastic support of the book and the *We Are the Troopers* documentary project.

The personal archives shared with me by many brought the stories to life, such as coach Jerry Davis's blue suitcase—full of hundreds of photographs, newspaper clippings, and various memorabilia—and players who've shared tattered, bloodstained jerseys and dented helmets and faded game-day programs. These preserved artifacts of those who lived the tale tell a more convincing history than words can.

Thank you to Deanna Lawrence for her undying support of the Trooper story, her steadfast work in spreading its word, and her guidance when I was starting out. Also Debbie Monagan, Joanne Frahn, and the team at Communica in Toledo have my gratitude for believing in the story and keeping the fire alive.

In their work in the documentary *We Are the Troopers*, Jonathon Kimble and Tom Sanders of Anserina Films have created a remarkable film and companion to this book.

Special thanks to authors Will Allison and Joe Oestreich for their advice when I was starting the publication process.

I'm also grateful for the diligence and expertise of production editor Cisca Schreefel and copyeditor Amy J. Schneider, whose herculean work cleaning up my messes as well as fact-checking the obscure history of the team and the era has brought clarity and integrity to the book.

Without the vision and support of Rica Allannic at the David Black Agency, the book wouldn't exist. Her guidance on the book's structure and character are imprinted on these pages. I'm also deeply grateful to my editor Brant Rumble for his numerous meticulous readings that brought out the heart of the story, as well as his savvy throughout production that ultimately carried the book over the goal line.

In many ways this book belongs to the coach and commissioner's son, Guy Stout. The vault of history he has preserved in his basement stands as a living museum to the Troopers, the National Women's Football League, and a son's admiration of his father. The exhaustive documentation in the form of NWFL meeting minutes, bylaws, player and franchise contracts, and championship trophies bears Guy's father's figurative and literal signatures. And beyond the tangible fruits of his work researching and preserving the history of the Troopers, I have Guy to thank for his storytelling and for his friendship.

I'm also grateful for the love and support of Deb, Eliot, and Claire. Despite your claims that the Troopers are my first family, I assure you that you are number one.

SOURCES

CHAPTER 1: THE GREAT BLACK SWAMP

Interviews: Mitchi Collette, Dr. Ted Ligabel
Hidden History of Toledo by Lou Hebert, 2019
Ohio: The History of a People by Andrew Cayton, 2002
Battle of Phillips Corners by Ohio History Connection, 2018
Brand Whitlock and the City Beautiful Movement in Toledo, Ohio by Shirley Leckie, 1982
Toledo: Future Great City of the World by Jesup Scott, 1937
Willys-Overland Company by Ohio History Central, Ohio History Connection, 2021
How Football Became Football: 150 Years of the Game's Evolution by Timothy Brown, 2020
Evolution of the Game: A Chronicle of American Football by Frank Francisco, 2016
Toledo Blade
"American Football and the 1970s Women's Movement" by Andrew Linden, May 2014

CHAPTER 2: THE PROMOTER

Interviews: Jennifer A. Carter, Bill Stout, Carl Hamilton
"How the NFL Fleeces Taxpayers" by Gregg Easterbrook, *The Atlantic*, 2013
New York Times
Sports and the Law: Major Legal Cases by Charles Quirk, 1999
A History of Women in Tackle Football by David R. Jackson, 2001
"The History of Women's Professional Football" by Stuart Kantor, 2001
"Let's Bang": Constructing, Reinforcing, and Embodying Orthodox Masculinity in Women's Full Contact, Tackle Football by Jennifer A. Carter, 2014
"No Kiddin'," *Morning Record*, September 9, 1967
Cleveland Plain Dealer

SOURCES

The Greatest Players in Women's Football History by Neal Rozendaal, 2021
The Women's Football Encyclopedia by Neal Rozendaal, 2016
The Mike Douglas Show, July 10, 1969

CHAPTER 3: THAT KIND OF CHARACTER

Interviews: Lee Hollar, Bill Stout, Sue Stout, Guy Stout, Rick Salem, Carl Hamilton, Jerry Davis, Jackie Allen, Deb Wright (Deb Brzozka), Pam Schwartz, Nanette Wolf, Diane Skiles, Debbie Skiles, Constance D'Angelis (Connie Miller), Karen Gould, Lynn Juress, Erick (Nancy) Erickson, Lora White (Lora Jean Smalley)
Detroit Free Press
Detroit News
"Introduction: 37 Words That Changed Sports," in *Title IX: A Brief History with Documents* by Susan Ware, 2007
Toledo Blade

CHAPTER 4: CHAOS

Interviews: Bill Stout, Sue Stout, Guy Stout, Stefanie Stout, Becky Stout, Vicky Stout, Rick Salem
Akron Beacon Journal
Cleveland Plain Dealer
Toledo Blade

CHAPTER 5: THE COMPROMISE

Interviews: Bill Stout, Sue Stout, Carl Hamilton, Judy Hamilton, Guy Stout
"The History of Women's Professional Football" by Stuart Kantor, 2001
Cleveland Plain Dealer
Akron Beacon Journal

CHAPTER 6: FIRST DOWN

Interviews: Lee Hollar, Judy Verbosky, Karen Kelly, Sheila Browne, Nanette Wolf, Constance D'Angelis (Connie Miller), Lynn Juress, Deb Wright (Deb Brzozka), Pam Schwartz, Jackie Allen, Peggy Dauer, Patsy Farrell
Cleveland Plain Dealer
Piqua Daily Call

SOURCES

CHAPTER 7: THEY'RE FOOTBALL PLAYERS

Interviews: Bill Stout, Carl Hamilton, Lee Hollar, Jackie Allen, Constance D'Angelis (Connie Miller), Pam Schwartz, Nanette Wolf, Peggy Dauer, Lora Jean Smalley, Patsy Farrell, Judy Verbosky, Karen Kelly
Cleveland Plain Dealer

CHAPTER 8: "THEY CAN'T CATCH ME, MOMMA!"

Interviews: Linda Jefferson, Sheila Browne, Frank Wallace, Lee Hollar, Constance D'Angelis (Connie Miller), Bill Stout, Carl Hamilton, Gloria Jimenez, Karen Gould, Terry Dale, Olivia Flores, Felissa Green, Pam Schwartz, Eunice White, Deb Wright (Deb Brzozka)
Ohio Interscholastic Track and Field Records by Ohio High School Athletic Association
Toledo Blade

CHAPTER 9: OWNERSHIP

Interviews: Bill Stout, Linda Jefferson, David Parker, Constance D'Angelis (Connie Miller), Lora White (Lora Jean Smalley), Lee Hollar, Nanette Wolf, Terry Dale, Karen Gould, Gloria Jimenez, Carl Hamilton, Jackie Allen, Deb Wright (Deb Brzozka)
Associated Press
Cleveland Plain Dealer
Detroit Free Press
Dallas Morning News

CHAPTER 10: WORLD CHAMPIONS

Interviews: Bill Stout, Linda Jefferson, Carl Hamilton, Constance D'Angelis (Connie Miller), Lora White (Lora Jean Smalley), Lee Hollar, Mary Meserole, Terry Dale, Gloria Jimenez, Jackie Allen, Deb Wright (Deb Brzozka), Eunice White
Associated Press
Cleveland Plain Dealer
Detroit Free Press
Dallas Morning News

CHAPTER 11: THE BOND

Interviews: Bill Stout, Linda Jefferson, Carl Hamilton, Lee Hollar, Mitchi Collette, Guy Stout, Sue Stout, Jerry Davis, Deb Wright (Deb Brzozka), Ken Dippman, Teri May (Teri Macias), Bronko Moonwater (Aldah Wilhelms)

Dayton Daily News
Toledo Blade
The Phil Donahue Show, March 23, 1973
womenSport magazine

CHAPTER 12: THE WORLD'S GREATEST FOOTBALL PLAYER

Interviews: Verna Henderson, Ken Dippman, Bill Stout, Carl Hamilton, Linda Jefferson, Ramella Smith, Judith Cook, Ruth Zuccarell, Guy Stout
People magazine
New York Times
Toledo Magazine
Toledo Blade
womenSport magazine

CHAPTER 13: MIRACLE

Interviews: Bill Stout, Guy Stout, Sue Stout, Stefanie Stout, Mitchi Collette, Carl Hamilton, Vicky Stout, Becky Stout, Ken Dippman
Toledo Blade
Detroit Free Press

CHAPTER 14: THE BRAWL

Interviews: Bill Stout, Guy Stout, Sue Stout, Barbara Church, Katie Graves, Judith Cook, Danise Dinardo, Denise Resin, Carl Hamilton, Ken Dippman, Pam Schwartz, Mitchi Collette, Jackie Allen, Ramella Smith, Gloria Jimenez, Eunice White, Linda Jefferson, Frank Wallace, Bronko Moonwater (Aldah Wilhelms)
Toledo Blade
Detroit Free Press
Detroit News
Houston Chronicle

CHAPTER 15: OBSTACLE

Interviews: Linda Jefferson, Guy Stout, Carl Hamilton, Sue Crawford
Toledo Blade
National Observer
New York Times

CHAPTER 16: THE UNTHINKABLE

Interviews: Bill Stout, Carl Hamilton, Jerry Davis, Mike Reynolds, Hal Reynolds, Pam Hardy, Joey Opfer, Cindee Herron, Doris Stokes, Cathie Schweitzer, Linda Jefferson, Barbara Church, Eunice White, Gloria Jimenez
Toledo Blade
Oklahoman
New York Times

CHAPTER 17: SHOWDOWN

Interviews: Bill Stout, Guy Stout, Carl Hamilton, Pam Schwartz, Gloria Jimenez, Frani Washington, Barbara Church, Bronko Moonwater (Aldah Wilhelms), Janelle Palmer, Deb Wright (Deb Schuster), Katie Graves, Mitchi Collette, Ken Dippman, Gloria Jimenez
Toledo Blade
ESPN The Magazine

CHAPTER 18: DEADLOCK

Interviews: Bill Stout, Guy Stout, Carl Hamilton, Gloria Jimenez, Mitchi Collette, Linda Jefferson, Eunice White, Deb Wright (Deb Schuster), Joey Opfer, Pam Hardy, Mike Reynolds, Hal Reynolds
Toledo Blade
Oklahoman

CHAPTER 19: BLIZZARD

Interviews: Bill Stout, Guy Stout, Deb Wright (Deb Schuster), Carl Hamilton, Mitchi Collette, Hal Reynolds, Mike Reynolds
Toledo Blade
Detroit Free Press
Smithsonian Magazine
Houstonia Magazine

CHAPTER 20: ANGELS IN THE BACKFIELD

Interviews: Carl Hamilton, Carla Miller, Joey Opfer, Guy Stout, Pam Hardy, Barbara Church, Verna Henderson, Linda Jefferson, Eunice White, Gloria Jimenez, Ruth Zuccarell, Mitchi Collette

SOURCES

Charlie's Angels, season 2, episode 17, 1977, ABC Television
Toledo Blade
Oklahoman

CHAPTER 21: THE RETURN

Interviews: Carl Hamilton, Carla Miller, Joey Opfer, Guy Stout, Pam Hardy, Barbara
      Church, Verna Henderson, Linda Jefferson, Eunice White, Doris Stokes, Ruth
      Zuccarell, Mitchi Collette
Toledo Blade
Oklahoman

CHAPTER 22: BROKEN BAND

Interviews: Bill Stout, Guy Stout, Hal Reynolds, Mike Reynolds, Joey Opfer, Mitchi
      Collette, Linda Jefferson, Iris Smith, Carl Hamilton, Carla Miller, Pam Schwartz
Toledo Blade
Port Clinton Times
The National Women's Football League Public Relations Manual by Bill Stout

CHAPTER 23: THE WOMEN OF TOMORROW

Interviews: Gloria Jimenez, Eunice White, Teri May (Teri Macias), Verna Henderson,
      Erick (Nancy) Erickson, Judy Verbosky, Beverly Severance, Carl Hamilton, Linda
      Jefferson, Mitchi Collette, Pam Schwartz, Carla Miller, Joey Opfer, Olivia Flores,
      Sue Stout, Guy Stout

EPILOGUE

Interviews: Bill Stout, Linda Jefferson, Jerry Davis

INDEX

INDEX